IN A FAR COUNTRY

IN
A FAR
COUNTRY

Jack London's
Tales of the West

EDITED AND WITH AN INTRODUCTION BY
DALE L. WALKER

Jameson Books ▪ OTTAWA, ILLINOIS

Special gratitude is due Mr. Milo Shepard and the Trust of Irving Shepard, Glen Ellen, California, for permission to reprint Chapter XV of The Star Rover, *copyright 1915, and the story, "Like Argus of the Ancient Times," copyright 1917, and for the encouragement of Mr. Shepard in preparation of this book.*

Distributed by Kampmann and Company, New York

All returns to Kampmann and Co. warehouse.

Jameson Books are available at special discounts for bulk purchases for sales promotions, premiums, fund-raising, or education use. Special editions or book excerpts can also be created to specification.

For details contact:
Special Sales Director
Jameson Books
P.O. Box 738
Ottawa, IL 61350

5 4 3 2 1

Printed in the United States of America

Designed by Irving Perkins

FOR RUSS KINGMAN
Keeper of the Flame

CONTENTS

California

Utah

Mexico

The Road

Far to the West

INTRODUCTION

"I am a Westerner despite my English name."

In those years from the century's leisurely turn to the blinking out of the lights in Europe, those years between the splendid little war and the war to end all wars, no man better epitomized the American West, both in his life and writings, than John Griffith "Jack" London (1876–1916).

He had all the requisites of the character of the American frontier spirit described by Frederick Jackson Turner in 1920: restless nervous energy, individualism, buoyancy and exuberance, coarseness and strength, acuteness and inquisitiveness. To these might be added a love of life but a recognition of its perils, injustices and evils; a natural generosity, a sense of humor, a firsthand knowledge of the meaning of work and sweat, and ambition.

In his fiction—an astonishing output for a professional writing life of but seventeen years (1899–1916)—Jack London wrote of a "West" that requires the fullest interpretation of the word. His were frontiers, plural. They ranged from revolutionary Mexico on the south to the white silences of the Yukon Territory, of Alaska and Canada on the north, with Western America between. Given this vast canvas, he wrote of things that were at once peculiarly Jack London's and commonest currency of western writers ever since: tales of heroic figures and heroic deeds and of figures and deeds that were malevolent; of the hostility of primitive environments to human intruders, of the clash of alien cultures—whether Indian and white in far-flung lands or capitalist and working class at home.

It is practically obligatory to say that Jack London was the most autobiographical of American writers. His fiction was almost in-

9

variably the product of his own life's experience. Of the twenty-two novels he wrote, the nearly two hundred short stories, it is difficult to find anything of consequence not grounded in London's frenetic, meteoric, forty-year life. While that hoary advice so often handed young writers ("write what you have experienced") is little more than a convenient old lie, American literature is the richer for London's hewing to it. (See the Jack London Chronology *herein for highlights of the author's life and career.)*

In this collection only the "Mountain Meadows Massacre" story is not drawn directly from the author's exprience. It is one of the rare pieces of historical fiction to be found in London's works, and derives from that strange and sadly neglected London novel, The Star Rover *(1915), which is made up of historically based episodes. Even so, London knew Utah. The father of Charmian Kittredge, London's second wife, was Union Army provost marshal at Fort Douglas, Utah Territory, and Jack and Charmian were in the state in 1905, on a lecture tour, and again in 1911 when headed east to New York.*

All else in this book, even the chilling little story "War" (we do not know precisely where or when it takes place but London knew war firsthand, in Manchuria in 1904 and in Mexico in 1914), is drawn from the author's extraordinary life.

The notes preceding each story are intended to "set the stage," and tell the context of it in London's life.

In the June, 1901, issue of Impressions, *London wrote: "This great, incoherent, amorphous West! Who could grip the spirit and essence of it, the luster and wonder, and bind it all, definitely and sanely, within the covers of a printed book?" He was writing of Frank Norris'* The Octopus, *but though his own writing career had just begun in earnest with the publication of his first book* (The Son of the Wolf), *and though it would be two years before publication of the novel that made him world-famous,* The Call of the Wild, *that gripping of the spirit and essence of the West was not to be Frank Norris' exclusive talent.*

Jack London, within the covers of over fifty books, gripped it and made it gripping for all time.

DALE L. WALKER
El Paso, Texas

THE
YUKON

GOLD HUNTERS OF THE NORTH

(*The Atlantic*, July, 1903)

This graceful and evocative tribute to the founding fathers of the Northlands saw publication simultaneously with London's immortal tale of the Yukon, *The Call of the Wild* (originally published serially in *The Saturday Evening Post*, June 20–July 18, 1903).

London knew the Yukon in its moment in the sun, the Klondike goldrush, firsthand. In July, 1897, he sailed to Juneau and landed in August on Dyea Beach. By September 8, London and his partners (including a certain Mr. Tarwater, who became the model for the old gentleman in the story "Like Argus of the Ancient Times," in this book) had struggled with their gear and supplies across the Dyea river, up from Sheep Camp to the Scales, above timberline to the foot of Chilkoot Pass, over the pass to Happy Camp and to Long Lake, and Deep Lake, and across the mammoth hogback to Lake Linderman—fighting fatigue every step of the way in the race against the coming winter when the Yukon would freeze solid and halt all movement north to Dawson—the *ne plus ultra* for the gold hunters.

By the end of September, having endured the fall blizzards and gale winds that keened across the lakes and rapids that stood between them and the Yukon, London and his party had made their way across Lake LeBarge (where, in Robert Service's poem, Sam McGee was cremated), then decided to avoid the hubbub ahead and to winter at Split-Up Island, eighty miles from Dawson.

London got to Dawson in October via the *Yukon Belle* and recorded a claim resulting from his panning on Henderson Creek, eighteen miles from Split-Up Island. He stayed in Dawson until December, then returned to his cabin on Split-Up for the winter. By the spring of 1898 he had developed scurvy, the common disease among the argonauts (in particular the *cheechakos*, or tenderfeet) who survived on a "three-B" diet—beans, bread, and bacon. He was able to return to Dawson in May when the Yukon ice broke, making a raft from the logs of his cabin with the help of his cabin-mate and some other miner friends.

But scurvy had defeated him. Ill and weak, London had to return "outside" and in late June he arrived in St. Michael, took the schooner *Bartlett* for Port Townsend, then—slowly recovering his health with a steady diet of antiscorbutics such as potatoes and canned tomatoes—stoked coal on a steamer that took him back to San Francisco.

London's year in the Northland produced no gold of the variety carried in a moosehide poke. But he mined his Yukon experiences the rest of his life and in "Gold Hunters of the North" he pays homage to those, from Baranov at Sitka in 1804 to Robert Henderson, "father of the Klondike," in '97, who knew and loved the land and laughed back at "the northland's hyperborean laugh" decades before the gold fever attracted the Jack Londons there.

GOLD HUNTERS OF THE NORTH

"Where the Northern Lights come down o' nights
to dance on the houseless snow."

IVAN, I FORBID you to go farther in this undertaking. Not a word about this, or we are all undone. Let the Americans and the English know that we have gold in these mountains, then we are ruined. They will rush in on us by thousands, and crowd us to the wall—to the death."

So spoke the old Russian governor, Baranov, at Sitka, in 1804, to one of his Slavonian hunters, who had just drawn from his pockets a handful of golden nuggets. Full well Baranov, fur trader and autocrat, understood and feared the coming of the sturdy, indomitable gold hunters of Anglo-Saxon stock. And thus he suppressed the news, as did the governors that followed him, so that when the United States bought Alaska in 1867, she bought it for its furs and fisheries, without a thought of its treasures underground.

No sooner, however, had Alaska become American soil than thousands of our adventurers were afoot and afloat for the north. They were the men of "the days of gold," the men of California, Fraser, Cassiar, and Cariboo. With the mysterious, infinite faith of the prospector, they believed that the gold streak, which ran through the Americas from Cape Horn to California, did not "peter out" in British Columbia. That it extended farther north, was their creed, and "Farther North!" became their cry. No time was lost, and in the early seventies, leaving the Treadwell and Silver Bow Basin to be discovered by those who came after, they went plunging on into the white unknown. North, farther north, they struggled, till their picks rang in the frozen beaches of the Arctic Ocean, and they shivered by driftwood fires on the ruby sands of Nome.

But first, in order that this colossal adventure may be fully grasped, the recentness and the remoteness of Alaska must be emphasized. The interior of Alaska and the contiguous Canadian territory was a vast wilderness. Its hundreds of thousands of square miles were as dark and chartless as Darkest Africa. In 1847, when the first Hudson Bay Company agents crossed over the Rockies from the Mackenzie to poach on the preserves of the Russian Bear, they thought that the Yukon flowed north and emptied into the Arctic Ocean. Hundreds of miles below, however, were the outposts of the Russian traders. They, in turn, did not know where the Yukon had its source, and it was not till later that Russ and Saxon learned that it was the same mighty stream they were occupying. And a little over ten years later, Frederick Whymper voyaged up the Great Bend to Fort Yukon under the Arctic Circle.

From fort to fort, from York Factory on Hudson's Bay to Fort Yukon in Alaska, the English traders transported their goods—a round trip requiring from a year to a year and a half. It was one of their deserters, in 1867, escaping down the Yukon to Bering Sea, who was the first white man to make the Northwest Passage by land from the Atlantic to the Pacific. It was at this time that the first accurate description of a fair portion of the Yukon was given by Dr. W. H. Ball, of the Smithsonian Institution. But even he had never seen its source, and it was not given him to appreciate the marvel of that great natural highway.

No more remarkable river in this one particular is there in the world—taking its rise in Crater Lake, thirty miles from the ocean, the Yukon flows for twenty-five hundred miles, through the heart of the continent, ere it empties into the sea. A portage of thirty miles, and then a highway for traffic one tenth the girth of the earth!

As late as 1869, Frederick Whymper, fellow of the Royal Geographical Society, stated on hearsay that the Chilcat Indians were believed occasionally to make a short portage across the Coast Range from salt water to the head-reaches of the Yukon. But it remained for a gold hunter, questing north, ever north, to be first of all white men to cross the terrible Chilcoot Pass, and tap the Yukon at its head. This happened only the other day, but the man has become a dim legendary hero. Holt was his name, and already the mists of antiquity have wrapped about the time of his passage. 1872, 1874, and 1878 are the dates variously given—a confusion which time will never clear.

Holt penetrated as far as the Hootalinqua, and on his return to the coast reported coarse gold. The next recorded adventurer is one Edward Bean, who in 1880 headed a party of twenty-five miners from Sitka into the uncharted land. and in the same year, other parties (now forgotten, for who remembers or ever hears the wanderings of the gold hunters?) crossed the Pass, built boats out of the standing timber, and drifted down the Yukon and farther north.

And then, for a quarter of a century, the unknown and unsung heroes grappled with the frost, and groped for the gold they were sure lay somewhere among the shadows of the Pole. In the struggle with the terrifying and pitiless natural forces, they returned to the primitive, garmenting themselves in the skins of wild beasts, and covering their feet with the walrus *mucluc* and the moosehide moccasin. They forgot the world and its ways, as the world had forgotten them; killed their meat as they found it; feasted in plenty and starved in famine, and searched unceasingly for the yellow lure. They crisscrossed the land in every direction, threaded countless unmapped rivers in precarious birch-bark canoes, and with snowshoes and dogs broke trail through thousands of miles of silent white, where man had never been. They struggled on, under the aurora borealis or the midnight sun, through temperatures that ranged from one hundred degrees above zero to eighty degrees below, living, in the grim humor of the land, on "rabbit tracks and salmon bellies."

To-day, a man may wander away from the trail for a hundred days, and just as he is congratulating himself that at last he is treading virgin soil, he will come upon some ancient and dilapidated cabin, and forget his disappointment in wonder at the man who reared the logs. Still, if one wanders from the trail far enough and deviously enough, he may chance upon a few thousand square miles which he may have all to himself. On the other hand, no matter how far and how deviously he may wander, the possibility always remains that he may stumble, not alone upon a deserted cabin, but upon an occupied one.

As an instance of this, and of the vastness of the land, no better case need be cited than that of Harry Maxwell. An able seaman, hailing from New Bedford, Massachusetts, his ship, the brig *Fannie E. Lee*, was pinched in the Arctic ice. Passing from whaleship to whaleship, he eventually turned up at Point Barrow in the summer of 1880. He was *north* of the Northland, and from this point of vantage he determined to pull south into the interior in search of gold. Across the mountains from Fort Macpherson, and a couple of hundred miles eastward from the Mackenzie, he built a cabin and established his headquarters. And here, for nineteen continuous years, he hunted his living and prospected. He ranged from the never opening ice to the north as far south as the Great Slave Lake. Here he met Warburton Pike, the author and explorer—an incident he now looks back upon as chief among the few incidents of his solitary life.

When this sailor-miner had accumulated $20,000 worth of dust he concluded that civilization was good enough for him, and proceeded "to pull for the outside." From the Mackenzie he went up the Little Peel to its headwaters, found a pass through the mountains, nearly starved to death on his way across to the Porcupine Hills, and eventually came out on the Yukon River, where he learned for the first time of the Yukon gold hunters and their discoveries. Yet for twenty years they had been working there, his next-door neighbors, virtually, in a land of such great spaces. At Victoria, British Columbia, previous to his going east over the Canadian Pacific (the existence of which he had just learned), he pregnantly remarked that he had faith in the Mackenzie watershed, and that he was going back after he had taken in the World's Fair and got a whiff or two of civilization.

Faith! It may or may not remove mountains, but it has certainly made the Northland. No Christian martyr ever possessed greater faith than did the pioneers of Alaska. They never doubted the bleak and barren land. Those who came remained, and more ever came. They could not leave. They "knew" the gold was there, and they persisted. Somehow, the romance of the land and the quest entered into their blood, the spell of it gripped hold of them and would not let them go. Man after man of them, after the most terrible privation and suffering, shook the muck of the country from his moccasins and departed for good. But the following spring always found him drifting down the Yukon on the tail of the ice jams.

Jack McQuestion aptly vindicates the grip of the North. After a residence of thirty years he insists that the climate is delightful, and declares that whenever he makes a trip to the States he is afflicted with homesickness. Needless to say, the North still has him and will keep tight hold of him until he dies. In fact, for him to die elsewhere would be inartistic and insincere. Of three of the "pioneer" pioneers, Jack McQuestion alone survives. In 1871, from one to seven years before Holt went over Chilcoot, in the company of Al Mayo and Arthur Harper, McQuestion came into the Yukon from the Northwest over the Hudson Bay Company route from the Mackenzie to Fort Yukon. The names of these three men, as their lives, are bound up in the history of the country, and so long as there be histories and charts, that long will the Mayo and McQuestion rivers and the Harper and Ladue town site of Dawson be remembered. As an agent of the Alaska Commercial Company, in 1873, McQuestion built Fort Reliance, six miles below the Klondike River. In 1898 the writer met Jack McQuestion at Minook, on the Lower Yukon. The old pioneer, though grizzled, was hale and hearty, and as optimistic as when he first journeyed into the land along the path of the Circle. And no man more beloved is there in all the North.

There will be great sadness there when his soul goes questing on over the Last Divide—"farther north," perhaps—who can tell?

Frank Dinsmore is a fair sample of the men who made the Yukon country. A Yankee, born in Auburn, Maine, the *Wanderlust* early laid him by the heels, and at sixteen he was heading west on the trail that led "farther north." He prospected in the Black Hills, Montana, and in the Cœur d'Alene, then heard the whisper of the North, and went up to Juneau on the Alaskan Panhandle. But the North still whispered, and more insistently, and he could not rest till he went over Chilcoot, and down into the mysterious Silent Land. This was in 1882, and he went down the chain of lakes, down the Yukon, up the Pelly, and tried his luck on the bars of McMillan River. In the fall, a perambulating skeleton, he came back over the Pass in a blizzard, with a rag of a shirt, tattered overalls, and a handful of raw flour.

But he was unafraid. That winter he worked for a grubstake in Juneau, and the next spring found the heels of his moccasins turned toward salt water and his face toward Chilcoot. This was repeated the next spring, and the following spring, and the spring after that, until, in 1885, he went over the Pass for good. There was to be no return for him until he found the gold he sought.

The years came and went, but he remained true to his resolve. For eleven long years, with snow-shoe and canoe, pickaxe and gold-pan, he wrote out his life on the face of the land. Upper Yukon, Middle Yukon, Lower Yukon—he prospected faithfully and well. His bed was anywhere. Winter or summer he carried neither tent nor stove, and his six-pound sleeping-robe of Arctic hare was the warmest covering he was ever known to possess. Rabbit tracks and salmon bellies were his diet with a vengeance, for he depended largely on his rifle and fishing-tackle. His endurance equaled his courage. On a wager he lifted thirteen fifty-pound sacks of flour and walked off with them. Winding up a seven-hundred-mile trip on the ice with a forty-mile run, he came into camp at six o'clock in the evening and found a "squaw dance" under way. He should have been exhausted. Anyway, his muclucs were frozen stiff. But he kicked them off and danced all night in stocking-feet.

At the last fortune came to him. The quest was ended, and he gathered up his gold and pulled for the outside. And his own end was as fitting as that of his quest. Illness came upon him down in San Francisco, and his splendid life ebbed slowly out as he sat in his big easy-chair, in the Commercial Hotel, the "Yukoner's home." The doctors came, discussed, consulted, the while he matured more plans of Northland adventure; for the North still gripped him and would not let him go. He grew weaker day by day, but each day he said, "To-morrow I'll be all right." Other old-timers, "out on furlough," came to see him. They wiped their eyes and swore under their breaths, then entered and talked largely and jovially about going in with him over the trail when spring came. But there in the big easy-chair it was that his Long Trail ended, and the life passed out of him still fixed on "farther north."

From the time of the first white man, famine loomed black and gloomy over the land. It was chronic with the Indians and Eskimos; it became chronic with the gold hunters. It was ever present, and so it came about that life was commonly expressed in terms of "grub"—was measured by cups of flour. Each winter, eight months long, the heroes of the frost faced starvation. It became the custom, as fall drew on, for partners to cut the cards or draw straws to determine which should hit the hazardous trail for salt water, and which should remain and endure the hazardous darkness of the Arctic night.

There was never food enough to winter the whole population. The A. C Company worked hard to freight up the grub, but the gold hunters came faster and dared more audaciously. When the A. C. Company added a new stern-wheeler to its fleet, men said, "Now we shall have plenty." But more gold hunters poured in over the passes to the south, more *voyageurs* and fur traders forced a way through the Rockies from the east, more seal hunters and coast adventurers poled up from Bering Sea on the west, more sailors deserted from the whale-ships to the north, and they all starved together in right brotherly fashion. More steamers were added, but the tide of prospectors welled always in advance. Then the N. A. T. & T. Company came upon the scene, and both companies added steadily to their fleets. But it was the same old story; famine would not depart. In fact, famine grew with the population, till, in the winter of 1897-1898, the United States government was forced to equip a reindeer relief expedition. As of old, that winter partners

cut the cards and drew straws, and remained or pulled for salt water
as chance decided. They were wise of old time, and had learned
never to figure on relief expeditions. They had heard of such things,
but no mortal man of them had ever laid eyes on one.

The hard luck of other mining countries pales into insignificance
before the hard luck of the North. And as for the hardship, it cannot
be conveyed by printed page or word of mouth. No man may know
who has not undergone. And those who have undergone, out of
their knowledge, claim that in the making of the world God grew
tired, and when he came to the last barrowload, "just dumped it
anyhow," and that was how Alaska happened to be. While no adequate conception of the life can be given to the stay-at-home, yet
the men themselves sometimes give a clew to its rigors. One old
Minook miner testified thus: "Haven't you noticed the expression
on the faces of us fellows? You can tell a newcomer the minute you
see him; he looks alive, enthusiastic, perhaps jolly. We old miners
are always grave, unless we're drinking."

Another old-timer, out of the bitterness of a "home-mood," imagined himself a Martian astronomer explaining to a friend, with the
aid of a powerful telescope, the institutions of the earth. "There are
the continents," he indicated; "and up there near the polar cap is
a country, frigid and burning and lonely and apart, called Alaska.
Now, in other countries and states there are great insane asylums,
but, though crowded, they are insufficient; so there is Alaska given
over to the worst cases. Now and then some poor insane creature
comes to his senses in those awful solitudes, and, in wondering joy,
escapes from the land and hastens back to his home. But most cases
are incurable. They just suffer along, poor devils, forgetting their
former life quite, or recalling it like a dream."—Again the grip of
the North, which will not let one go,—for *most cases are incurable.*

For a quarter of a century the battle with frost and famine went
on. The very severity of the struggle with Nature seemed to make
the gold hunters kindly toward one another. The latch-string was
always out, and the open land was the order of the day. Distrust
was unknown, and it was no hyperbole for a man to take the last
shirt off his back for a comrade. Most significant of all, perhaps, in
this connection, was the custom of the old days, that when August

the first came around, the prospectors who had failed to locate "pay dirt" were permitted to go upon the ground of their more fortunate comrades and take out enough for the next year's grub-stake.

In 1885 rich bar-washing was done on the Stewart River, and in 1886 Cassiar Bar was struck just below the mouth of the Hootal-inqua. It was at this time that the first moderate strike was made on Forty Mile Creek, so called because it was judged to be that distance below Fort Reliance of Jack McQuestion fame. A prospector named Williams started for the outside with dogs and Indians to carry the news, but suffered such hardship on the summit of Chilcoot that he was carried dying into the store of Captain John Healy at Dyea. But he had brought the news through—*coarse gold!* Within three months more than two hundred miners had passed in over Chilcoot, stampeding for Forty Mile. Find followed find—Sixty Mile, Miller, Glacier, Birch, Franklin, and the Koyokuk. But they were all moderate discoveries, and the miners still dreamed and searched for the fabled stream, "Too Much Gold," where gold was so plentiful that gravel had to be shovelled into the sluice-boxes in order to wash it.

And all the time the Northland was preparing to play its own huge joke. It was a great joke, albeit an exceeding bitter one, and it has led the old-timers to believe that the land is left in darkness the better part of the year because God goes away and leaves it to itself. After all the risk and toil and faithful endeavor, it was destined that few of the heroes should be in at the finish when Too Much Gold turned its yellow treasure to the stars.

First, there was Robert Henderson—and this is true history. Henderson had faith in the Indian River district. For three years, by himself, depending mainly on his rifle, living on straight meat a large portion of the time, he prospected many of the Indian River tributaries, just missed finding the rich creeks, Sulphur and Do-minion, and managed to make grub (poor grub) out of Quartz Creek and Australia Creek. Then he crossed the divide between Indian River and Klondike, and on one of the "feeders" of the latter found eight cents to the pan. This was considered excellent in those simple days. Naming the creek "Gold Bottom," he recrossed the divide and got three men, Munson, Dalton, and Swanson, to return with him. The four took out $750. And be it emphasized, and emphasized again, *that this was the first Klondike gold ever shovelled in and washed out*. And be it also emphasized, *that Robert Henderson was the discoverer of Klondike, all lies and hearsay tales to the contrary*.

Running out of grub, Henderson again recrossed the divide, and went down the Indian River and up the Yukon to Sixty Mile. Here Joe Ladue ran the trading post, and here Joe Ladue had originally grub-staked Henderson. Henderson told his tale, and a dozen men (all it contained) deserted the Post for the scene of his find. Also, Henderson persuaded a party of prospectors, bound for Stewart River, to forgo their trip and go down and locate with him. He loaded his boat with supplies, drifted down the Yukon to the mouth of the Klondike, and towed and poled up the Klondike to Gold Bottom. But at the mouth of the Klondike he met George Carmack, and thereby hangs the tale.

Carmack was a squawman. He was familiarly known as "Siwash" George—a derogatory term which had arisen out of his affinity for the Indians. At the time Henderson encountered him he was catching salmon with his Indian wife and relatives on the site of what was to become Dawson, the Golden City of the Snows. Henderson, bubbling over with good-will, open-handed, told Carmack of his discovery. But Carmack was satisfied where he was. He was possessed by no overweening desire for the strenuous life. Salmon were good enough for him. But Henderson urged him to come on and locate, until, when he yielded, he wanted to take the whole tribe along. Henderson refused to stand for this, said that he must give the preference over Siwashes to his old Sixty Mile friends, and, it is rumored, said some things about Siwashes that were not nice.

The next morning Henderson went on alone up the Klondike to Gold Bottom. Carmack, by this time aroused, took a short cut afoot for the same place. Accompanied by his two Indian brothers-in-law, Skookum Jim and Tagish Charley, he went up Rabbit Creek (now Bonanza), crossed into Gold Bottom, and staked near Henderson's discovery. On the way up he had panned a few shovels on Rabbit Creek, and he showed Henderson "colors" he had obtained. Henderson made him promise, if he found anything on the way back, that he would send up one of the Indians with the news. Henderson also agreed to pay for this service, for he seemed to feel that they were on the verge of something big, and he wanted to make sure.

Carmack returned down Rabbit Creek. While he was taking a sleep on the bank about half a mile below the mouth of what was to be known as Eldorado, Skookum Jim tried his luck, and from surface prospects got from ten cents to a dollar to the pan. Carmack and his brothers-in-law staked and "hit the high places" for Forty Mile, where they filed on the claims before Captain Constantine, and renamed the creek Bonanza. And Henderson was forgotten. No word of it reached him. Carmack broke his promise.

Weeks afterward, when Bonanza and Eldorado were staked from end to end and there was no more room, a party of late comers pushed over the divide and down to Gold Bottom, where they found Henderson still at work. When they told him they were from Bonanza, he was nonplussed. He had never heard of such a place. But when they described it, he recognized it as Rabbit Creek. Then they told him of its marvelous richness, and, as Tappan Adney relates, when Henderson realized what he had lost through Carmack's treachery, "he threw down his shovel and went and sat on the bank, so sick at heart that it was some time before he could speak."

Then there were the rest of the old-timers, the men of Forty Mile and Circle City. At the time of the discovery, nearly all of them were over to the west at work in the old diggings or prospecting for new ones. As they said of themselves, they were the kind of men who are always caught out with forks when it rains soup. In the stampede that followed the news of Carmack's strike very few old miners took part. They were not there to take part. But the men who did go on the stampede were mainly the worthless ones, the newcomers, and the camp hangers-on. And while Bob Henderson plugged away to the east, and the heroes plugged away to the west, the greenhorns and rounders went up and staked Bonanza.

But the Northland was not yet done with its joke. When fall came on and the heroes returned to Forty Mile and to Circle City, they listened calmly to the up-river tales of Siwash discoveries and loafers' prospects, and shook their heads. They judged by the caliber of the men interested, and branded it a bunco game. But glowing reports continued to trickle down the Yukon, and a few of the old-timers went up to see. They looked over the ground—the unlikeliest place for gold in all their experience—and they went down the river again, "leaving it to the Swedes."

Again the Northland turned the tables. The Alaskan gold hunter is proverbial, not so much for his unveracity, as for his inability to tell the precise truth. In a country of exaggerations, he likewise is prone to hyperbolic description of things actual. But when it came to Klondike, he could not stretch the truth as fast as the truth itself stretched. Carmack first got a dollar pan. He lied when he said it was two dollars and a half. And when those who doubted him did get two-and-a-half pans, they said they were getting an ounce, and lo! ere the lie had fairly started on its way, they were getting, not one ounce, but five ounces. This they claimed was six ounces; but when they filled a pan of dirt to prove the lie, they washed out twelve ounces. And so it went. They continued valiantly to lie, but the truth continued to outrun them.

But the Northland's hyperborean laugh was not yet ended. When Bonanza was staked from mouth to source, those who failed "to get in," disgruntled and sore, went up the "pups" and feeders. Eldorado was one of these feeders, and many men, after locating on it, turned their backs upon their claims and never gave them a second thought. One man sold a half-interest in five hundred feet of it for a sack of flour. Other owners wandered around trying to bunco men into buying them out for a song. And then Eldorado "showed up." It was far, far richer than Bonanza, with an average value of a thousand dollars a foot to every foot of it.

A Swede named Charley Anderson had been at work on Miller Creek the year of the strike, and arrived in Dawson with a few hundred dollars. Two miners, who had staked No. 29 Eldorado, decided that he was the proper man upon whom to "unload." He was too canny to approach sober, so at considerable expense they got him drunk. Even then it was hard work, but they kept him befuddled for several days, and finally inveigled him into buying No. 29 for $750. When Anderson sobered up, he wept at his folly, and pleaded to have his money back. But the men who had duped him were hard-hearted. They laughed at him, and kicked themselves for not having tapped him for a couple of hundred more. Nothing remained for Anderson but to work the worthless ground. This he did, and out of it he took over three-quarters of a million of dollars.

It was not till Frank Dinsmore, who already had big holdings on Birch Creek, took a hand, that the old-timers developed faith in the new diggings. Dinsmore received a letter from a man on the spot, calling it "the biggest thing in the world," and harnessed his dogs and went up to investigate. And when he sent a letter back, saying that he had "never seen anything like it," Circle City for the first time believed, and at once was precipitated one of the wildest stampedes the country had ever seen or ever will see. Every dog was taken, many went without dogs, and even the women and children and weaklings hit the three hundred miles of ice through the long Arctic night for the biggest thing in the world. It is related that but twenty people, mostly cripples and unable to travel, were left in Circle City when the smoke of the last sled disappeared up the Yukon.

Since that time gold has been discovered in all manner of places, under the grass roots of the hillside benches, in the bottom of Monte Cristo Island, and in the sands of the sea at Nome. And now the gold hunter who knows his business shuns the "favorable looking" spots, confident in his hard-won knowledge that he will find the most gold in the least likely place. This is sometimes adduced to support the theory that the gold hunters, rather than the explorers, are the men who will ultimately win to the Pole. Who knows? It is in their blood, and they are capable of it.

THE TASTE OF THE MEAT

(Cosmopolitan, June, 1911)

For the romantic view of the *cheechako* against the odds in the Yukon there are no better tales than those in the little-known Jack London book *Smoke Bellew* (Century Co., 1912), the individual chapters of which ("The Taste of the Meat" is the opening chapter of the book) can be read as stories or the whole as a novel.

Christopher Bellew is a Lord Fauntleroyish literary dilettante who "never had to sweat" until joining the Klondike goldrush almost on a lark. The details of the packers who crossed Dyea Flats and made the Chilkoot climb to a thousand feet above the timberline "on a mountain's backbone" are authentic and a part of London's own experience in 1897. And while it is unlikely there were "sourdough" (veterans of the Northland) women anything like Joy Gastell, there were plenty of men who "rubbed the velvet" off their strength and rubbed it to the bone, returning to Dyea Beach to hail a steamer back to Portland or San Francisco, leaving the misery to others to endure.

Incidentally, London loved to play with names, places, and incidents in his fiction, and "Gillet Bellamy" and the literary magazine "The Billow" are London's inside jokes for Gelett Burgess (who wrote the "I never saw a Purple Cow" quatrain) and the innovative San Francisco literary and social journal *The Wave,* among the contributors to which were Ambrose Bierce, Frank Norris, Burgess—and Jack London.

THE TASTE OF THE MEAT

IN THE BEGINNING he was Christopher Bellew. By the time he was at college he had become Chris Bellew. Later, in the Bohemian crowd of San Francisco, he was called Kit Bellew. And in the end he was known by no other name than Smoke Bellew. And this history of the evolution of his name is the history of his evolution. Nor would it have happened had he not had a fond mother and an iron uncle, and had he not received a letter from Gillet Bellamy.

"I have just seen a copy of *The Billow*," Gillet wrote from Paris. "Of course O'Hara will succeed with it. But he's missing some tricks." Here followed details in the improvement of the budding society weekly. "Go down and see him. Let him think they're your own suggestions. Don't let him know they're from me. If you do, he'll make me Paris correspondent, which I can't afford, because I'm getting real money for my stuff from the big magazines. Above all, don't forget to make him fire that dub who's doing the musical and art criticism. Another thing. San Francisco has always had a literature of her own. But she hasn't any now. Tell him to kick around and get some gink to turn out a live serial, and to put into it the real romance and glamour and color of San Francisco."

And down to the office of *The Billow* went Kit Bellew faithfully to instruct. O'Hara listened. O'Hara debated. O'Hara agreed. O'Hara fired the dub who wrote criticisms. Further, O'Hara had a way with him, the very way that was feared by Gillet in distant Paris. When O'Hara wanted anything, no friend could deny him. He was sweetly and compellingly irresistible. Before Kit Bellew could escape from the office, he had become an associate editor, had agreed to write weekly columns of criticism till some decent pen was found, and had pledged himself to write a weekly instalment of ten thousand words on the San Francisco serial—and all this without pay. *The Billow* wasn't paying yet, O'Hara explained; and just as convincingly had he exposited that there was only one man in San Francisco capable of writing the serial and that man Kit Bellew.

"Oh, Lord, I'm the gink!" Kit had groaned to himself afterward on the narrow stairway.

And thereat had begun his servitude to O'Hara and the insatiable columns of *The Billow*. Week after week he held down an office chair, stood off creditors, wrangled with printers, and turned out twenty-five thousand words of all sorts. Nor did his labors lighten. *The Billow* was ambitious. It went in for illustration. The processes were expensive. It never had any money to pay Kit Bellew, and by the same token it was unable to pay for any additions to the office staff. Luckily for Kit, he had his own income. Small it was, compared with some, yet it was large enough to enable him to belong to several clubs and maintain a studio in the Latin quarter. In point of fact, since his associate-editorship, his expenses had decreased prodigiously. He had no time to spend money. He never saw the studio any more, nor entertained the local Bohemians with his famous chafing-dish suppers. Yet he was always broke, for *The Billow*, in perennial distress, absorbed his cash as well as his brains. There were the illustrators, who periodically refused to illustrate; the printers who periodically refused to print; and the office-boy, who frequently refused to officiate. At such times O'Hara looked at Kit, and Kit did the rest.

When the steamship *Excelsior* arrived from Alaska, bringing the news of the Klondike strike that set the country mad, Kit made a purely frivolous proposition.

"Look here, O'Hara," he said. "This gold rush is going to be big—the days of '49 over again. Suppose I cover it for *The Billow?* I'll pay my own expenses."

O'Hara shook his head. "Can't spare you from the office, Kit. Then there's that serial. Besides, I saw Jackson not an hour ago. He's starting for the Klondike tomorrow, and he's agreed to send a weekly letter and photos. I wouldn't let him get away till he promised. And the beauty of it is that it doesn't cost us anything."

The next Kit heard of the Klondike was when he dropped into the club that afternoon and in an alcove off the library encountered his uncle.

"Hello, avuncular relative," Kit greeted, sliding into a leather chair and spreading out his legs. "Won't you join me?"

He ordered a cocktail, but the uncle contented himself with a thin native claret he invariably drank. He glanced with irritated disapproval at the cocktail and on to his nephew's face. Kit saw a lecture gathering.

"I've only a minute," he announced hastily. "I've got to run and take in that Keith exhibition at Ellery's and do half a column on it."

"What's the matter with you?" the other demanded. "You're pale. You're a wreck."

Kit's only answer was a groan.

"I'll have the pleasure of burying you. I can see that."

Kit shook his head sadly. "No destroying worm, thank you. Cremation for mine."

John Bellew came of the old hard and hardy stock that had crossed the plains by ox-team in the fifties, and in him was this same hardness and the hardness of a childhood spent in the conquering of a new land. "You're not living right, Christopher. I'm ashamed of you."

"Primrose path, eh?" Kit chuckled.

The older man shrugged his shoulders.

"Shake not your gory locks at me, avuncular. I wish it were the primrose path. But that's all cut out. I have no time."

"Then what in—?"

"Overwork."

John Bellew laughed harshly and incredulously.

"Honest."

Again came the laughter.

"Men are the products of their environment," Kit proclaimed, pointing at the other's glass. "Your mirth is thin and bitter as your drink."

"Overwork!" was the sneer. "You never earned a cent in your life."

"You bet I have, only I never got it. I'm earning five hundred a week right now, and doing four men's work."

"Pictures that won't sell? Or—er—fancy work of some sort? Can you swim?"

"I used to."

"Sit a horse?"

"I have essayed that adventure."

John Bellow snorted with disgust. "I'm glad your father didn't live to see you in all the glory of your gracelessness," he said. "Your father was a man, every inch of him. Do you get it? A man. I think he'd have whaled all this musical and artistic tomfoolery out of you."

"Alas! these degenerate days," Kit sighed.

"I could understand it, and tolerate it," the other went on savagely, "if you succeeded at it. You've never earned a cent in your life, not done a tap of man's work. What earthly good are you, anyway? You were well put up, yet even at university you didn't play football. You didn't row. You didn't—"

"I boxed and fenced—some."

"When did you box last?"

"Not since, but I was considered an excellent judge of time and distance, only I was—er—"

"Go on."

"Considered desultory."

"Lazy, you mean."

"I always imagined it was an euphemism."

"My father, sir, your grandfather, old Isaac Bellew, killed a man with a blow of his fist when he was sixty-nine years old."

"The man?"

"No, you graceless scamp! But you'll never kill a mosquito at sixty-nine."

"The times have changed, O my avuncular! They send men to prison for homicide now."

"Your father rode one hundred and eighty-five miles, without sleeping, and killed three horses."

"Had he lived today he'd have snored over the same course in a Pullman."

The older man was on the verge of choking with wrath, but swallowed it down and managed to articulate, "How old are you?"

"I have reason to believe—"

"I know. Twenty-seven. You finished college at twenty-two. You've dabbled and played and frilled for five years. Before God and man, of what use are you? When I was your age I had one suit of underclothes. I was riding with the cattle in Coluso. I was hard as rocks, and I could sleep on a rock. I lived on jerked beef and bear meat. I am a better man physically right now than you are. You weigh about one hundred sixty-five. I can throw you right now, or thrash you with my fists."

"It doesn't take a physical prodigy to mop up cocktails or pink tea," Kit murmured deprecatingly. "Don't you see, my avuncular, the times have changed. Besides, I wasn't brought up right. My dear fool of a mother—"

John Bellew started angrily.

"—as you once described her, was too good to me, kept me in cotton wool and all the rest. Now, if when I was a youngster I had taken some of those intensely masculine vacations you go in for—I wonder why you didn't invite me sometimes? You took Hal and Robbie all over the Sierras on that Mexico trip."

"I guess you were too Lord-Fauntleroyish."

"Your fault, avuncular, and my dear—er—mother's. How was I to know the hard? I was only a chee-ild. What was there left but etchings and pictures and fans? Was it my fault that I never had to sweat?"

The older man looked at his nephew with unconcealed disgust. He had no patience with levity from the lips of softness. "Well, I'm going to take another one of those what you call masculine vacations. Suppose I asked you to come along?"

"Rather belated, I must say. Where is it?"

"Hal and Robert are going in to Klondike, and I'm going to see them across the pass and down to the lakes, then return—"

He got no further, for the young man had sprung forward and gripped his hand. "My preserver!"

John Bellew was immediately suspicious. He had not dreamed the invitation would be accepted. "You don't mean it?" he said.

"When do we start?"

"It will be a hard trip. You'll be in the way."

"No, I won't. I'll work. I've learned to work since I went on *The Billow*."

"Each man has to take a year's supplies in with him. There'll be such a jam the Indian packers won't be able to handle it. Hal and Robert will have to pack their outfits across themselves. That's what I'm going along for—to help them pack. If you come you'll have to do the same."

"Watch me."

"You can't pack," was the objection.

"When do we start?"

"Tomorrow."

"You needn't take it to yourself that your lecture on the hard has done it," Kit said, at parting. "I just had to get away, somewhere, anywhere, from O'Hara."

"Who is O'Hara? A Jap?"

"No; he's an Irishman, and a slave-driver, and my best friend. He's the editor and proprietor and all-around big squeeze of *The Billow*. What he says goes. He can make ghosts walk."

That night Kit Bellew wrote a note to O'Hara. "It's only a several weeks' vacation," he explained. "You'll have to get some gink to dope out instalments for that serial. Sorry, old man, but my health demands it. I'll kick in twice as hard when I get back."

Kit Bellew landed through the madness of the Dyea beach congested with the thousand-pound outfits of thousands of men. This immense mass of luggage and food, flung ashore in mountains by the steamers, was beginning slowly to dribble up the Dyea Valley and across Chilkoot. It was a portage of twenty-eight miles, and could be accomplished only on the backs of men. Despite the fact that the Indian packers had jumped the freight from eight cents a pound to forty, they were swamped with the work, and it was plain that winter would catch the major portion of the outfits on the wrong side of the divide.

Tenderest of the tenderfeet was Kit. Like many hundreds of others, he carried a big revolver swung on a cartridge-belt. Of this his uncle, filled with memories of old lawless days, was likewise guilty. But Kit Bellew was romantic. He was fascinated by the froth and sparkle of the gold rush, and viewed its life and movement with an artist's eyes. He did not take it seriously. As he said on the steamer, it was not his funeral. He was merely on a vacation, and intended to peep over the top of the pass for a "look see" and then return.

Leaving his party on the sand to wait for the putting ashore of the freight, he strolled up the beach toward the old trading-post. He did not swagger, though he noticed that many of the be-revolvered individuals did. A strapping, six-foot Indian passed him, carrying an unusually large pack. Kit swung in behind, admiring the splendid calves of the man, and the grace and ease with which he moved along under his burden. The Indian dropped his pack on the scales in front of the post, and Kit joined the group of admiring gold-rushers who surrounded him. The pack weighed one hundred and twenty-five pounds, which fact was uttered back and forth in tones of awe. It was going some, Kit decided, and he wondered if he could lift such a weight, much less walk off with it.

"Going to Lake Linderman with it, old man?" he asked.

The Indian, welling with pride, grunted an affirmative.

"How much you make that one pack?"

"Fifty dollars."

Here Kit slid out of the conversation. A young woman, standing in the doorway, had caught his eye. Unlike other women landing from the steamers, she was neither short-skirted nor bloomer-clad. She was dressed as any woman traveling anywhere would be dressed. What struck him was the justness of her being there, a feeling that somehow she belonged. Moreover, she was young and pretty. The bright beauty and color of her oval face held him, and he looked overlong—looked till she resented, and her own eyes, long lashed and dark, met his in cool survey. From his face, they traveled in evident amusement down to the big revolver at his thigh. Then her eyes came back to his, and in them was amused contempt. It struck him like a blow. She turned to the man beside her and indicated Kit. The man glanced him over with the same amused contempt.

"Chekako," the girl said.

The man, who looked like a tramp in his cheap overalls and dilapidated woolen jacket, grinned dryly, and Kit felt withered, though he knew not why. But anyway she was an unusually pretty girl, he decided, as the two moved off. He noted the way of her walk, and recorded the judgment that he would recognize it after the lapse of a thousand years.

"Did you see that man with the girl?" Kit's neighbor asked him excitedly. "Know who he is?"

Kit shook his head.

"Cariboo Charley. He was just pointed out to me. He struck it big on Klondike. Old-timer. Been on the Yukon a dozen years. He's just come out."

"What does 'chekako' mean?" Kit asked.

"You're one; I'm one," was the answer.

"Maybe I am, but you've got to search me. What does it mean?"

"Tenderfoot."

On his way back to the beach, Kit turned the phrase over and over. It rankled to be called tenderfoot by a slender chit of a woman. Going into a corner among the heaps of freight, his mind still filled

with the vision of the Indian with the redoubtable pack, Kit essayed
to learn his own strength. He picked out a sack of flour which he
knew weighed an even hundred pounds. He stepped astride it,
reached down, and strove to get it on his shoulder. His first conclusion was that one hundred pounds were real heavy. His next was
that his back was weak. His third was an oath, and it occurred at
the end of five futile minutes, when he collapsed on top of the
burden with which he was wrestling. He mopped his forehead, and
across a heap of grub-sacks saw John Bellew gazing at him, wintry
amusement in his eyes.

"God!" proclaimed that apostle of the hard. "Out of our loins has
come a race of weaklings. When I was sixteen I toyed with things
like that."

"You forget, avuncular," Kit retorted, "that I wasn't raised on
bear-meat."

"And I'll toy with it when I'm sixty."

"You've got to show me."

John Bellew did. He was forty-eight, but he bent over the sack,
applied a tentative, shifting grip that balanced it, and with a quick
heave stood erect, the sack of flour on his shoulder.

"Knack, my boy, knack—and a spine."

Kit took off his hat reverently. "You're a wonder, avuncular, a
shining wonder. D'ye think I can learn the knack?"

John Bellew shrugged his shoulders. "You'll be hitting the back
trail before we get started."

"Never you fear," Kit groaned. "There's O'Hara, the roaring lion,
down there. I'm not going back till I have to."

Kit's first pack was a success. Up to Finnegan's Crossing they had
managed to get Indians to carry the twenty-five-hundred-pound
outfit. From that point their own backs must do the work. They
planned to move forward at the rate of a mile a day. It looked
easy—on paper. Since John Bellew was to stay in camp and do the
cooking, he would be unable to make more than an occasional pack;
so to each of the three young men fell the task of carrying eight
hundred pounds one mile each day. If they made fifty-pound sacks,
it meant a daily walk of sixteen miles loaded and of fifteen miles
light—"Because we don't back-trip the last time," Kit explained the
pleasant discovery. Eighty-pound packs meant nineteen miles travel
each day; and hundred-pound packs meant only fifteen miles.

"I don't like walking," said Kit. "Therefore I shall carry one hundred pounds." He caught the grin of incredulity on his uncle's face, and added hastily: "Of course I shall work up to it. A fellow's got to learn the ropes and tricks. I'll start with fifty."

He did, and ambled gaily along the trail. He dropped the sack at the next camp-site and ambled back. It was easier than he had thought. But two miles had rubbed off the velvet of his strength and exposed the underlying softness. His second pack was sixty-five pounds. It was more difficult, and he no longer ambled. Several times, following the custom of all packers, he sat down on the ground, resting the pack behind him on a rock or stump. With the third pack he became bold. He fastened the straps to a ninety-five-pound sack of beans and started. At the end of a hundred yards he felt that he must collapse. He sat down and mopped his face.

"Short hauls and short rests," he muttered. "That's the trick."

Sometimes he did not make a hundred yards, and each time he struggled to his feet for another short haul the pack became undeniably heavier. He panted for breath, and the sweat streamed from him. Before he had covered a quarter of a mile he stripped off his woolen shirt and hung it on a tree. A little later he discarded his hat. At the end of half a mile he decided he was finished. He had never exerted himself so in his life, and he knew that he was finished. As he sat and panted, his gaze fell upon the big revolver and the heavy cartridge-belt.

"Ten pounds of junk!" he sneered, as he unbuckled it.

He did not bother to hang it on a tree, but flung it into the underbrush. And as the steady tide of packers flowed by him, up trail and down, he noted that the other tenderfeet were beginning to shed their shooting-irons.

His short hauls decreased. At times a hundred feet was all he could stagger, and then the ominous pounding of his heart against his eardrums and the sickening totteriness of his knees compelled him to rest. And his rests grew longer. But his mind was busy. It was a twenty-eight-mile portage, which represented as many days, and this by all accounts was the easiest part of it. "Wait till you get to Chilkoot," others told him as they rested and talked, "where you climb with hands and feet."

"They ain't going to be no Chilkoot," was his answer. "Not for me. Long before that I'll be at peace in my little couch beneath the moss."

A slip and a violent, wrenching effort at recovery frightened him. He felt that everything inside him had been torn asunder.

"If ever I fall down with this on my back, I'm a goner," he told another packer.

"That's nothing," came the answer. "Wait till you hit the Canyon. You'll have to cross a raging torrent on a sixty-foot pine-tree. No guide-ropes, nothing, and the water boiling at the sag of the log to your knees. If you fall with a pack on your back, there's no getting out of the straps. You just stay there and drown."

"Sounds good to me," he retorted; and out of the depths of his exhaustion he almost meant it.

"They drown three or four a day there," the man assured him. "I helped fish a German out of there. He had four thousand in greenbacks on him."

"Cheerful, I must say," said Kit, battling his way to his feet and tottering on.

He and the sack of beans became a perambulating tragedy. It reminded him of the old man of the sea who sat on Sindbad's neck. And this was one of those intensely masculine vacations, he meditated. Compared with it, the servitude to O'Hara was sweet. Again and again he was nearly seduced by the thought of abandoning the sack of beans in the brush and of sneaking around the camp to the beach and catching a steamer for civilization.

But he didn't. Somewhere in him was the strain of the hard, and he repeated over and over to himself that what other men could do he could. It became a nightmare chant, and he gibbered it to those that passed him on the trail. At other times, resting he watched and envied the stolid mule-footed Indians that plodded by under heavier packs. They never seemed to rest, but went on and on with a steadiness and certitude that were to him appalling.

He sat and cursed—he had no breath for it when under way—and fought the temptation to sneak back to San Francisco. Before the mile pack was ended he ceased cursing and took to crying. The tears were tears of exhaustion and of disgust with self. If ever a man was a wreck, he was. As the end of the pack came in sight, he strained himself in desperation, gained the camp-site, and pitched forward on his face, the beans on his back. It did not kill him, but he lay for fifteen minutes before he could summon sufficient shreds of strength to release himself from the straps. Then he became deathly sick, and was so found by Robbie, who had similar troubles of his own. It was this sickness of Robbie that braced Kit up.

"What other men can do we can do," he told Robbie, though down in his heart he wondered whether or not he was bluffing.

"And I am twenty-seven years old and a man," he privately assured himself many times in the days that followed. There was need for it. At the end of a week, though he had succeeded in moving his eight hundred pounds forward a mile a day, he had lost fifteen pounds of his own weight. His face was lean and haggard. All resilience had gone out of his body and mind. He no longer walked, but plodded. And on the back-trips, traveling light, his feet dragged almost as much as when he was loaded.

He had become a work animal. He fell asleep over his food, and his sleep was heavy and beastly, save when he was aroused, screaming in agony, by the cramps in his legs. Every part of him ached. He tramped on raw blisters; yet even this was easier than the fearful bruising his feet received on the water-rounded rocks of the Dyea Flats, across which the trail led for two miles. These two miles represented thirty-eight miles of traveling. His shoulders and chest, galled by the pack-straps, made him think, and for the first time with understanding, of the horses he had seen on city streets.

When they had moved the outfit across the foot-logs at the mouth of the Canyon, they made a change in their plans. Word had come across the pass that at Lake Linderman the last available trees for building boats were being cut. The two cousins, with tools, whipsaw, blankets, and grub on their backs, went on, leaving Kit and his uncle to hustle along the outfit. John Bellew now shared the cooking with Kit, and both packed shoulder to shoulder. Time was flying, and on the peaks the first snow was falling. To be caught on the wrong side of the pass meant a delay of nearly a year. The older man put his iron back under a hundred pounds. Kit was shocked, but he gritted his teeth and fastened his own straps to a hundred pounds. It hurt, but he had learned the knack, and his body, purged of all softness and fat, was beginning to harden up with lean and bitter muscle. Also, he observed and devised. He took note of the head-straps worn by the Indians and manufactured one for himself which he used in addition to the shoulder-straps. It made things easier, so that he began the practice of piling any light, cumbersome piece of luggage on top. Thus he was soon able to bend along with a hundred pounds in the straps, fifteen or twenty more lying loosely on top the pack and against his neck, an ax or a pair of oars in one hand, and in the other the nested cooking-pails of the camp.

But work as they would, the toil increased. The trail grew more rugged; their packs grew heavier; and each day saw the snow-line dropping down the mountains, while freight jumped to sixty cents. No word came from the cousins beyond, so they knew they must be at work chopping down the standing trees and whipsawing them into boat-planks. John Bellew grew anxious. Capturing a bunch of Indians back-tripping from Lake Linderman, he persuaded them to put their straps on the outfit. They charged thirty cents a pound to carry it to the summit of Chilkoot, and it nearly broke him. As it was, some four hundred pounds of clothes-bags and camp outfit were not handled. He remained behind to move it along, despatching Kit with the Indians. At the summit Kit was to remain, slowly moving his ton until overtaken by the four hundred pounds with which his uncle guaranteed to catch him.

Kit plodded along the trail with his Indian packers. In recognition of the fact that it was to be a long pack, straight to the top of Chilkoot, his own load was only eighty pounds. The Indians plodded under their loads, but it was a quicker gait than he had practised. Yet he felt no apprehension, and by now had come to deem himself almost the equal of an Indian.

At the end of a quarter of a mile he desired to rest. But the Indians kept on. He stayed with them, and kept his place in the line. At the half-mile he was convinced that he was incapable of another step, yet he gritted his teeth, kept his place, and at the end of the mile was amazed that he was still alive. Then, in some strange way, came the thing called second wind, and the next mile was almost easier than the first. The third mile nearly killed him, but, though half delirious with pain and fatigue, he never whimpered. And then, when he felt he must surely faint, came the rest. Instead of sitting in the straps, as was the custom of the white packers, the Indians slipped out of the shoulder- and head-straps and lay at ease, talking and smoking. A full half-hour passed before they made another start. To Kit's surprise, he found himself a fresh man, and "long hauls and long rests" became his newest motto.

The pitch of Chilkoot was all he had heard of it, and many were the occasions when he climbed with hands as well as feet. But when he reached the crest of the divide in the thick of a driving snow-squall, it was in the company of his Indians, and his secret pride was that he had come through with them and never squealed and never lagged. To be almost as good as an Indian was a new ambition to cherish.

When he had paid off the Indians and seen them depart, a stormy darkness was falling, and he was left alone, a thousand feet above timber-line, on the backbone of a mountain. Wet to the waist, famished and exhausted, he would have given a year's income for a fire and a cup of coffee. Instead, he ate half a dozen cold flapjacks and crawled into the folds of the partly unrolled tent. As he dozed off he had time for only one fleeting thought, and he grinned with vicious pleasure at the picture of John Bellew in the days to follow, masculinely back-tripping his four hundred pounds up Chilkoot. As for himself, even though burdened with two thousand pounds, he was bound down the hill.

In the morning, stiff from his labors and numb with the frost, he rolled out of the canvas, ate a couple of pounds of uncooked bacon, buckled the straps on a hundred pounds, and went down the rocky way. Several hundred yards beneath, the trail led across a small glacier and down to Crater Lake. Other men packed across the glacier. All that day he dropped his packs at the glacier's upper edge, and by virtue of the shortness of the pack, he put his straps on one hundred and fifty pounds each load. His astonishment at being able to do it never abated. For two dollars he bought from an Indian three leathery sea-biscuits, and out of these, and a huge quantity of raw bacon, made several meals. Unwashed, unwarmed, his clothing wet with sweat, he slept another night in the canvas.

In the early morning he spread a tarpaulin on the ice, loaded it with three quarters of a ton, and started to pull. Where the pitch of the glacier accelerated, his load likewise accelerated, overran him, scooped him in on top, and ran away with him.

A hundred packers, bending under their loads, stopped to watch him. He yelled frantic warnings, and those in his path stumbled and staggered clear. Below, on the lower edge of the glacier, was pitched a small tent, which seemed leaping toward him, so rapidly did it grow larger. He left the beaten track where the packers' trail swerved to the left, and struck a patch of fresh snow. This arose about him in frosty smoke, while it reduced his speed. He saw the tent the instant he struck it, carrying away the corner guys, bursting in the front flaps, and fetching up inside, still on top of the tarpaulin and in the midst of his grub-sacks. The tent rocked drunkenly, and in the frosty vapor he found himself face to face with a startled young woman who was sitting up in her blankets—the very one who had called him a tenderfoot at Dyea.

"Did you see my smoke?" he queried cheerfully.

She regarded him with disapproval.

"Talk about your magic carpets!" he went on.

Her coolness was a challenge. "It was a mercy you did not overturn the stove," she said.

He followed her glance and saw a sheet-iron stove and a coffee-pot, attended by a young squaw. He sniffed the coffee and looked back to the girl.

"I'm a chekako," he said.

Her bored expression told him that he was stating the obvious. But he was unabashed.

"I've shed my shooting-irons," he added.

Then she recognized him, and her eyes lighted. "I never thought you'd get this far," she informed him.

Again, and greedily, he sniffed the air. "As I live, coffee!" He turned and directly addressed her: "I'll give you my little finger—cut it off right now; I'll do anything; I'll be your slave for a year and a day or any other old time, if you'll give me a cup out of that pot."

And over the coffee he gave his name and learned hers—Joy Gastell. Also, he learned that she was an old-timer in the country. She had been born in a trading-post on the Great Slave, and as a child had crossed the Rockies with her father and come down to the Yukon. She was going in, she said, with her father, who had been delayed by business in Seattle and who had then been wrecked on the ill-fated *Chanter* and carried back to Puget Sound by the rescuing steamer.

In view of the fact that she was still in her blankets he did not make it a long conversation, and, heroically declining a second cup of coffee, he removed himself and his heaped and shifted baggage from her tent. Further, he took several conclusions away with him: she had a fetching name and fetching eyes; could not be more than twenty, or twenty-one or -two; her father must be French; she had a will of her own; temperament to burn; and she had been educated elsewhere than on the frontier.

Over the ice-scoured rocks and above the timberline, the trail ran around Crater Lake and gained the rocky defile that led toward Happy Camp and the first scrub-pines. To pack his heavy outfit around would take days of heart-breaking toil. On the lake was a canvas boat employed in freighting. Two trips with it, in two hours, would see him and his ton across. But he was broke, and the ferryman charged forty dollars a ton.

"You've got a gold-mine, my friend, in that kinky boat," Kit said to the ferryman. "Do you want another gold-mine?"

"Show me," was the answer.

"I'll sell it to you for the price of ferrying my outfit. It's an idea, not patented, and you can jump the deal as soon as I tell you it. Are you game?"

The ferryman said he was, and Kit liked his looks.

"Very well. You see that glacier. Take a pick-ax and wade into it. In a day you can have a decent groove from top to bottom. See the point? The Chilkoot and Crater Lake Consolidated Chute Corporation, Limited. You can charge fifty cents a hundred, get a hundred tons a day, and have no work to do but collect the coin."

Two hours later, Kit's ton was across the lake, and he had gained three days on himself. And when John Bellew overtook him, he was well along toward Deep Lake, another volcanic pit filled with glacial water.

The last pack, from Long Lake to Linderman, was three miles, and the trail, if trail it could be called, rose up over a thousand-foot hogback, dropped down a scramble of slippery rocks, and crossed a wide stretch of swamp. John Bellew remonstrated when he saw Kit rise with a hundred pounds in the straps and pick up a fifty-pound sack of flour and place it on top of the pack against the back of his neck.

"Come on, you chunk of the hard," Kit retorted. "Kick in on your bear-meat fodder and your one suit of underclothes."

But John Bellew shook his head. "I'm afraid I'm getting old, Christopher."

"You're only forty-eight. Do you realize that my grandfather, sir, your father, old Isaac Bellew, killed a man with his fist when he was sixty-nine years old?"

John Bellew grinned and swallowed his medicine.

"Avuncular, I want to tell you something important. I was raised a Lord Fauntleroy, but I can outpack you, outwalk you, put you on your back, or lick you with my fists right now."

John Bellew thrust out his hand and spoke solemnly. "Christopher, my boy, I believe you can do it. I believe you can do it with that pack on your back at the same time. You've made good, boy, though it's too unthinkable to believe."

Kit made the round trip of the last pack four times a day, which is to say that he daily covered twenty-four miles of mountain climbing, twelve miles of it under one hundred and fifty pounds. He was proud, hard, and tired, but in splendid physical condition. He ate and slept as he had never eaten and slept in his life, and as the end of the work came in sight, he was almost half sorry.

One problem half bothered him. He had learned that he could fall with a hundred-weight on his back and survive; but he was confident that if he fell with that additional fifty pounds across the back of his neck, it would break it clean. Each trail through the swamp was quickly churned bottomless by the thousands of packers, who were compelled continually to make new trails. It was while pioneering such a new trail that he solved the problem of the extra fifty.

The soft, lush surface gave way under him, he floundered, and pitched forward on his face. The fifty pounds crushed his face into the mud and went clear without snapping his neck. With the remaining hundred pounds on his back, he arose on hands and knees. But he got no farther. One arm sank to the shoulder, pillowing his cheek in the slush. As he drew this arm clear, the other sank to the shoulder. In this position it was impossible to slip the straps, and the hundred-weight on his back would not let him rise. On hands and knees, sinking first one arm and then the other, he made an effort to crawl to where the small sack of flour had fallen. But he exhausted himself without advancing, and so churned and broke the grass surface that a tiny pool of water began to form in perilous proximity to his mouth and nose.

He tried to throw himself on his back with the pack underneath, but this resulted in sinking both arms to the shoulders and gave him a foretaste of drowning. With exquisite patience, he slowly withdrew one sucking arm and then the other and rested them flat on the surface for the support of his chin. Then he began to call for help. After a time he heard the sound of feet sucking through the mud as some one advanced from behind.

"Lend a hand, friend," he said. "Throw out a life-line or something."

It was a woman's voice that answered, and he recognized it.

"If you'll unbuckle the straps I can get up."

The hundred pounds rolled into the mud with a soggy noise, and he slowly gained his feet.

"A pretty predicament," Miss Gastell laughed, at sight of his mud-covered face.

"Not at all," he replied airily. "My favorite physical-exercise stunt. Try it some time. It's great for the pectoral muscles and the spine." He wiped his face, flinging the slush from his hand with a snappy jerk.

"Oh!" she cried in recognition. "It's Mr.—ah—Mr. Smoke Bellew."

"I thank you gravely for your timely rescue and for that name," he answered. "I have been doubly baptized. Henceforth I shall insist always on being called Smoke Bellew. It is a strong name, and not without significance."

He paused, and then voice and expression became suddenly fierce.

"Do you know what I'm going to do?" he demanded. "I'm going back to the States. I am going to get married. I am going to raise a large family of children. And then, as the evening shadows fall, I shall gather those children about me and relate the sufferings and hardships I endured on the Chilkoot Trail. And if they don't cry—I repeat, if they don't cry, I'll lambaste the stuffing out of them."

The arctic winter came down apace. Snow that had come to stay lay six inches on the ground, and the ice was forming in quiet ponds, despite the fierce gales that blew. It was in the late afternoon, during a lull in such a gale, that Kit and John Bellew helped the cousins load the boat and watched it disappear down the lake in a snow-squall.

"And now a night's sleep and an early start in the morning," said John Bellew. "If we aren't stormbound at the summit we'll make Dyea tomorrow night, and if we have luck in catching a steamer we'll be in San Francisco in a week."

"Enjoyed your vacation?" Kit asked absently.

Their camp for that last night at Linderman was a melancholy remnant. Everything of use, including the tent, had been taken by the cousins. A tattered tarpaulin, stretched as a wind-break, partially sheltered them from the driving snow. Supper they cooked on an open fire in a couple of battered and discarded camp utensils. All that was left them were their blankets and food for several meals.

Only once during supper did Kit speak. "Avuncular," he said, "after this I wish you'd call me Smoke. I've made some smoke on this trail, haven't I?"

A few minutes later he wandered away in the direction of the village of tents that sheltered the goldrushers who were still packing or building their boats. He was gone several hours, and when he returned and slipped into his blankets John Bellew was asleep.

In the darkness of a gale-driven morning, Kit crawled out, built a fire in his stocking feet, by which he thawed out his frozen shoes, then boiled coffee and fried bacon. It was a chilly, miserable meal. As soon as it was finished, they strapped their blankets. As John Bellew turned to lead the way toward the Chilkoot Trail, Kit held out his hand.

"Good-by, avuncular," he said.

John Bellew looked at him and swore in his surprise.

"Don't forget, my name's Smoke," Kit chided.

"But what are you going to do?"

Kit waved his hand in a general direction northward over the storm-lashed lake. "What's the good of turning back after getting this far?" he asked. "Besides, I've got my taste of meat, and I like it. I'm going on."

"You're broke," protested John Bellew. "You have no outfit."

"I've got a job. Behold your nephew, Christopher Smoke Bellew! He's got a job. He's a gentleman's man. He's got a job at a hundred and fifty per month and grub. He's going down to Dawson with a couple of dudes and another gentleman's man—camp-cook, boat-man, and general all-around hustler. And O'Hara and *The Billow* can go to the devil. Good-by."

But John Bellew was dazed, and could only mutter, "I don't understand."

"They say the bald-face grizzlies are thick in the Yukon Basin," Kit explained. "Well, I've got only one suit of underclothes, and I'm going after the bear-meat, that's all."

IN A FAR COUNTRY

(Overland Monthly, June, 1899)

Here is a long stride from the carefree and good-humored adventures of Smoke Bellew. Carter Weatherbee and Percy Cuthfert, in this grim tale of *cheechakos*, are, like Smoke, "effete scions of civilization," but with dooming differences: the clerkish Weatherbee has no romance in his soul, and the "master of arts" and dabbler in oils and literature, Cuthfert, mistakes sentimentality for the spirit of romance and adventure. Both are shirks and grumblers; neither pulls his load. They are perfect victims for that "joint child of the Great Cold and the Great Silence," Fear of the North.

London believed there was a Code of the North, made poignant in its import by the sheer cosmic power of a land which barely countenanced any life at all in its awesome whiteness, quiet and cold, and rejected out-of-hand any humankind with marks of weakness. Jacques Baptiste and Sloper (a character based on a real-life Klondike comrade of London's, Ira Merritt Sloper, a wiry soldier-of-fortune who also figures in "Like Argus of the Ancient Times") live by the Code and manage to abide. But Cuthfert and Weatherbee break the Code—indeed, recognize no Code—and their fates are Darwinian and inexorable.

An obscure but historically accurate feature of this story is that these argonauts are not Chilkoot-bound as the avenue to the gold-fields of the Klondike; they are taking another route—via Edmonton to Lake Athabaska, across the Great Slave Lake and the Great Bear Lake, over the Mackenzie River to the Rat River, which feeds the

Porcupine River, which feeds, at last, the Yukon. They set out to reach Dawson via the longest and worst possible route. Goldrush chronicler Pierre Berton (in his *Klondike Fever*, 1968) describes the travail of two partners who had come almost four thousand miles up blizzard-swept mountain trails, through uncharted rapids and forest-country from Edmonton to a lonely cabin in the wilderness on the Porcupine. "When they were found," Berton writes, "they were frozen rock-solid beside a stew kettle hanging above a long-dead fire. The pot contained a pair of partly cooked moccasins embedded in a cake of ice. The rest was ashes."

These men may have been the prototypes for Cuthbert and Weatherbee.

London knew some of the problems of cabin fever from his experiences on Split-Up Island in the winter of 1897-98—lethargy, boredom, scurvy, among them, and he may have known of the fates of men similar to these "Kilkenny Cats," Cuthfert and Weatherbee.

In a May, 1899, letter to a friend, London saw no middle ground for "In a Far Country." He said, "It is either bosh, or good; either the worst or the best of the series I have turned out" for the *Overland*.

IN A FAR COUNTRY

WHEN A MAN journeys into a far country, he must be prepared to forget many of the things he has learned, and to acquire such customs as are inherent with existence in the new land; he must abandon the old ideals and the old gods, and oftentimes he must reverse the very codes by which his conduct has hitherto been shaped. To those who have the protean faculty of adaptability, the novelty of such change may even be a source of pleasure; but to those who happen to be hardened to the ruts in which they were created, the pressure of the altered environment is unbearable, and they chafe in body and in spirit under the new restrictions which they do not understand. This chafing is bound to act and react, producing divers evils and leading to various misfortunes. It were better for the man who cannot fit himself to the new groove to return to his own country; if he delay too long he will surely die.

The man who turns his back upon the comforts of an elder civilization, to face the savage youth, the primordial simplicity of the North, may estimate success at an inverse ratio to the quantity and quality of his hopelessly fixed habits. He will soon discover, if he be a fit candidate, that the material habits are the less important. The exchange of such things as a dainty menu for rough fare, of the stiff leather shoe for the soft, shapeless moccasin, of the feather bed for a couch in the snow, is after all a very easy matter. But his pinch will come in learning properly to shape his mind's attitude toward all things, and especially toward his fellow man. For the courtesies of ordinary life, he must substitute unselfishness, forbearance, and tolerance. Thus, and thus only, can he gain that pearl of great price—true comradeship. He must not say "Thank you;" he must mean it without opening his mouth, and prove it by responding in kind. In short, he must substitute the deed for the word, the spirit for the letter.

When the world rang with the tale of Arctic gold, and the lure of the North gripped the heartstrings of men, Carter Weatherbee threw up his snug clerkship, turned the half of his savings over to his wife, and with the remainder bought an outfit. There was no romance in his nature—the bondage of commerce had crushed all that; he was simply tired of the ceaseless grind, and wished to risk great hazards in view of corresponding returns. Like many another fool, disdaining the old trails used by the Northland pioneers for a score of years, he hurried to Edmonton in the spring of the year; and there, unluckily for his soul's welfare, he allied himself with a party of men.

There was nothing unusual about this party, except its plans. Even its goal, like that of all other parties, was the Klondike. But the route it had mapped out to attain that goal took away the breath of the hardiest native, born and bred to the vicissitudes of the Northwest. Even Jacques Baptiste, born of a Chippewa woman and a renegade *voyageur* (having raised his first whimpers in a deerskin lodge north of the sixty-fifth parallel, and had the same hushed by blissful sucks of raw tallow), was surprised. Though he sold his services to them and agreed to travel even to the never-opening ice, he shook his head ominously whenever his advice was asked.

Percy Cuthfert's evil star must have been in the ascendant, for he, too, joined this company of argonauts. He was an ordinary man, with a bank account as deep as his culture, which is saying a good deal. He had no reason to embark on such a venture—no reason in the world, save that he suffered from an abnormal development of sentimentality. He mistook this for the true spirit of romance and adventure. Many another man has done the like, and made as fatal a mistake.

The first break-up of spring found the party following the ice-run of Elk River. It was an imposing fleet, for the outfit was large, and they were accompanied by a disreputable contingent of half-breed *voyageurs* with their women and children. Day in and day out, they labored with the bateaux and canoes, fought mosquitoes and other kindred pests, or sweated and swore at the portages. Severe toil like this lays a man naked to the very roots of his soul, and ere Lake Athabasca was lost in the south, each member of the party had hoisted his true colors.

The two shirks and chronic grumblers were Carter Weatherbee and Percy Cuthfert. The whole party complained less of its aches and pains than did either of them. Not once did they volunteer for the thousand and one petty duties of the camp. A bucket of water to be brought, an extra armful of wood to be chopped, the dishes to be washed and wiped, a search to be made through the outfit for some suddenly indispensable article—and these two effete scions of civilization discovered sprains or blisters requiring instant attention. They were the first to turn in at night, with a score of tasks yet undone; the last to turn out in the morning, when the start should be in readiness before the breakfast was begun. They were the first to fall to at meal-time, the last to have a hand in the cooking; the first to dive for a slim delicacy, the last to discover they had added to their own another man's share. If they toiled at the oars, they slyly cut the water at each stroke and allowed the boat's momentum to float up the blade. They thought nobody noticed; but their comrades swore under their breaths and grew to hate them, while Jacques Baptiste sneered openly and damned them from morning till night. But Jacques Baptiste was no gentleman.

At the Great Slave, Hudson Bay dogs were purchased, and the fleet sank to the guards with its added burden of dried fish and pemmican. Then canoe and bateau answered to the swift current of the Mackenzie, and they plunged into the Great Barren Ground. Every lively-looking "feeder" was prospected, but the elusive "pay-dirt" danced ever to the north. At the Great Bear, overcome by the common dread of the Unknown Lands, their *voyageurs* began to desert, and Fort of Good Hope saw the last and bravest bending to the tow-lines as they bucked the current down which they had so treacherously glided. Jacques Baptiste alone remained. Had he not sworn to travel even to the never-opening ice?

The lying charts, compiled in main from hearsay, were now constantly consulted. And they felt the need of hurry, for the sun had already passed its northern solstice and was leading the winter south again. Skirting the shores of the bay, where the Mackenzie disembogues into the Arctic Ocean, they entered the mouth of the Little Peel River. Then began the arduous up-stream toil, and the two Incapables fared worse than ever. Tow-line and pole, paddle and tump-line, rapids and portages—such tortures served to give the one a deep disgust for great hazards, and printed for the other a fiery text on the true romance of adventure. One day they waxed mutinous, and being vilely cursed by Jacques Baptiste, turned, as worms sometimes will. But the half-breed thrashed the twain, and sent them, bruised and bleeding, about their work. It was the first time either had been man-handled.

Abandoning their river craft at the headwaters of the Little Peel, they consumed the rest of the summer in the great portage over the Mackenzie watershed to the West Rat. This little stream fed the Porcupine, which in turned joined the Yukon where that mighty highway of the North countermarches on the Arctic Circle. But they had lost in the race with winter, and one day they tied their rafts to the thick eddy-ice and hurried their goods ashore. That night the river jammed and broke several times; the following morning it had fallen asleep for good.

"We can't be more'n four hundred miles from the Yukon," concluded Sloper, multiplying his thumb nails by the scale of the map. The council, in which the two Incapables had whined to excellent disadvantage, was drawing to a close.

"Hudson Bay Post, long time ago. No use um now." Jacques Baptiste's father had made the trip for the Fur Company in the old days, incidentally marking the trail with a couple of frozen toes.

"Sufferin' cracky!" cried another of the party. "No whites?"

"Nary white," Sloper sententiously affirmed; "but it's only five hundred more up the Yukon to Dawson. Call it a rough thousand from here."

Weatherbee and Cuthfert groaned in chorus.

"How long'll that take, Baptiste?"

The half-breed figured for a moment. "Workum like hell, no man play out, ten—twenty—forty—fifty days. Um babies come" (designating the Incapables), "no can tell. Mebbe when hell freeze over; mebbe not then."

The manufacture of snowshoes and moccasins ceased. Somebody called the name of an absent member, who came out of an ancient cabin at the edge of the camp-fire and joined them. The cabin was one of the many mysteries which lurk in the vast recesses of the North. Built when and by whom, no man could tell. Two graves in the open, piled high with stones, perhaps contained the secret of those early wanderers. But whose hand had piled the stones?

The moment had come. Jacques Baptiste paused in the fitting of a harness and pinned the struggling dog in the snow. The cook made mute protest for delay, threw a handful of bacon into a noisy pot of beans, then came to attention. Sloper rose to his feet. His body was a ludicrous contrast to the healthy physiques of the Incapables. Yellow and weak, fleeing from a South American feverhole, he had not broken his flight across the zones, and was still able to toil with men. His weight was probably ninety pounds, with the heavy hunting-knife thrown in, and his grizzled hair told of a prime which had ceased to be. The fresh young muscles of either Weatherbee or Cuthfert were equal to ten times the endeavor of his; yet he could walk them into the earth in a day's journey. And all this day he had whipped his stronger comrades into venturing a thousand miles of the stiffest hardship man can conceive. He was the incarnation of the unrest of his race, and the old Teutonic stubbornness, dashed with the quick grasp and action of the Yankee, held the flesh in the bondage of the spirit.

"All those in favor of going on with the dogs as soon as the ice sets, say ay."

"Ay!" rang out eight voices—voices destined to string a trail of oaths along many a hundred miles of pain.

"Contrary minded?"

"No!" For the first time the Incapables were united without some compromise of personal interests.

"And what are you going to do about it?" Weatherbee added belligerently.

"Majority rule! Majority rule!" clamored the rest of the party.

"I know the expedition is liable to fall through if you don't come," Sloper replied sweetly; "but I guess, if we try real hard, we can manage to do without you. What do you say, boys?"

The sentiment was cheered to the echo.

"But I say, you know," Cuthfert ventured apprehensively; "what's a chap like me to do?"

"Ain't you coming with us?"

"No-o."

"Then do as you damn well please. We won't have nothing to say."

"Kind o' calkilate yuh might settle it with that canoodlin' pardner of yourn," suggested a heavy-going Westerner from the Dakotas, at the same time pointing out Weatherbee. "He'll be shore to ask yuh what yur a-goin' to do when it comes to cookin' an' gatherin' the wood."

"Then we'll consider it all arranged," concluded Sloper. "We'll pull out tomorrow, if we camp within five miles—just to get every-thing in running order and remember if we've forgotten anything."

The sleds groaned by on their steel-shod runners, and the dogs strained low in the harnesses in which they were born to die. Jacques Baptiste paused by the side of Sloper to get a last glimpse of the cabin. The smoke curled up pathetically from the Yukon stovepipe. The two Incapables were watching them from the doorway.

Sloper laid his hand on the other's shoulder.

"Jacques Baptiste, did you ever hear of the Kilkenny cats?"

The half-breed shook his head.

"Well, my friend and good comrade, the Kilkenny cats fought till neither hide, nor hair, nor yowl, was left. You understand?—till nothing was left. Very good. Now, these two men don't like work. They won't work. We know that. They'll be all alone in that cabin all winter—a mighty long, dark winter. Kilkenny cats—well?"

The Frenchman in Baptiste shrugged his shoulders, but the Indian in him was silent. Nevertheless, it was an eloquent shrug, pregnant with prophecy.

Things prospered in the little cabin at first. The rough badinage of their comrades had made Weatherbee and Cuthfert conscious of the mutual responsibility which had devolved upon them; besides, there was not so much work after all for two healthy men. And the removal of the cruel whip-hand, or in other words the bulldozing half-breed, had brought with it a joyous reaction. At first, each strove to outdo the other, and they performed petty tasks with an unction which would have opened the eyes of their comrades who were now wearing out bodies and souls on the Long Trail.

All care was banished. The forest, which shouldered in upon them from three sides, was an inexhaustible woodyard. A few yards from their door slept the Porcupine, and a hole through its winter robe formed a bubbling spring of water, crystal clear and painfully cold. But they soon grew to find fault with even that. The hole would persist in freezing up, and thus gave them many a miserable hour of ice-chopping. The unknown builders of the cabin had extended the side-logs so as to support a cache at the rear. In this was stored the bulk of the party's provisions. Food was there, without stint, for three times the men who were fated to live upon it. But the most of it was the kind which built up brawn and sinew, but did not tickle the palate. True, there was sugar in plenty for two ordinary men; but these two were little else than children. They early discovered the virtues of hot water judiciously saturated with sugar, and they prodigally swam their flapjacks and soaked their crusts in the rich, white syrup. Then coffee and tea, and especially the dried fruits, made disastrous inroads upon it. The first words they had were over the sugar question. And it is a really serious thing when two men, wholly dependent upon each other for company, begin to quarrel.

Weatherbee loved to discourse blatantly on politics, while Cuthfert, who had been prone to clip his coupons and let the commonwealth jog on as best it might, either ignored the subject or delivered himself of startling epigrams. But the clerk was too obtuse to appreciate the clever shaping of thought, and this waste of ammunition irritated Cuthfert. He had been used to blinding people by his brilliancy, and it worked him quite a hardship, this loss of an audience. He felt personally aggrieved and unconsciously held his mutton-head companion responsible for it.

Save existence, they had nothing in common—came in touch on no single point. Weatherbee was a clerk who had known naught but clerking all his life; Cuthfert was a master of arts, a dabbler in oils, and had written not a little. The one was a lower-class man who considered himself a gentleman, and the other was a gentleman who knew himself to be such. From this it may be remarked that a man can be a gentleman without possessing the first instinct of true comradeship. The clerk was as sensuous as the other was æsthetic, and his love adventures, told at great length and chiefly coined from his imagination, affected the supersensitive master of arts in the same way as so many whiffs of sewer gas. He deemed the clerk a filthy, uncultured brute, whose place was in the muck with the swine, and told him so; and he was reciprocally informed that he was a milk-and-water sissy and a cad. Weatherbee could not have defined "cad" for his life; but it satisfied its purpose, which after all seems the main point in life.

Weatherbee flatted every third note and sang such songs as "The Boston Burglar" and "The Handsome Cabin Boy," for hours at a time, while Cuthfert wept with rage, till he could stand it no longer and fled into the outer cold. But there was no escape. The intense frost could not be endured for long at a time, and the little cabin crowded them—beds, stove, table, and all—into a space of ten by twelve. The very presence of either became a personal affront to the other, and they lapsed into sullen silences which increased in length and strength as the days went by. Occasionally, the flash of an eye or the curl of a lip got the better of them, though they strove to wholly ignore each other during these mute periods. And a great wonder sprang up in the breast of each, as to how God had ever come to create the other.

With little to do, time became an intolerable burden to them. This naturally made them still lazier. They sank into a physical lethargy which there was no escaping, and which made them rebel at the performance of the smallest chore. One morning when it was his turn to cook the common breakfast, Weatherbee rolled out of his blankets, and to the snoring of his companion, lighted first the slush-lamp and then the fire. The kettles were frozen hard, and there was no water in the cabin with which to wash. But he did not mind that. Waiting for it to thaw, he sliced the bacon and plunged into the hateful task of breakfast-making. Cuthfert had been slyly watching through his half-closed lids. Consequently there was a scene, in which they fervently blessed each other, and agreed, thenceforth, that each do his own cooking. A week later, Cuthfert neglected his morning ablutions, but none the less complacently ate the meal which he had cooked. Weatherbee grinned. After that the foolish custom of washing passed out of their lives.

As the sugar-pile and other little luxuries dwindled, they began to be afraid they were not getting their proper shares, and in order that they might not be robbed, they fell to gorging themselves. The luxuries suffered in this gluttonous contest, as did also the men. In the absence of fresh vegetables and exercise, their blood became impoverished, and a loathsome, purplish rash crept over their bodies. Yet they refused to heed the warning. Next, their muscles and joints began to swell, the flesh turning black, while their mouths, gums, and lips took on the color of rich cream. Instead of being drawn together by their misery, each gloated over the other's symptoms as the scurvy took its course.

They lost all regard for personal appearance, and for that matter, common decency. The cabin became a pigpen, and never once were the beds made or fresh pine boughs laid underneath. Yet they could not keep to their blankets, as they would have wished; for the frost was inexorable, and the fire box consumed much fuel. The hair on their heads and faces grew long and shaggy, while their garments would have disgusted a ragpicker. But they did not care. They were sick, and there was no one to see; besides, it was very painful to move about.

To all this was added a new trouble—the Fear of the North. This Fear was the joint child of the Great Cold and the Great Silence, and was born in the darkness of December, when the sun dipped below the southern horizon for good. It affected them according to their natures. Weatherbee fell prey to the grosser superstitions, and did his best to resurrect the spirits which slept in the forgotten graves. It was a fascinating thing, and in his dreams they came to him from out of the cold, and snuggled into his blankets, and told him of their toils and troubles ere they died. He shrank away from the clammy contact as they drew closer and twined their frozen limbs about him, and when they whispered in his ear of things to come, the cabin rang with his frightened shrieks. Cuthfert did not understand—for they no longer spoke—and when thus awakened he invariably grabbed for his revolver. Then he would sit up in bed, shivering nervously, with the weapon trained on the unconscious dreamer. Cuthfert deemed the man going mad, and so came to fear for his life.

His own malady assumed a less concrete form. The mysterious artisan who had laid the cabin, log by log, had pegged a wind-vane to the ridge-pole. Cuthfert noticed it always pointed south, and one day, irritated by its steadfastness of purpose, he turned it toward the east. He watched eagerly, but never a breath came by to disturb it. Then he turned the vane to the north, swearing never again to touch it till the wind did blow. But the air frightened him with its unearthly calm, and he often rose in the middle of the night to see if the vane had veered—ten degrees would have satisfied him. But no, it poised above him as unchangeable as fate. His imagination ran riot, till it became to him a fetich. Sometimes he followed the path it pointed across the dismal dominions, and allowed his soul to become saturated with the Fear. He dwelt upon the unseen and the unknown till the burden of eternity appeared to be crushing him. Everything in the Northland had that crushing effect—the absence of life and motion; the darkness, the infinite peace of the brooding land; the ghastly silence, which made the echo of each heart-beat a sacrilege; the solemn forest which seemed to guard an awful, inexpressible something, which neither word nor thought could compass.

The world he had so recently left, with its busy nations and great enterprises, seemed very far away. Recollections occasionally obtruded—recollections of marts and galleries and crowded thoroughfares, of evening dress and social functions, of good men and dear women he had known—but they were dim memories of a life he had lived long centuries agone, on some other planet. This phantasm was the Reality. Standing beneath the wind-vane, his eyes fixed on the polar skies, he could not bring himself to realize that the Southland really existed, that at that very moment it was a-roar with life and action. There was no Southland, no men being born of women, no giving and taking in marriage. Beyond his bleak sky-line there stretched vast solitudes, and beyond these still vaster solitudes. There were no lands of sunshine, heavy with the perfume of flowers. Such things were only old dreams of paradise. The sunlands of the West and the spicelands of the East, the smiling Arcadias and blissful Islands of the Blest—ha! ha! His laughter split the void and shocked him with its unwonted sound. There was no sun. This was the Universe, dead and cold and dark, and he its only citizen. Weatherbee? At such moments Weatherbee did not count. He was a Caliban, a monstrous phantom, fettered to him for untold ages, the penalty of some forgotten crime.

He lived with Death among the dead, emasculated by the sense of his own insignificance, crushed by the passive mastery of the slumbering ages. The magnitude of all things appalled him. Everything partook of the superlative save himself—the perfect cessation of wind and motion, the immensity of the snow-covered wilderness, the height of the sky and the depth of the silence. That wind-vane—if it would only move. If a thunderbolt would fall, or the forest flare up in flame. The rolling up of the heavens as a scroll, the crash of Doom—anything, anything! But no, nothing moved; the Silence crowded in, and the Fear of the North laid icy fingers on his heart.

Once, like another Crusoe, by the edge of the river he came upon a track—the faint tracery of a showshoe rabbit on the delicate snow-crust. It was a revelation. There was life in the Northland. He would follow it, look upon it, gloat over it. He forgot his swollen muscles, plunging through the deep snow in an ecstasy of anticipation. The forest swallowed him up, and the brief midday twilight vanished; but he pursued his quest till exhausted nature asserted itself and laid him helpless in the snow. There he groaned and cursed his folly, and knew the track to be the fancy of his brain; and late that night he dragged himself into the cabin on hands and knees, his cheeks frozen and a strange numbness about his feet. Weatherbee grinned malevolently, but made no offer to help him. He thrust needles into his toes and thawed them out by the stove. A week later mortification set in.

But the clerk had his own troubles. The dead men came out of their graves more frequently now, and rarely left him, waking or sleeping. He grew to wait and dread their coming, never passing the twin cairns without a shudder. One night they came to him in his sleep and led him forth to an appointed task. Frightened into inarticulate horror, he awoke between the heaps of stones and fled wildly to the cabin. But he had lain there for some time, for his feet and cheeks were also frozen.

Sometimes he became frantic at their insistent presence, and danced about the cabin, cutting the empty air with an axe, and smashing everything within reach. During these ghostly encounters, Cuthfert huddled into his blankets and followed the madman about with a cocked revolver, ready to shoot him if he came too near. But, recovering from one of these spells, the clerk noticed the weapon trained upon him. His suspicions were aroused, and thenceforth he, too, lived in fear of his life. They watched each other closely after that, and faced about in startled fright whenever either passed behind the other's back. This apprehensiveness became a mania which controlled them even in their sleep. Through mutual fear they tacitly let the slush-lamp burn all night, and saw to a plentiful supply of bacon-grease before retiring. The slightest movement on the part of one was sufficient to arouse the other, and many a still watch their gazes countered as they shook beneath their blankets with fingers on the trigger-guards.

What with the Fear of the North, the mental strain, and the ravages of the disease, they lost all semblance of humanity, taking on the appearance of wild beasts, hunted and desperate. Their cheeks and noses, as an aftermath of the freezing, had turned black. Their frozen toes had begun to drop away at the first and second joints. Every movement brought pain, but the fire box was insatiable, wringing a ransom of torture from their miserable bodies. Day in, day out, it demanded its food—a veritable pound of flesh—and they dragged themselves into the forest to chop wood on their knees. Once, crawling thus in search of dry sticks, unknown to each other they entered a thicket from opposite sides. Suddenly, without warning, two peering death's-heads confronted each other. Suffering had so transformed them that recognition was impossible. They sprang to their feet, shrieking with terror, and dashed away on their mangled stumps; and falling at the cabin door, they clawed and scratched like demons till they discovered their mistake.

Occasionally they lapsed normal, and during one of these sane intervals, the chief bone of contention, the sugar, had been divided equally between them. They guarded their separate sacks, stored up in the cache, with jealous eyes; for there were but a few cupfuls left, and they were totally devoid of faith in each other. But one day Cuthfert made a mistake. Hardly able to move, sick with pain, with his head swimming and eyes blinded, he crept into the cache, sugar cannister in hand, and mistook Weatherbee's sack for his own.

January had been born but a few days when this occurred. The sun had some time since passed its lowest southern declination, and at meridian now threw flaunting streaks of yellow light upon the northern sky. On the day following his mistake with the sugarbag, Cuthfert found himself feeling better, both in body and in spirit. As noontime drew near and the day brightened, he dragged himself outside to feast on the evanescent glow, which was to him an earnest of the sun's future intentions. Weatherbee was also feeling somewhat better, and crawled out beside him. They propped themselves in the snow beneath the moveless wind-vane, and waited.

The stillness of death was about them. In other climes, when nature falls into such moods, there is a subdued air of expectancy, a waiting for some small voice to take up the broken strain. Not so in the North. The two men had lived seeming æons in this ghostly peace. They could remember no song of the past; they could conjure no song of the future. This unearthly calm had always been—the tranquil silence of eternity.

Their eyes were fixed upon the north. Unseen, behind their backs, behind the towering mountains to the south, the sun swept toward the zenith of another sky than theirs. Sole spectators of the mighty canvas, they watched the false dawn slowly grow. A faint flame began to glow and smoulder. It deepened in intensity, ringing the changes of reddish-yellow, purple, and saffron. So bright did it become that Cuthfert thought the sun must surely be behind it—a miracle, the sun rising in the north! Suddenly, without warning and without fading, the canvas was swept clean. There was no color in the sky. The light had gone out of the day. They caught their breaths in half-sobs. But lo! the air was a-glint with particles of scintillating frost, and there, to the north, the wind-vane lay in vague outline on the snow. A shadow! A shadow! It was exactly midday. They jerked their heads hurriedly to the south. A golden rim peeped over the mountain's snowy shoulder, smiled upon them an instant, then dipped from sight again.

There were tears in their eyes as they sought each other. A strange softening came over them. They felt irresistibly drawn toward each other. The sun was coming back again. It would be with them to-morrow, and the next day, and the next. And it would stay longer every visit, and a time would come when it would ride their heaven day and night, never once dropping below the sky-line. There would be no night. The ice-locked winter would be broken; the winds would blow and the forests answer; the land would bathe in the blessed sunshine, and life renew. Hand in hand, they would quit this horrid dream and journey back to the Southland. They lurched blindly forward, and their hands met—their poor maimed hands, swollen and distorted beneath their mittens.

But the promise was destined to remain unfulfilled. The North-land is the Northland, and men work out their souls by strange rules, which other men, who have not journeyed into far countries, cannot come to understand.

An hour later, Cuthfert put a pan of bread into the oven, and fell to speculating on what the surgeons could do with his feet when he got back. Home did not seem so very far away now. Weatherbee was rummaging in the cache. Of a sudden, he raised a whirlwind of blasphemy, which in turn ceased with startling abruptness. The other man had robbed his sugar-sack. Still, things might have happened differently, had not the two dead men come out from under the stones and hushed the hot words in his throat. They led him quite gently from the cache, which he forgot to close. That consummation was reached; that something they had whispered to him in his dreams was about to happen. They guided him gently, very gently, to the woodpile, where they put the axe in his hands. Then they helped him shove open the cabin door, and he felt sure they shut it after him—at least he heard it slam and the latch fall sharply into place. And he knew they were waiting just without, waiting for him to do his task.

"Carter! I say, Carter!"

Percy Cuthfert was frightened at the look on the clerk's face, and he made haste to put the table between them.

Carter Weatherbee followed, without haste and without enthusiasm. There was neither pity nor passion in his face, but rather the patient, stolid look of one who has certain work to do and goes about it methodically.

"I say, what's the matter?"

The clerk dodged back, cutting off his retreat to the door, but never opening his mouth.

"I say, Carter, I say; let's talk. There's a good chap."

The master of arts was thinking rapidly, now, shaping a skillful flank movement on the bed where his Smith & Wesson lay. Keeping his eyes on the madman, he rolled backward on the bunk, at the same time clutching the pistol.

"Carter!"

The powder flashed full in Weatherbee's face, but he swung his weapon and leaped forward. The axe bit deeply at the base of his spine, and Percy Cuthfert felt all consciousness of his lower limbs leave him. Then the clerk fell heavily upon him, clutching him by the throat with feeble fingers. The sharp bite of the axe had caused Cuthfert to drop the pistol, and as his lungs panted for release, he fumbled aimlessly for it among the blankets. Then he remembered. He slid a hand up the clerk's belt to the sheath-knife; and they drew very close to each other in that last clinch.

Percy Cuthfert felt his strength leave him. The lower portion of his body was useless. The inert weight of Weatherbee crushed him—crushed him and pinned him there like a bear under a trap. The cabin became filled with a familiar odor, and he knew the bread to be burning. Yet what did it matter? He would never need it. And there were all of six cupfuls of sugar in the cache—if he had foreseen this he would not have been so saving the last several days. Would the wind-vane ever move? It might even be veering now. Why now? Had he not seen the sun today? He would go and see. No; it was impossible to move. He had not thought the clerk so heavy a man.

How quickly the cabin cooled! The fire must be out. The cold was forcing in. It must be below zero already, and the ice creeping up the inside of the door. He could not see it, but his past experience enabled him to gauge its progress by the cabin's temperature. The lower hinge must be white ere now. Would the tale of this ever reach the world? How would his friends take it? They would read it over their coffee, most likely, and talk it over at the clubs. He could see them very clearly. "Poor Old Cuthfert," they murmured; "not such a bad sort of a chap, after all." He smiled at their eulogies, and passed on in search of a Turkish bath. It was the same old crowd upon the streets. Strange, they did not notice his moosehide moccasins and tattered German socks! He would take a cab. And after a bath a shave would not be bad. No; he would eat first. Steak, and potatoes, and green things—how fresh it all was! And what was that? Squares of honey, streaming liquid amber! But why did they bring so much? Ha! ha! he could never eat it all. Shine! Why certainly. He put his foot on the box. The bootblack looked curiously up at him, and he remembered his moosehide moccasins and went away hastily.

Hark! The wind-vane must be surely spinning. No; a mere singing in his ears. That was all—a mere singing. The ice must have passed the latch by now. More likely the upper hinge was covered. Between the moss-chinked roof-poles, little points of frost began to appear. How slowly they grew! No; not so slowly. There was a new one, and there another. Two—three—four; they were coming too fast to count. There were two growing together. And there, a third had joined them. Why, there were no more spots. They had run together and formed a sheet.

Well, he could have company. If Gabriel ever broke the silence of the North, they would stand together, hand in hand, before the great White Throne. And God would judge them, God would judge them!

Then Percy Cuthfert closed his eyes and dropped off to sleep.

TO BUILD A FIRE

(The Century Magazine, August, 1908)

Of all of Jack London's prodigious flow of fiction in his brief but spectacular writing career (the years 1899 to 1916), "To Build a Fire" has had almost a life of its own. *Two* lives, in fact.

The original version of the story was published in *The Youth's Companion* in 1902 and London regarded that first incarnation of it as a "juvenile." It had a happy ending, too, something required by the magazine.

Beyond acknowledging to *Century* editor R. C. Gilder the origin of the story, London himself paid it little mind: it was a 7,500-word tale and *Century* bought it for $400 after *Success* magazine, an ironic market, to be sure, rejected it as "too gruesome." The sale was made at a propitious time for London, at the critical moment when he was financing the repair of the *Snark*, his fifty-seven-foot, $30,000 ketch, which he sailed on April 23, 1907, from San Francisco to Hawaii on the first leg of his intended round-the-world voyage. The *Snark* turned out to be, at least at the start of the voyage, a nightmare instead of a dream—it leaked like a sieve, the expensive reserve engines failed, the watertight compartments shipped water, the copper hull sheathing had to be replaced. At Pearl Harbor, with the *Snark* being repaired, re-crewed and refitted, London wrote or completed six short stories, including "To Build a Fire," and began work on his splendid autobiographical novel, *Martin Eden.*

Whatever London's own view of it, "To Build a Fire" has become an enduring American classic of short fiction. It has been depthfully analyzed by literary scholars and its rhythmic, portentous opening passage quoted countless times as an example of the conveyance of mood and atmosphere through simple, stark language.

Readers who remember Jack London from their youth usually identify him with this story and *The Call of the Wild*.

The unnamed protagonist here is also a *cheechako* but how different he is from Smoke Bellew and the "Kilkenny Cats" of "In a Far Country"! His only mistake is that he has not taken the advice of the oldtimer at Sulphur Creek who tried to tell him how cold it could get in the Klondike and why he should never travel alone. The nameless man is neither good nor bad, neither brilliant nor a fool; he is merely human. He handles himself well in a grave situation but "never sees beyond the surface of things" and, without the luxury of the instinct that permits the wolf-dog to survive, he is doomed by his inadequacies and what James McClintock (in *White Logic*, 1975) calls "his masculine pride in his rationality."

Whoever he was, we know him, we have sympathy and empathy for him: He mirrors us far more than Smoke, Cuthfert, or Weatherbee.

TO BUILD A FIRE

DAY HAD BROKEN cold and gray, exceedingly cold and gray, when the man turned aside from the main Yukon trail and climbed the high earth-bank, where a dim and little-traveled trail led eastward through the fat spruce timberland. It was a steep bank, and he paused for breath at the top, excusing the act to himself by looking at his watch. It was nine o'clock. There was no sun nor hint of sun, though there was not a cloud in the sky. It was a clear day, and yet there seemed an intangible pall over the face of things, a subtle gloom that made the day dark, and that was due to the absence of sun. This fact did not worry the man. He was used to the lack of sun. It had been days since he had seen the sun, and he knew that a few more days must pass before that cheerful orb, due south, would just peep above the sky-line and dip immediately from view.

The man flung a look back along the way he had come. The Yukon lay a mile wide and hidden under three feet of ice. On top of this ice were as many feet of snow. It was all pure white, rolling in gentle, undulations where the ice-jams of the freeze-up had formed. North and south, as far as his eye could see, it was unbroken white, save for a dark hair-line that curved and twisted from around the spruce-covered island to the south, and that curved and twisted away into the north, where it disappeared behind another spruce-covered island. This dark hair-line was the trail—the main trail—that led south five hundred miles to the Chilkoot Pass, Dyea, and salt water; and that led north seventy miles to Dawson, and still on to the north a thousand miles to Nulato, and finally to St. Michael on Bering Sea, a thousand miles and half a thousand more.

But all this—the mysterious, far-reaching hair-line trail, the absence of sun from the sky, the tremendous cold, and the strangeness and weirdness of it all—made no impression on the man. It was not because he was long used to it. He was a newcomer in the land, a *chechaquo,* and this was his first winter. The trouble with him was that he was without imagination. He was quick and alert in the things of life, but only in the things, and not in the signficances. Fifty degrees below zero meant eighty-odd degrees of frost. Such fact impressed him as being cold and uncomfortable, and that was all. It did not lead him to meditate upon his frailty in general, able only to live within certain narrow limits of heat and cold; and from there on it did not lead him to the conjectural field of immortality and man's place in the universe. Fifty degrees below zero stood for a bite of frost that hurt and that must be guarded against by the use of mittens, ear-flaps, warm moccasins, and thick socks. Fifty degrees below zero was to him just precisely fifty degrees below zero. That there should be anything more to it than that was a thought that never entered his head.

As he turned to go on, he spat speculatively. There was a sharp, explosive crackle that startled him. He spat again. And again, in the air, before it could fall to the snow, the spittle crackled. He knew that at fifty below spittle crackled on the snow, but this spittle had crackled in the air. Undoubtedly it was colder than fifty below—how much colder he did not know. But the temperature did not matter. He was bound for the old claim on the left fork of Henderson Creek, where the boys were already. They had come over across the divide from the Indian Creek country, while he had come the roundabout way to take a look at the possibilities of getting out logs in the spring from the islands in the Yukon. He would be in to camp by six o'clock; a bit after dark, it was true, but the boys would be there, a fire would be going, and a hot supper would be ready. As for lunch, he pressed his hand against the protruding bundle under his jacket. It was also under his shirt, wrapped up in a handkerchief and lying against the naked skin. It was the only way to keep the biscuits from freezing. He smiled agreeably to himself as he thought of those biscuits, each cut open and sopped in bacon grease, and each enclosing a generous slice of fried bacon.

He plunged in among the big spruce trees. The trail was faint. A foot of snow had fallen since the last sled had passed over, and he was glad he was without a sled, travelling light. In fact, he carried nothing but the lunch wrapped in the handkerchief. He was surprised, however, at the cold. It certainly was cold, he concluded, as he rubbed his numb nose and cheek-bones with his mittened hand. He was a warm-whiskered man, but the hair on his face did not protect the high cheek-bones and the eager nose that thrust itself aggressively into the frosty air.

At the man's heels trotted a dog, a big native husky, the proper wolf-dog, gray-coated and without any visible or temperamental difference from its brother, the wild wolf. The animal was depressed by the tremendous cold. It knew that it was no time for traveling. Its instinct told a truer tale than was told to the man by the man's judgment. In reality, it was not merely colder than fifty below zero; it was colder than sixty below, than seventy below. It was seventy-five below zero. Since the freezing-point is thirty-two above zero, it meant that one hundred and seven degrees of frost obtained. The dog did not know anything about thermometers. Possibly in its brain there was no sharp consciousness of a condition of very cold such as was in the man's brain. But the brute had its instinct. It experienced a vague but menacing apprehension that subdued it and made it slink along at the man's heels, and that made it question eagerly every unwonted movement of the man as if expecting him to go into camp or to seek shelter somewhere and build a fire. The dog had learned fire, and it wanted fire, or else to burrow under the snow and cuddle its warmth away from the air.

The frozen moisture of its breathing had settled on its fur in a fine powder of frost, and especially were its jowls, muzzle, and eyelashes whitened by its crystalled breath. The man's red beard and mustache were likewise frosted, but more solidly, the deposit taking the form of ice and increasing with every warm, moist breath he exhaled. Also, the man was chewing tobacco, and the muzzle of ice held his lips so rigidly that he was unable to clear his chin when he expelled the juice. The result was that a crystal beard of the color and solidity of amber was increasing its length on his chin. If he fell down it would shatter itself, like glass, into brittle fragments. But he did not mind the appendage. It was the penalty all tobacco-chewers paid in that country, and he had been out before in two cold snaps. They had not been so cold as this, he knew, but by the spirit thermometer at Sixty Mile he knew they had been registered at fifty below and at fifty-five.

He held on through the level stretch of woods for several miles, crossed a wide flat of niggerheads, and dropped down a bank to the frozen bed of a small stream. This was Henderson Creek, and he knew he was ten miles from the forks. He looked at his watch. It was ten o'clock. He was making four miles an hour, and he calculated that he would arrive at the forks at half-past twelve. He decided to celebrate that event by eating his lunch there.

The dog dropped in again at his heels, with a tail drooping discouragement, as the man swung along the creek-bed. The furrow of the old sled-trail was plainly visible, but a dozen inches of snow covered the marks of the last runners. In a month no man had come up or down that silent creek. The man held steadily on. He was not much given to thinking, and just then particularly he had nothing to think about save that he would eat lunch at the forks and that at six o'clock he would be in camp with the boys. There was nobody to talk to; and, had there been, speech would have been impossible because of the ice-muzzle on his mouth. So he continued monotonously to chew tobacco and to increase the length of his amber beard.

Once in a while the thought reiterated itself that it was very cold and that he had never experienced such cold. As he walked along he rubbed his cheek-bones and nose with the back of his mittened hand. He did this automatically, now and again changing hands.

But rub as he would, the instant he stopped his cheek-bones went numb, and the following instant the end of his nose went numb. He was sure to frost his cheeks; he knew that, and experienced a pang of regret that he had not devised a nose-strap of the sort Bud wore in cold snaps. Such a strap passed across the cheeks, as well, and saved them. But it didn't matter much, after all. What were frosted cheeks? A bit painful, that was all; they were never serious.

Empty as the man's mind was of thoughts, he was keenly obser-vant, and he noticed the changes in the creek, the curves and bends and timber-jams, and always he sharply noted where he placed his feet. Once, coming around a bend, he shied abruptly, like a startled horse, curved away from the place where he had been walking, and retreated several paces back along the trail. The creek he knew was frozen clear to the bottom—no creek could contain water in that arctic winter—but he knew also that there were springs that bubbled out from the hillsides and ran along under the snow and on top of the ice of the creek. He knew that the coldest snaps never froze these springs, and he knew likewise their danger. They were traps. They hid pools of water under the snow that might be three inches deep, or three feet. Sometimes a skin of ice half an inch thick covered them, and in turn was covered by the snow. Sometimes they were alternate layers of water and ice-skin, so that when one broke through he kept on breaking through for a while, sometimes wetting himself to the waist.

That was why he had shied in such panic. He had felt the give under his feet and heard the crackle of a snow-hidden ice-skin. And to get his feet wet in such a temperature meant trouble and danger. At the very least it meant delay, for he would be forced to stop and build a fire, and under its protection to bare his feet while he dried his socks and moccasins. He stood and studied the creek-bed and its banks, and decided that the flow of water came from the right. He reflected awhile, rubbing his nose and cheeks, then skirted to the left, stepping gingerly and testing the footing for each step. Once clear of the danger, he took a fresh chew of tobacco and swung along at his four-mile gait.

In the course of the next two hours he came upon several similar traps. Usually the snow above the hidden pools had a sunken, can-died appearance that advertised the danger. Once again, however, he had a close call; and once, suspecting danger, he compelled the dog to go on in front. The dog did not want to go. It hung back until the man shoved it forward, and then it went quickly across the white, unbroken surface. Suddenly it broke through, floundered to one side, and got away to firmer footing. It had wet its forefeet and legs, and almost immediately the water that clung to it turned to ice. It made quick efforts to lick the ice off its legs, then dropped down in the snow and began to bite out the ice that had formed between the toes. This was a matter of instinct. To permit the ice to remain would mean sore feet. It did not know this. It merely obeyed the mysterious prompting that arose from the deep crypts of its being. But the man knew, having achieved a judgment on the subject, and he removed the mitten from his right hand and helped tear out the ice-particles. He did not expose his fingers more than a minute, and was astonished at the swift numbness that smote them. It certainly was cold. He pulled on the mitten hastily, and beat the hand savagely across his chest.

At twelve o'clock the day was at its brightest. Yet the sun was too far south on its winter journey to clear the horizon. The bulge of the earth intervened between it and Henderson Creek, where the man walked under a clear sky at noon and cast no shadow. At half-past twelve, to the minute, he arrived at the forks of the creek. He was pleased at the speed he had made. If he kept it up, he would certainly be with the boys by six. He unbuttoned his jacket and shirt and drew forth his lunch. The action consumed no more than a quarter of a minute, yet in that brief moment the numbness laid hold of the exposed fingers. He did not put the mitten on, but, instead, struck the fingers a dozen sharp smashes against his leg. Then he sat down on a snow-covered log to eat. The sting that followed upon the striking of his fingers against his leg ceased so quickly that he was startled. He had had no chance to take a bite of biscuit. He struck the fingers repeatedly and returned them to the mitten, baring the other hand for the purpose of eating. He tried to take a mouthful, but the ice-muzzle prevented. He had forgotten to build a fire and thaw out. He chuckled at his foolishness, and as he chuckled he noted the numbness creeping into the exposed fingers. Also, he noted that the stinging which had first come to his toes when he sat down was already passing away. He wondered whether the toes were warm or numb. He moved them inside the moccasins and decided that they were numb.

He pulled the mitten on hurriedly and stood up. He was a bit frightened. He stamped up and down until the sting returned into the feet. It certainly was cold, was his thought. That man from Sulphur Creek had spoken the truth when telling how cold it sometimes got in the country. And he had laughed at him at the time! That showed one must not be too sure of things. There was no mistake about it, it *was* cold. He strode up and down, stamping his feet and threshing his arms, until reassured by the returning warmth. Then he got out matches and proceeded to make a fire. From the undergrowth, where high water of the previous spring had lodged a supply of seasoned twigs, he got his fire-wood. Working carefully from a small beginning, he soon had a roaring fire, over which he thawed the ice from his face and in the protection of which he ate his biscuits. For the moment the cold of space was outwitted. The dog took satisfaction in the fire, stretching out close enough for warmth and far enough away to escape being singed.

When the man had finished, he filled his pipe and took his comfortable time over a smoke. Then he pulled on his mittens, settled the earflaps of his cap firmly about his ears, and took the creek trail up the left fork. The dog was disappointed and yearned back toward the fire. This man did not know cold. Possibly all the generations of his ancestry had been ignorant of cold, of real cold, of cold one hundred and seven degrees below freezing-point. But the dog knew; all its ancestry knew, and it had inherited the knowledge. And it knew that it was not good to walk abroad in such fearful cold. It was the time to lie snug in a hole in the snow and wait for a curtain of cloud to be drawn across the face of outer space whence this cold came. On the other hand, there was no keen intimacy between the dog and the man. The one was the toil-slave of the other, and the only caresses it had ever received were the caresses of the whip-lash and of harsh and menacing throat-sounds that threatened the whip-lash. So the dog made no effort to communicate its apprehension to the man. It was not concerned in the welfare of the man; it was for its own sake that it yearned back toward the fire. But the man whistled, and spoke to it with the sound of whip-lashes, and the dog swung in at the man's heels and followed after.

The man took a chew of tobacco and proceeded to start a new amber beard. Also, his moist breath quickly powdered with white his mustache, eyebrows, and lashes. There did not seem to be so many springs on the left fork of the Henderson, and for half an hour the man saw no signs of any. And then it happened. At a place where there were no signs, where the soft, unbroken snow seemed to advertise solidity beneath, the man broke through. It was not deep. He wet himself to the knees before he floundered out to the firm crust.

He was angry, and cursed his luck aloud. He had hoped to get into camp with the boys at six o'clock, and this would delay him an hour, for he would have to build a fire and dry out his foot-gear. This was imperative at that low temperature—he knew that much; and he turned aside to the bank, which he climbed. On top, tangled in the underbrush about the trunks of several small spruce trees, was a high-water deposit of dry fire-wood—sticks and twigs, principally, but also larger portions of seasoned branches and fine, dry, last-year's grasses. He threw down several large pieces on top of the snow. This served for a foundation and prevented the young flame from drowning itself in the snow it otherwise would melt. The flame he got by touching a match to a small shred of birch-bark that he took from his pocket. This burned even more readily than paper. Placing it on the foundation, he fed the young flame with wisps of dry grass and with the tiniest dry twigs.

He worked slowly and carefully, keenly aware of his danger. Gradually, as the flame grew stronger, he increased the size of the twigs with which he fed it. He squatted in the snow, pulling the twigs out from their entanglement in the brush and feeding directly to the flame. He knew there must be no failure. When it is seventy-five below zero, a man must not fail in his first attempt to build a fire—that is, if his feet are wet. If his feet are dry, and he fails, he can run along the trail for half a mile and restore his circulation. But the circulation of wet and freezing feet cannot be restored by running when it is seventy-five below. No matter how fast he runs, the wet feet will freeze the harder.

All this the man knew. The old-timer on Sulphur Creek had told him about it the previous fall, and now he was appreciating the advice. Already all sensation had gone out of his feet. To build the fire he had been forced to remove his mittens, and the fingers had quickly gone numb. His pace of four miles an hour had kept his heart pumping blood to the surface of his body and to all the extremities. But the instant he stopped, the action of the pump eased down. The cold of space smote the unprotected tip of the planet, and he, being on that unprotected tip, received the full force of the blow. The blood of his body recoiled before it. The blood was alive, like the dog, and like the dog it wanted to hide away and cover itself up from the fearful cold. So long as he walked four miles an hour, he pumped that blood, willy-nilly, to the surface; but now it ebbed away and sank down into the recesses of his body. The extremities were the first to feel its absence. His wet feet froze the faster, and his exposed fingers numbed the faster, though they had not yet begun to freeze. Nose and cheeks were already freezing, while the skin of all his body chilled as it lost its blood.

But he was safe. Toes and nose and cheeks would be only touched by the frost, for the fire was beginning to burn with strength. He was feeding it with twigs the size of his finger. In another minute he would be able to feed it with branches the size of his wrist, and then he could remove his wet foot-gear, and, while it dried, he could keep his naked feet warm by the fire, rubbing them at first, of course, with snow. The fire was a success. He was safe. He remembered the advice of the old-timer on Sulphur Creek, and smiled. The old-timer had been very serious in laying down the law that no man must travel alone in the Klondike after fifty below. Well, here he was; he had had the accident; he was alone; and he had saved himself. Those old-timers were rather womanish, some of them, he thought. All a man had to do was to keep his head, and he was all right. Any man who was a man could travel alone. But it was surprising, the rapidity with which his cheeks and nose were freezing. And he had not thought his fingers could go lifeless in so short a time. Lifeless they were, for he could scarcely make them move together to grip a twig, and they seemed remote from his body and from him. When he touched a twig, he had to look and see whether or not he had hold of it. The wires were pretty well down between him and his finger-ends.

All of which counted for little. There was the fire, snapping and crackling and promising life with every dancing flame. He started to untie his moccasins. They were coated with ice; the thick German socks were like sheaths of iron halfway to the knees; and the moccasin strings were like rods of steel all twisted and knotted as by some conflagration. For a moment he tugged with his numb fingers, then, realizing the folly of it, he drew his sheath-knife.

But before he could cut the strings, it happened. It was his own fault or, rather, his mistake. He should not have built the fire under the spruce tree. He should have built it in the open. But it had been easier to pull the twigs from the brush and drop them directly on the fire. Now the tree under which he had done this carried a weight of snow on its boughs. No wind had blown for weeks, and each bough was fully freighted. Each time he had pulled a twig he had communicated a slight agitation to the tree—an imperceptible agitation, so far as he was concerned, but an agitation sufficient to bring about the disaster. High up in the tree one bough capsized its load of snow. This fell on the boughs beneath, capsizing them. This process continued, spreading out and involving the whole tree. It grew like an avalanche, and it descended without warning upon the man and the fire, and the fire was blotted out! Where it had burned was a mantle of fresh and disordered snow.

The man was shocked. It was as though he had just heard his own sentence of death. For a moment he sat and stared at the spot where the fire had been. Then he grew very calm. Perhaps the old-timer on Sulphur Creek was right. If he had only had a trail-mate he would have been in no danger now. The trail-mate could have built the fire. Well, it was up to him to build the fire over again, and this second time there must be no failure. Even if he succeeded, he would most likely lose some toes. His feet must be badly frozen by now, and there would be some time before the second fire was ready.

Such were his thoughts, but he did not sit and think them. He was busy all the time they were passing through his mind. He made a new foundation for a fire, this time in the open, where no treacherous tree could blot it out. Next, he gathered dry grasses and tiny twigs from the high-water flotsam. He could not bring his fingers together to pull them out, but he was able to gather them by the handful. In this way he got many rotten twigs and bits of green moss that were undesirable, but it was the best he could do. He worked methodically, even collecting an armful of the larger branches to be used later when the fire gathered strength. And all the while the dog sat and watched him, a certain yearning wistfulness in its eyes, for it looked upon him as the fire-provider, and the fire was slow in coming.

When all was ready, the man reached in his pocket for a second piece of birch-bark. He knew the bark was there, and, though he could not feel it with his fingers, he could hear its crisp rustling as he fumbled for it. Try as he would, he could not clutch hold of it. And all the time, in his consciousness, was the knowledge that each instant his feet were freezing. This thought tended to put him in a panic, but he fought against it and kept calm. He pulled on his mittens with his teeth, and threshed his arms back and forth, beating his hands with all his might against his sides. He did this sitting down, and he stood up to do it; and all the while the dog sat in the snow, its wolf-brush of a tail curled around warmly over its forefeet, its sharp wolf-ears pricked forward intently as it watched the man. And the man, as he beat and threshed with his arms and hands, felt a great surge of envy as he regarded the creature that was warm and secure in its natural covering.

After a time he was aware of the first faraway signals of sensation in his beaten fingers. The faint tingling grew stronger till it evolved into a stinging ache that was excruciating, but which the man hailed with satisfaction. He stripped the mitten from his right hand and fetched forth the birch-bark. The exposed fingers were quickly going numb again. Next he brought out his bunch of sulphur matches. But the tremendous cold had already driven the life out of his fingers. In his effort to separate one match from the others, the whole bunch fell in the snow. He tried to pick it out of the snow, but failed. The dead fingers could neither touch nor clutch. He was very careful. He drove the thought of his freezing feet, and nose, and cheeks, out of his mind, devoting his whole soul to the matches. He watched, using the sense of vision in place of that of touch, and when he saw his fingers on each side the bunch, he closed them—that is, he willed to close them, for the wires were down, and the fingers did not obey. He pulled the mitten on the right hand, and beat it fiercely against his knee. Then, with both mittened hands, he scooped the bunch of matches, along with much snow, into his lap. Yet he was no better off.

After some manipulation he managed to get the bunch between the heels of his mittened hands. In this fashion he carried it to his mouth. The ice crackled and snapped when by a violent effort he opened his mouth. He drew the lower jaw in, curled the upper lip out of the way, and scraped the bunch with his upper teeth in order to separate a match. He succeeded in getting one, which he dropped on his lap. He was no better off. He could not pick it up. Then he devised a way. He picked it up in his teeth and scratched it on his leg. Twenty times he scratched before he succeeded in lighting it. As it flamed he held it with his teeth to the birch-bark. But the burning brimstone went up his nostrils and into his lungs, causing him to cough spasmodically. The match fell into the snow and went out.

The old-timer on Sulphur Creek was right, he thought in the moment of controlled despair that ensued: after fifty below, a man should travel with a partner. He beat his hands, but failed in exciting any sensation. Suddenly he bared both hands, removing the mittens with his teeth. He caught the whole bunch between the heels of his hands. His arm-muscles not being frozen enabled him to press the hand-heels tightly against the matches. Then he scratched the bunch along his leg. It flared into flame, seventy sulphur matches at once! There was no wind to blow them out. He kept his head to one side to escape the strangling fumes, and held the blazing bunch to the birch-bark. As he so held it, he became aware of sensation in his hand. His flesh was burning. He could smell it. Deep down below the surface he could feel it. The sensation developed into pain that grew acute. And still he endured it, holding the flame of the matches clumsily to the bark that would not light readily because his own burning hands were in the way, absorbing most of the flame.

At last, when he could endure no more, he jerked his hands apart. The blazing matches fell sizzling into the snow, but the birch-bark was alight. He began laying dry grasses and the tiniest twigs on the flame. He could not pick and choose, for he had to lift the fuel between the heels of his hands. Small pieces of rotten wood and green moss clung to the twigs, and he bit them off as well as he could with his teeth. He cherished the flame carefully and awkwardly. It meant life, and it must not perish. The withdrawal of blood from the surface of his body now made him begin to shiver, and he grew more awkward. A large piece of green moss fell squarely on the little fire. He tried to poke it out with his fingers, but his shivering frame made him poke too far, and he disrupted the nucleus of the little fire, the burning grasses and tiny twigs separating and scattering. He tried to poke them together again, but in spite of the tenseness of the effort, his shivering got away with him, and the twigs were hopelessly scattered. Each twig gushed a puff of smoke and went out. The fire-provider had failed. As he looked apathetically about him, his eyes chanced on the dog, sitting across the ruins of the fire from him, in the snow, making restless, hunching movements, slightly lifting one forefoot and then the other, shifting its weight back and forth on them with wistful eagerness.

The sight of the dog put a wild idea into his head. He remembered the tale of the man, caught in a blizzard, who killed a steer and crawled inside the carcass, and so was saved. He would kill the dog and bury his hands in the warm body until the numbness went out of them. Then he could build another fire. He spoke to the dog, calling it to him; but in his voice was a strange note of fear that frightened the animal, who had never known the man to speak in such way before. Something was the matter, and its suspicious nature sensed danger—it knew not what danger, but somewhere, somehow, in its brain arose an apprehension of the man. It flattened its ears down at the sound of the man's voice, and its restless, hunching movements and the liftings and shiftings of its forefeet became more pronounced; but it would not come to the man. He got on his hands and knees and crawled toward the dog. This unusual posture again excited suspicion, and the animal sidled mincingly away.

The man sat up in the snow for a moment and struggled for calmness. Then he pulled on his mittens, by means of his teeth, and got upon his feet. He glanced down at first in order to assure himself that he was really standing up, for the absence of sensation in his feet left him unrelated to the earth. His erect position in itself started to drive the webs of suspicion from the dog's mind; and when he spoke peremptorily, with the sound of whiplashes in his voice, the dog rendered its customary allegiance and came to him. As it came within reaching distance, the man lost his control. His arms flashed out to the dog, and he experienced genuine surprise when he discovered that his hands could not clutch, that there was neither bend nor feeling in the fingers. He had forgotten for the moment that they were frozen and that they were freezing more and more. All this happened quickly, and before the animal could get away, he encircled its body with his arms. He sat down in the snow, and in this fashion held the dog, while it snarled and whined and struggled.

But it was all he could do, hold its body encircled in his arms and sit there. He realized that he could not kill the dog. There was no way to do it. With his helpless hands he could neither draw nor hold his sheath-knife nor throttle the animal. He released it, and it plunged wildly away, with tail between its legs, and still snarling. It halted forty feet away and surveyed him cautiously, with ears sharply pricked forward. The man looked down at his hands in order to locate them, and found them hanging on the ends of his arms. It struck him as curious that one should have to use his eyes in order to find out where his hands were. He began threshing his arms back and forth, beating the mittened hands against his sides. He did this for five minutes, violently, and his heart pumped enough blood up to the surface to put a stop to his shivering. But no sensation was aroused in the hands. He had an impression that they hung like weights on the ends of his arms, but when he tried to run the impression down, he could not find it.

A certain fear of death, dull and oppressive, came to him. This fear quickly became poignant as he realized that it was no longer a mere matter of freezing his fingers and toes, or of losing his hands and feet, but that it was a matter of life and death with the chances against him. This threw him into a panic, and he turned and ran up the creek-bed along the old, dim trail. The dog joined in behind and kept up with him. He ran blindly, without intention, in fear such as he had never known in his life. Slowly, as he ploughed and floundered through the snow, he began to see things again—the banks of the creek, the old timber-jams, the leafless aspens, and the sky. The running made him feel better. He did not shiver Maybe, if he ran on, his feet would thaw out; and, anyway, if he ran far enough, he would reach camp and the boys. Without doubt he would lose some fingers and toes and some of his face; but the boys would take care of him, and save the rest of him when he got there.

And at the same time there was another thought in his mind that said he would never get to the camp and the boys; that it was too many miles away, that the freezing had too great a start on him, and that he would soon be stiff and dead. This thought he kept in the background and refused to consider. Sometimes it pushed itself forward and demanded to be heard, but he thrust it back and strove to think of other things.

It struck him as curious that he could run at all on feet so frozen that he could not feel them when they struck the earth and took the weight of his body. He seemed to himself to skim along above the surface, and to have no connection with the earth. Somewhere he had once seen a winged Mercury, and he wondered if Mercury felt as he felt when skimming over the earth.

His theory of running until he reached camp and the boys had one flaw in it: he lacked the endurance. Several times he stumbled, and finally he tottered, crumpled up, and fell. When he tried to rise, he failed. He must sit and rest, he decided, and next time he would merely walk and keep on going. As he sat and regained his breath, he noted that he was feeling quite warm and comfortable. He was not shivering, and it even seemed that a warm glow had come to his chest and trunk. And yet, when he touched his nose or cheeks, there was no sensation. Running would not thaw them out. Nor would it thaw out his hands and feet. Then the thought came to him that the frozen portions of his body must be extending. He tried to keep this thought down, to forget it, to think of something else; he was aware of the panicky feeling that it caused, and he was afraid of the panic. But the thought asserted itself, and persisted, until it produced a vision of his body totally frozen. This was too much, and he made another wild run along the trail. Once he slowed down to a walk, but the thought of the freezing extending itself made him run again.

And all the time the dog ran with him, at his heels. When he fell down a second time, it curled its tail over its forefeet and sat in front of him, facing him, curiously eager and intent. The warmth and security of the animal angered him, and he cursed it till it flattened down its ears appeasingly. This time the shivering came more quickly upon the man. He was losing in his battle with the frost. It was creeping into his body from all sides. The thought of it drove

him on, but he ran no more than a hundred feet, when he staggered
and pitched headlong. It was his last panic. When he had recovered
his breath and control, he sat up and entertained in his mind the
conception of meeting death with dignity. However, the conception
did not come to him in such terms. His idea of it was that he had
been making a fool of himself, running around like a chicken with
its head cut off—such was the simile that occurred to him. Well,
he was bound to freeze anyway, and he might as well take it decently.
With this new-found peace of mind came the first glimmerings of
drowsiness. A good idea, he thought, to sleep off to death. It was
like taking an anæsthetic. Freezing was not so bad as people thought.
There were lots worse ways to die.

He pictured the boys finding his body next day. Suddenly he
found himself with them, coming along the trail and looking for
himself. And, still with them, he came around a turn in the trail
and found himself lying in the snow. He did not belong with himself
any more, for even then he was out of himself, standing with the
boys and looking at himself in the snow. It certainly was cold, was
his thought. When he got back to the States he could tell the folks
what real cold was. He drifted on from this to a vision of the old-
timer on Sulphur Creek. He could see him quite clearly, warm and
comfortable, and smoking a pipe.

"You were right, old hoss; you were right," the man mumbled
to the old-timer on Sulphur Creek.

Then the man drowsed off into what seemed to him the most
comfortable and satisfying sleep he had ever known. The dog sat
facing him and waiting. The brief day drew to a close in a long, slow
twilight. There were no signs of a fire to be made, and, besides,
never in the dog's experience had it known a man to sit like that
in the snow and make no fire. As the twilight drew on, its eager
yearning for the fire mastered it, and with a great lifting and shifting
of its forefeet, it whined softly, then flattened its ears down in
anticipation of being chidden by the man. But the man remained
silent. Later, the dog whined loudly. And still later it crept close
to the man and caught the scent of death. This made the animal
bristle and back away. A little longer it delayed, howling under the
stars that leaped and danced and shone brightly in the cold sky.
Then it turned and trotted up the trail in the direction of the camp
it knew, where were the other food-providers and fire-providers.

LIKE ARGUS OF THE ANCIENT TIMES

(*Hearst's Magazine*, March, 1917)

"Klondike Fever" was not only an affliction of youth. Here is mettlesome John Tarwater, age seventy, cackling a fragment of a goldhunters' chantey and rearing up for a final adventure rather than living on the dole with his daughter and dreaming of his lost youth. This man, soon to be known from the Chilkoot to Tarwater Hill as "Father Christmas" and "Old Hero," knows the gold-fever intimately: he had all its symptoms a half-century ago when he sold off his Michigan homestead for four yoke of oxen and a wagon to head for the California placer diggings.

The story, posthumously published, was one of London's last (he died at age forty on November 22, 1916) and Irving Stone, London's most popular biographer (*Sailor on Horseback*, 1938), cites "Like Argus of the Ancient Times" as an example of the author "rearing up for one last show of strength."

During his packing up Chilkoot Pass in August, 1897, London and his partners, Fred Thompson, Jim Goodman, and Merritt Sloper, met an old man from Santa Rosa, California, named Tarwater and took him into their party. Thompson, who kept a diary of his Klondike adventures, wrote that Tarwater was helpful at cooking, repairing shoes, and packing. What became of the old man is not known—a mystery London may have had in mind in writing this tale in which he depicts himself as Liverpool, Fred Thompson as

Charles Crayton, Jim Goodman as Big Bill Wilson, and Sloper as Anson.

As early as 1906 London's work began to reveal his interest in the fledgling science of psychology, but it was not until the eve of his death that these delvings became almost desperate in their fervor. Richard O'Connor (in his *Jack London*, 1964) wrote of London seeking "at the last moment to make the transition from Marxist to Freudian and to thereby save himself, like a man sliding down the face of a cliff and grabbing at rocks and bushes to save his fall."

There is ample evidence in this story of the influence on London of his reading of the 1916 edition of Carl Gustav Jung's *Psychology of the Unconscious*, edited by Beatrice M. Hinkle. Hinkle's introductory essay captivated London with her contrast of Freud and Jung's concepts, especially of dreams and dream symbols. In Jung he discovered the substance for his lifelong interest in atavism and atavistic dreams (which is the theme of London's *Before Adam* and other works).

"I tell you," he said to his wife Charmian, at this late point of his life (quoted in her *The Book of Jack London*, 1920), "I am standing on the edge of a world so new, so wonderful, that I am almost afraid to look over into it."

But look he did and, says James McClintock in his superb study of London's short stories, *White Logic* (1975), found in Jung's definition of the libido some unique human quality, a sort of cosmic energy which he invested in John Tarwater in the form of a fever and which permitted the old hero to withstand the crushing forces of nature to which lesser men invariably and inexorably succumbed.

LIKE ARGUS OF THE ANCIENT TIMES

IT WAS THE summer of 1897, and there was trouble in the Tarwater family. Grandfather Tarwater, after remaining properly subdued and crushed for a quiet decade, had broken out again. This time it was the Klondike fever. His first and one unvarying symptom of such attacks was song. One chant only he raised, though he remembered no more than the first stanza and but three lines of that.

And the family knew his feet were itching and his brain was tingling with the old madness, when he lifted his hoarse-cracked voice, now falsetto-cracked, in:

> Like Argus of the ancient times,
> We leave this modern Greece,
> Tum-tum, tum-tum, tum, tum, tum-tum,
> To shear the Golden Fleece.

Ten years earlier he had lifted the chant, sung to the air of the "Doxology," when afflicted with the fever to go goldmining in Patagonia. The multitudinous family had sat upon him, but had had a hard time doing it. When all else had failed to shake his resolution, they had applied lawyers to him, with the threat of getting out guardianship papers and of confining him in the state asylum for the insane—which was reasonable for a man who had, a quarter of a century before, speculated away all but ten meager acres of a California principality, and who had displayed no better business acumen ever since.

The application of lawyers to John Tarwater was like the application of a mustard plaster. For, in his judgment, they were the gentry, more than any other, who had skinned him out of the broad Tarwater acres. So, at the time of his Patagonian fever, the very thought of so drastic a remedy was sufficient to cure him. He quickly demonstrated he was not crazy by shaking the fever from him and agreeing not to go to Patagonia.

Next, he demonstrated how crazy he really was, by deeding over to his family, unsolicited, the ten acres on Tarwater Flat, the house, barn, outbuildings, and water-rights. Also did he turn over the eight hundred dollars in bank that was the long-saved salvage of his wrecked fortune. But for this the family found no cause for committal to the asylum, since such committal would necessarily invalidate what he had done.

"Grandfather is sure peeved," said Mary, his oldest daughter, herself a grandmother, when her father quit smoking.

All he had retained for himself was a span of old horses, a mountain buckboard, and his one room in the crowded house. Further, having affirmed that he would be beholden to none of them, he got the contract to carry the United States mail, twice a week, from Kelterville up over Tarwater Mountain to Old Almaden—which was a sporadically worked quicksilver mine in the upland cattle country. With his old horses it took all his time to make the two weekly round trips. And for ten years, rain or shine, he had never missed a trip. Nor had he failed once to pay his week's board into Mary's hand. This board he had insisted on, in the convalescence from his Patagonian fever, and he had paid it strictly though he had given up tobacco in order to be able to do it.

"Huh!" he confided to the ruined water wheel of the old Tarwater Mill, which he had built from the standing timber and which had ground wheat for the first settlers. "Huh! They'll never put me in the poor farm so long as I support myself. And without a penny to my name it ain't likely any lawyer fellows'll come snoopin' around after me."

And yet, precisely because of these highly rational acts, it was held that John Tarwater was mildly crazy!

The first time he had lifted the chant of "Like Argus of the Ancient Times," had been in 1849, when, twenty-two years of age, violently attacked by the California fever, he had sold two hundred and forty Michigan acres, forty of it cleared, for the price of four yoke of oxen and a wagon, and had started across the Plains.

"And we turned off at Fort Hall, where the Oregon emigration went north'ard, and swung south for Californy," was his way of concluding the narrative of that arduous journey. "And Bill Ping and me used to rope grizzlies out of the underbrush of Cache Slough in the Sacramento Valley."

Years of freighting and mining had followed, and, with a stake gleaned from the Merced placers, he satisfied the land-hunger of his race and time by settling in Sonoma County.

During the ten years of carrying the mail across Tarwater Township, up Tarwater Valley, and over Tarwater Mountain, most all of which land had once been his, he had spent his time dreaming of winning back that land before he died. And now, his huge gaunt form more erect than it had been for years, with a glinting of blue fires in his small and close-set eyes, he was lifting his ancient chant again.

"There he goes now—listen to him," said William Tarwater.

"Nobody at home," laughed Harris Topping, day laborer, husband of Annie Tarwater, and father of her nine children.

The kitchen door opened to admit the old man, returning from feeding his horses. The song had ceased from his lips; but Mary was irritable from a burnt hand and a grandchild whose stomach refused to digest properly diluted cow's milk.

"Now there ain't no use you carryin' on that way, father," she tackled him. "The time's past for you to cut and run for a place like the Klondike, and singing won't buy you nothing."

"Just the same," he answered quietly. 'I bet I could go to that Klondike place and pick up enough gold to buy back the Tarwater lands."

"Old fool!" Annie contributed.

"You couldn't buy them back for less 'n three hundred thousand and then some," was William's effort at squelching him.

"Then I could pick up three hundred thousand, and then some, if I was only there," the old man retorted placidly.

"Thank God, you can't walk there, or you'd be startin', I know," Mary cried. "Ocean travel costs money."

"I used to have money," her father said humbly.

"Well, you ain't got any now—so forget it," William advised. "Them times is past, like roping bear with Bill Ping. There ain't no more bear."

"Just the same—"

But Mary cut him off. Seizing the day's paper from the kitchen table, she flourished it savagely under her aged progenitor's nose.

"What do those Klondikers say? There it is in cold print. Only the young and robust can stand the Klondike. It's worse than the north pole. And they've left their dead a-plenty there themselves. Look at their pictures. You're forty years older'n the oldest of them."

John Tarwater did look, but his eyes strayed to other photographs on the highly sensational front page.

"And look at the photys of them nuggets they brought down," he said. "I know gold. Didn't I gopher twenty thousand outa the Merced? And wouldn't it a-ben a hundred thousand if that cloud-burst hadn't busted my wing-dam? Now if I was only in the Klondike—"

"Crazy as a loon," William sneered in open aside to the rest.

"A nice way to talk to your father," Old Man Tarwater censured mildly. "My father'd have walloped the tar out of me with a single-tree if I'd spoke to him that way."

"But you *are* crazy, father—" William began.

"Reckon you're right, son. And that's where my father wasn't crazy. He'd a-done it."

"The old man's been reading some of them magazine articles about men who succeeded after forty," Annie gibed.

"And why not, daughter?" he asked. "And why can't a man succeed after he's seventy? I was only seventy this year. And mebbe I could succeed if only I could get to the Klondike—"

"Which you ain't going to get to," Mary shut him off.

"Oh, well, then," he sighed, "seein's I ain't, I might just as well go to bed."

He stood up, tall, gaunt, great-boned and gnarled, a splendid ruin of a man. His ragged hair and whiskers were not gray but snowy white, as were the tufts of hair that stood out on the backs of his huge bony fingers. He moved toward the door, opened it, sighed, and paused with a backward look.

"Just the same," he murmured plaintively, "the bottoms of my feet is itching something terrible."

Long before the family stirred next morning, his horses fed and harnessed by lantern light, breakfast cooked and eaten by lamplight, Old Man Tarwater was off and away down Tarwater Valley on the road to Kelterville. Two things were unusual about this usual trip which he had made a thousand and forty times since taking the mail contract. He did not drive to Kelterville, but turned off on the main road south to Santa Rosa. Even more remarkable than this was the paper-wrapped parcel between his feet. It contained his one decent black suit, which Mary had been long reluctant to see him wear any more, not because it was shabby, but because, as he guessed what was at the back of her mind, it was decent enough to bury him in.

And at Santa Rosa, in a second-hand clothes shop, he sold the suit outright for two dollars and a half. From the same obliging shopman he received four dollars for the wedding ring of his long-dead wife. The span of horses and the wagon he disposed of for seventy-five dollars, although twenty-five was all he received down in cash. Chancing to meet Alton Granger on the street, to whom never before had he mentioned the ten dollars loaned him in '74, he reminded Alton Granger of the little affair, and was promptly paid. Also, of all unbelievable men to be in funds, he so found the town drunkard for whom he had bought many a drink in the old and palmy days. And from him John Tarwater borrowed a dollar. Finally, he took the afternoon train to San Francisco.

A dozen days later, carrying a half-empty canvas sack of blankets and old clothes, he landed on the beach of Dyea in the thick of the great Klondike Rush. The beach was screaming bedlam. Ten thousand tons of outfit lay heaped and scattered, and twice ten thousand men struggled with it and clamored about it. Freight, by Indian-back, over Chilcoot to Lake Linderman, had jumped from sixteen to thirty cents a pound, which latter was a rate of six hundred dollars a ton. And the sub-arctic winter gloomed near at hand. All knew it, and all knew that of the twenty thousand of them very few would get across the passes, leaving the rest to winter and wait for the late spring thaws.

Such the beach old John Tarwater stepped upon; and straight across the beach and up the trail toward Chilcoot he headed, cackling his ancient chant, a very Grandfather Argus himself, with no outfit worry in the world, for he did not possess any outfit. That night he slept on the flats, five miles above Dyea, at the head of canoe navigation. Here the Dyea River became a rushing mountain torrent, plunging out of a dark canyon from the glaciers that fed it far above.

And here, early next morning, he beheld a little man weighing no more than a hundred, staggering along a foot-log under all of a hundred pounds of flour strapped on his back. Also, he beheld the little man stumble off the log and fall face-downward in a quiet eddy where the water was two feet deep and proceed quietly to drown. It was no desire of his to take death so easily, but the flour on his back weighed as much as he and would not let him up.

"Thank you, old man," he said to Tarwater, when the latter had dragged him up into the air and ashore.

While he unlaced his shoes and ran the water out, they had further talk. Next, he fished out a ten-dollar gold-piece and offered it to his rescuer.

Old Tarwater shook his head and shivered, for the ice-water had wet him to his knees.

"But I reckon I wouldn't object to settin' down to a friendly meal with you."

"Ain't had breakfast?" the little man, who was past forty and who had said his name was Anson, queried with a glance frankly curious.

"Nary bite," John Tarwater answered.

"Where's your outfit? Ahead?"

"Nary outfit."

"Expect to buy your grub on the Inside?"

"Nary a dollar to buy it with, friend. Which ain't so important as a warm bite of breakfast right now."

In Anson's camp, a quarter of a mile on, Tarwater found a slender, red-whiskered young man of thirty cursing over a fire of wet willow wood. Introduced as Charles, he transferred his scowl and wrath to Tarwater, who, genially oblivious, devoted himself to the fire, took advantage of the chill morning breeze to create a draught which the other had left stupidly blocked by stones, and soon developed less smoke and more flame. The third member of the party, Bill Wilson, or Big Bill as they called him, came in with a hundred-and-forty-pound pack; and what Tarwater esteemed to be a very rotten breakfast was dished out by Charles. The mush was half cooked and mostly burnt, the bacon was charred carbon, and the coffee was unspeakable.

Immediately the meal was wolfed down, the three partners took their empty packstraps and headed down trail to where the remainder of their outfit lay at the last camp a mile away. And old Tarwater became busy. He washed the dishes, foraged dry wood, mended a broken packstrap, put an edge on the butcher-knife and camp-ax, and repacked the picks and shovels into a more carryable parcel.

What had impressed him during the brief breakfast was the sort of awe in which Anson and Big Bill stood of Charles. Once, during the morning, while Anson took a breathing spell after bringing in another hundred-pound pack, Tarwater delicately hinted his impression.

"You see, it's this way," Anson said. "We've divided our leadership. We've all got specialties. Now I'm a carpenter. When we get to Lake Linderman, and the trees are chopped and whipsawed into planks, I'll boss the building of the boat. Big Jim is a logger and miner. So he'll boss getting out the logs and all mining operations. Most of our outfit's ahead. We went broke paying the Indians to pack that much of it to the top of Chilcoot. Our last partner is up there with it, moving it along by himself down the other side. His name's Liverpool, and he's a sailor. So, when the boat's built, he's the boss of the outfit to navigate the lakes and rapids to Klondike."

"And Charles—this Mr. Clayton—what might his specialty be?" Tarwater asked.

"He's the business man. When it comes to business and organization he's boss."

"Hum," Tarwater pondered. "Very lucky to get such a bunch of specialties into one outfit."

"More than lucky," Anson agreed. "It was all accident, too. Each of us started alone. We met on the steamer coming up from San Francisco, and formed the party.—Well, I got to be goin'. Charles is liable to get kicking because I ain't packing my share. Just the same, you can't expect a hundred-pound man to pack as much as a hundred-and-sixty-pounder."

"Stick around and cook us something for dinner," Charles, on his next load in and noting the effects of the old man's handiness, told Tarwater.

And Tarwater cooked a dinner that was a dinner, washed the dishes, had real pork and beans for supper, and bread baked in a frying-pan that was so delectable that the three partners nearly foundered themselves on it. Supper dishes washed, he cut shavings and kindling for a quick and certain breakfast fire, showed Anson a trick with foot-gear that was invaluable to any hiker, sang his "Like Argus of the Ancient Times," and told them of the great emigration across the Plains in Forty-nine.

"My goodness, the first cheerful and hearty-like camp since we hit the beach," Big Jim remarked as he knocked out his pipe and began pulling off his shoes for bed.

"Kind of made things easy, boys, eh?" Tarwater queried genially.

All nodded. "Well, then, I got a proposition, boys. You can take it or leave it, but just listen kindly to it. You're in a hurry to get in before the freeze-up. Half the time is wasted over the cooking by one of you that he might be puttin' in packin' outfit. If I do the cookin' for you, you all'll get on that much faster. Also, the cookin'll be better, and that'll make you pack better. And I can pack quite a bit myself in between times, quite a bit, yes, sir, quite a bit."

Big Bill and Anson were just beginning to nod their heads in agreement, when Charles stopped them.

"What do you expect of us in return?" he demanded of the old man.

"Oh, I leave it up to the boys."

"That ain't business," Charles reprimanded sharply. "You made the proposition. Now finish it."

"Well, it's this way—"

"You expect us to feed you all winter, eh?" Charles interrupted.

"No, siree, I don't. All I reckon is a passage to Klondike in your boat would be mighty square of you."

"You haven't an ounce of grub, old man. You'll starve to death when you get there."

"I've been feedin' some long time pretty succesful," Old Tarwater replied, a whimsical light in his eyes. "I'm seventy, and ain't starved to death never yet."

"Will you sign a paper to the effect that you shift for yourself as soon as you get to Dawson?" the business one demanded.

"Oh, sure," was the response.

Again Charles checked his two partners' expressions of satisfaction with the arrangement.

"One other thing, old man. We're a party of four, and we all have a vote on questions like this. Young Liverpool is ahead with the main outfit. He's got a say so, and he isn't here to say it."

"What kind of a party might he be?" Tarwater inquired.

"He's a rough-neck sailor, and he's got a quick, bad temper."

"Some turbulent," Anson contributed.

"And the way he can cuss is simply God-awful," Big Jim testified.

"But he's square," Big Jim added.

Anson nodded heartily to this appraisal.

"Well, boys," Tarwater summed up, "I set out for Californy and I got there. And I'm going to get to Klondike. Ain't a thing can stop me, ain't a thing. I'm going to get three hundred thousand outa the ground, too. Ain't a thing can stop me, ain't a thing, because I just naturally need the money. I don't mind a bad temper so long's the boy is square. I'll take my chance, an' I'll work along with you till we catch up with him. Then, if he says no to the proposition, I reckon I'll lose. But somehow I just can't see 'm sayin' no, because that'd mean too close up to freeze-up and too late for me to find another chance like this. And, as I'm sure going to get to Klondike, it's just plumb impossible for him to say no."

Old John Tarwater became a striking figure on a trail unusually replete with striking figures. With thousands of men, each back-tripping half a ton of outfit, retracing every mile of the trail twenty times, all came to know him and to hail him as "Father Christmas." And as he worked ever he raised his chant with his age-falsetto voice. None of the three men he had joined could complain about his work. True, his joints were stiff—he admitted to a trifle of rheumatism. He moved slowly, and seemed to creak and crackle when he moved; but he kept on moving. Last into the blankets at night, he was first out in the morning, so that the other three had hot coffee before their one before-breakfast pack. And, between breakfast and dinner and between dinner and supper, he always managed to back-trip for several packs himself. Sixty pounds was the limit of his burden, however. He could manage seventy-five, but he could not keep it up. Once, he tried ninety, but collapsed on the trail and was seriously shaky for a couple of days afterward.

Work! On a trail where hard-working men learned for the first time what work was, no man worked harder in proportion to this strength than Old Tarwater. Driven desperately on by the near-thrust of winter, and lured madly on by the dream of gold, they worked to their last ounce of strength and fell by the way. Others, when failure made certain, blew out their brains. Some went mad, and still others, under the irk of the man-destroying strain, broke partnerships and dissolved life-time friendships with fellows just as good as themselves and just as strained and mad.

Work! Old Tarwater could shame them all, despite his creaking and crackling and the nasty hacking cough he had developed. Early and late, on trail or in camp beside the trail, he was ever in evidence, ever busy at something, ever responsive to the hail of "Father

Christmas." Weary backtrippers would rest their packs on a log or rock alongside of where he rested his, and would say: "Sing us that song of yourn, dad, about Forty-Nine." And, when he had wheezingly complied, they would arise under their loads, remark that it was real heartening, and hit the forward trail again.

"If ever a man worked his passage and earned it," Big Jim confided to his two partners, "that man's our old Skeezicks."

"You bet," Anson confirmed. "He's a valuable addition to the party, and I, for one, ain't at all disagreeable to the notion of making him a regular partner—"

"None of that!" Charles Crayton cut in. "When we get to Dawson we're quit of him—that's the agreement. We'd only have to bury him if we let him stay on with us. Besides, there's going to be a famine, and every ounce of grub'll count. Remember, we're feeding him out of our own supply all the way in. And if we run short in the pinch next year, you'll know the reason. Steamboats can't get up grub to Dawson till the middle of June, and that's nine months away."

"Well, you put as much money and outfit in as the rest of us," Big Bill conceded, "and you've a say according."

"And I'm going to have my say," Charles asserted with increasing irritability. "And it's lucky for you with your fool sentiments that you've got somebody to think ahead for you, else you'd all starve to death. I tell you that famine's coming. I've been studying the situation. Flour will be two dollars a pound, or ten, and no sellers. You mark my words."

Across the rubble-covered flats, up the dark canyon to Sheep Camp, past the overhanging and ever-threatening glaciers to the Scales, and from the Scales up the steep pitches of ice-scoured rock where packers climbed with hands and feet, Old Tarwater camp-cooked and packed and sang. He blew across Chilcoot Pass, above timber-line, in the first swirl of autumn snow. Those below, without firewood, on the bitter rim of Crater Lake, heard from the driving obscurity above them a weird voice chanting:

> Like Argus of the ancient times,
> We leave this modern Greece,
> Tum-tum, tum-tum, tum, tum, tum-tum,
> To shear the Golden Fleece.

And out of the snow flurries they saw appear a tall, gaunt form, with whiskers of flying white that blended with the storm, bending under a sixty-pound of camp dunnage.

"Father Christmas!" was the hail. And then: "Three rousing cheers for Father Christmas!"

Two miles beyond Crater Lake lay Happy Camp—so named because here was found the uppermost fringe of the timber-line, where men might warm themselves by fire again. Scarcely could it be called timber, for it was a dwarf rock-spruce that never raised its loftiest branches higher than a foot above the moss, and that twisted and groveled like a pig-vegetable under the moss. Here, on the trail leading into Happy Camp, in the first sunshine of half a dozen days, Old Tarwater rested his pack against a huge bowlder and caught his breath. Around this bowlder the trail passed, laden men toiling slowly forward and men with empty pack-straps limping rapidly back for fresh loads. Twice Old Tarwater essayed to rise and go on, and each time, warned by his shakiness, sank back to recover more strength. From around the bowlder he heard voices in greeting, recognized Charles Crayton's voice, and realized that at last they had met up with Young Liverpool. Quickly, Charles plunged into business, and Tarwater heard with great distinctness every word of Charles' unflattering description of him and of the proposition to give him passage to Dawson.

"A damn fool proposition," was Liverpool's judgment, when Charles had concluded. "An old granddad of seventy! If he's on his last legs, why in hell did you hook up with him? If there's going to be a famine, and it looks like it, we need every ounce of grub for ourselves. We only outfitted for four, not five."

"It's all right," Tarwater heard Charles assuring the other. "Don't get excited. The old codger agreed to leave the final decision to you when we caught up with you. All you've got to do is put your foot down and say no."

"You mean it's up to me to turn the old one down, after your encouraging him and taking advantage of his work clear from Dyea here?"

"It's a hard trail, Liverpool, and only the men that are hard will get through," Charles strove to palliate.

"And I'm to do the dirty work?" Liverpool complained, while Tarwater's heart sank.

"That's just about the size of it," Charles said. "You've got the deciding."

Then Old Tarwater's heart uprose again as the air was rent by a cyclone of profanity, from the midst of which crackled sentences like: "Dirty skunks! . . . See you in hell first! . . . My mind's made up! . . . Hell's fire and corruption! . . . The old codger goes down the Yukon with us, stack on that, my hearty! . . . Hard? You don't know what hard is unless I show you! . . . I'll bust the whole outfit to hell and gone if any of you try to side-track him! . . . Just try to sidetrack him, that's all, and you'll think the day of Judgment and all God's blastingness has hit the camp in one chunk!"

Such was the invigoratingness of Liverpool's flow of speech that, quite without consciousness of effort, the old man arose easily under his load and strode on toward Happy Camp.

From Happy Camp to Long Lake, from Long Lake to Deep Lake, and from Deep Lake up over the enormous hog-back and down to Linderman, the man-killing race against winter kept on. Men broke their hearts and backs and wept beside the trail in sheer exhaustion. But winter never faltered. The fall gales blew, and amid bitter soaking rains and ever increasing snow flurries, Tarwater and the party to which he was attached piled the last of their outfit on the beach.

There was no rest. Across the lake, a mile above a roaring torrent, they located a patch of spruce and built their saw-pit. Here, by hand, with an inadequate whipsaw, they sawed the spruce-trunks into lumber. They worked night and day. Thrice, on the night-shift, underneath in the saw-pit, Old Tarwater fainted. By day he cooked as well, and, in the betweenwhiles, helped Anson in the building of the boat beside the torrent as the green planks came down.

The days grew shorter. The wind shifted into the north and blew unending gales. In the mornings the weary men crawled from their blankets and in their socks thawed out their frozen shoes by the fire Tarwater always had burning for them. Ever arose the increasing tale of famine on the Inside. The last grub steamboats up from

Bering Sea were stalled by low water at the beginning of the Yukon Flats hundred of miles north of Dawson. In fact, they lay at the old Hudson Bay Company's post at Fort Yukon inside the Arctic Circle. Flour in Dawson was up to two dollars a pound but no one would sell. Bonanza and Eldorado Kings, with money to burn, were leaving for the Outside because they could buy no grub. Miners' Committees were confiscating all grub and putting the population on strict rations. A man who held out an ounce of grub was shot like a dog. A score had been so executed already.

And, under a strain which had broken so many younger men, Old Tarwater began to break. His cough had become terrible, and had not his exhausted comrades slept like the dead, he would have kept them awake nights. Also, he began to take chills, so that he dressed up to go to bed. When he had finished so dressing, not a rag of garment remained in his clothes bag. All he possessed was on his back and swathed around his gaunt old form.

"Gee!" said Big Bill. "If he puts all he's got on now, when it ain't lower than twenty above, what'll he do later on when it goes down to fifty and sixty below?"

They lined the rough-made boat down the mountain torrent, nearly losing it a dozen times, and rowed across the south end of Lake Linderman in the thick of a fall blizzard. Next morning they planned to load and start, squarely into the teeth of the north, on their perilous traverse of half a thousand miles of lakes and rapids and box canyons. But before he went to bed that night, Young Liverpool was out over the camp. He returned to find his whole party asleep. Rousing Tarwater, he talked with him in low tones.

"Listen, dad," he said. "You've got a passage in our boat, and if ever a man earned a passage you have. But you know yourself you're pretty well along in years, and your health right now ain't exciting. If you go on with us you'll croak surer'n hell.—Now wait till I finish, dad. The price for a passage has jumped to five hundred dollars. I've been throwing my feet and I've hustled a passenger. He's an official of the Alaska Commercial and just has to get in. He's bid up to six hundred to go with me in our boat. Now the passage is yours. You sell it to him, poke the six hundred into your jeans, and pull South for California while the goin's good. You can be in Dyea in two days, and in California in a week more. What d'ye say?"

Tarwater coughed and shivered for a space, ere he could get freedom of breath for speech.

"Son," he said, "I just want to tell you one thing. I drove my four yoke of oxen across the Plains in Forty-nine and lost nary a one. I drove them plumb to Californy, and I freighted with them afterward out of Sutter's Fort to American Bar. Now I'm going to Klondike. Ain't nothing can stop me, ain't nothing at all. I'm going to ride that boat, with you at the steering sweep, clean to Klondike, and I'm going to shake three hundred thousand out of the moss-roots. That being so, it's contrary to reason and common sense for me to sell out my passage. But I thank you kindly, son, I thank you kindly."

The young sailor shot out his hand impulsively and gripped the old man's.

"By God, dad!" he cried. "You're sure going to go then. You're the real stuff." He looked with undisguised contempt across the sleepers to where Charles Crayton snored in his red beard. "They don't seem to make your kind any more, dad."

Into the north they fought their way, although old-timers, coming out, shook their heads and prophesied they would be frozen in on the lakes. That the freeze-up might come any day was patent, and delays of safety were no longer considered. For this reason, Liverpool decided to shoot the rapid stream connecting Linderman to Lake Bennett with the fully loaded boat. It was the custom to line the empty boats down and to portage the cargoes across. Even then, many empty boats had been wrecked. But the time was past for such precaution.

"Climb out, dad," Liverpool commanded, as he prepared to swing from the bank and enter the rapids.

Old Tarwater shook his white head.

"I'm sticking to the outfit," he declared. "It's the only way to get through. You see, son, I'm going to Klondike. If I stick by the boat, then the boat just naturally goes to Klondike, too. If I get out, then most likely you'll lose the boat."

"Well, there's no use in overloading," Charles announced, springing abruptly out on the bank as the boat cast off.

"Next time you wait for my orders!" Liverpool shouted ashore as the current gripped the boat. "And there won't be any more walking around rapids and losing time waiting to pick you up!"

What took them ten minutes by river, took Charles half an hour by land, and while they waited for him at the head of Lake Bennett they passed the time of day with several dilapidated oldtimers on their way out. The famine news was graver than ever. The Northwest Mounted Police, stationed at the foot of Lake Marsh where the gold-rushers entered Canadian territory, were refusing to let a man past who did not carry with him seven hundred pounds of grub. In Dawson City a thousand men, with dog-teams, were waiting the freeze-up to come out over the ice. The trading companies could not fill their grub-contracts, and partners were cutting the cards to see which should go and which should stay and work the claims.

"That settles it," Charles announced, when he learned of the action of the mounted police on the boundary. "Old Man, you might as well start back now."

"Climb aboard!" Liverpool commanded. "We're going to Klondike, and old dad is going along."

A shift of gale to the south gave them a fair wind down Lake Bennett, before which they ran under a huge sail made by Liverpool. The heavy weight of outfit gave such ballast that he cracked on as a daring sailor should when moments counted. A shift of four points into the southwest, coming just at the right time as they entered upon Caribou Crossing, drove them down that connecting link to lakes Tagish and Marsh. In stormy sunset and twilight they made the dangerous crossing of Great Windy Arm, wherein they beheld two other boat-loads of gold-rushers capsize and drown.

Charles was for beaching for the night, but Liverpool held on, steering down Tagish by the sound of the surf on the shoals and by the occasional shore-fires that advertised wrecked or timid argonauts. At four in the morning, he aroused Charles. Old Tarwater, shiveringly awake, heard Liverpool order Crayton aft beside him at the steering-sweep, and also heard the one-sided conversation.

"Just listen, friend Charles, and keep your own mouth shut," Liverpool began. "I want you to get one thing into your head and keep it there: *old dad's going by the police. Understand? He's going by.* When they examine our outfit, old dad's got a fifth share in it, savvee? That'll put us all 'way under what we ought to have, but we can bluff it through. Now get this, and get it hard: *there ain't going to be any fall-down on this bluff—*"

"If you think I'd give away on the old codger—" Charles began indignantly.

"You thought that," Liverpool checked him, "because I never mentioned any such thing. Now—get me and get me hard: I don't care what you've been thinking. It's what you're going to think. We'll make the police post some time this afternoon, and we've got to get ready to pull the bluff without a hitch, and a word to the wise is plenty."

"If you think I've got it in my mind—" Charles began again.

"Look here," Liverpool shut him off. "I don't know what's in your mind. I don't want to know. I want you to know what's in my mind. If there's any slip-up, if old dad gets turned back by the police, I'm going to pick out the first quiet bit of landscape and take you ashore on it. And then I'm going to beat you up to the Queen's taste. Get me, and get me hard. It ain't going to be any half-way beating, but a real, two-legged, two-fisted, he-man beating. I don't expect I'll kill you, but I'll come damn near to half-killing you."

"But what can I do?" Charles almost whimpered.

"Just one thing," was Liverpool's final word. "You just pray. You pray so hard that old dad gets by the police that he does get by. That's all. Go back to your blankets."

Before they gained Lake Le Barge, the land was sheeted with snow that would not melt for half a year. Nor could they lay their boat at will against the bank, for the rim-ice was already forming. Inside the mouth of the river, just ere it entered Lake Le Barge, they found a hundred storm-bound boats of the argonauts. Out of the north, across the full sweep of the great lake, blew an unending snow gale. Three mornings they put out and fought it and the cresting seas it drove that turned to ice as they fell in-board. While the others broke their hearts at the oars, Old Tarwater managed to keep up just sufficient circulation to survive by chopping ice and throwing it overboard.

Each day for three days, beaten to helplessness, they turned tail on the battle and ran back into the sheltering river. By the fourth day, the hundred boats had increased to three hundred, and the two thousand argonauts on board knew that the great gale heralded the freeze-up of Le Barge. Beyond, the rapid rivers would continue to run for days, but unless they got beyond, and immediately, they were doomed to be frozen in for six months to come.

"This day we go through," Liverpool announced. "We turn back for nothing. And those of us that dies at the oars will live again and go on pulling."

And they went through, winning half the length of the lake by nightfall and pulling on through all the night hours as the wind went down, falling asleep at the oars and being rapped awake by Liverpool, toiling on through an age-long nightmare while the stars came out and the surface of the lake turned to the unruffledness of a sheet of paper and froze skin-ice that tinkled like broken glass as their oarblades shattered it.

As day broke clear and cold, they entered the river, with behind them a sea of ice. Liverpool examined his aged passenger and found him helpless and almost gone. When he rounded the boat to against the rim-ice to build a fire and warm up Tarwater inside out, Charles protested against such loss of time.

"This ain't business, so don't you come horning in," Liverpool informed him. "I'm running the boat trip. So you just climb out and chop firewood, and plenty of it. I'll take care of dad. You, Anson, make a fire on the bank. And you, Bill, set up the Yukon stove in the boat. Old dad ain't as young as the rest of us, and for the rest of this voyage he's going to have a fire on board to sit by."

All of which came to pass; and the boat, in the grip of the current, like a river steamer with smoke rising from the two joints of stovepipe, grounded on shoals, hung up on split currents, and charged rapids and canyons, as it drove deeper into the Northland winter. The Big and Little Salmon rivers were throwing mush-ice into the main river as they passed, and, below the riffles, anchor-ice arose from the river bottom and coated the surface with crystal scum. Night and day the rim-ice grew, till, in quiet places, it extended out a hundred yards from shore. And Old Tarwater, with all his clothes on, sat by the stove and kept the fire going. Night and day, not daring to stop for fear of the imminent freeze-up, they dared to run, an increasing mushiness of ice running with them.

"What ho, old hearty?" Liverpool would call out at times.

"Cheer O," Old Tarwater had learned to respond.

"What can I ever do for you, son, in payment?" Tarwater, stoking the fire, would sometimes ask Liverpool beating now one released hand and now the other as he fought for circulation where he steered in the freezing sternsheets.

"Just break out that regular song of yours, old Forty-Niner," was the invariable reply.

And Tarwater would lift his voice in the cackling chant, as he lifted it at the end, when the boat swung in through driving cake-ice and moored to the Dawson City bank, and all waterfront Dawson pricked its ears to hear the triumphant pæan:

> Like Argus of the ancient times,
> We leave this modern Greece,
> Tum-tum, tum-tum, tum, tum, tum-tum,
> To shear the Golden Fleece.

Charles did it, but he did it so discreetly that none of his party, least of all the sailor, ever learned of it. He saw two great open barges being filled up with men, and, on inquiry, learned that these were grubless ones being rounded up and sent down the Yukon by the Committee of Safety. The barges were to be towed by the last little steamboat in Dawson, and the hope was that Fort Yukon, where lay the stranded steamboats, would be gained before the river froze. At any rate, no matter what happened to them, Dawson would be relieved of their grub-consuming presence. So to the Committee of Safety Charles went, privily to drop a flea in its ear concerning Tarwater's grubless, moneyless, and aged condition. Tarwater was one of the last gathered in, and when Young Liverpool returned to the boat, from the bank he saw the barges in a run of cake-ice, disappearing around the bend below Moosehide Mountain.

Running in cake-ice all the way, and several times escaping jams in the Yukon Flats, the barges made their hundreds of miles of progress farther into the north and froze up cheek by jowl with the grub-fleet. Here, inside the Arctic Circle Old Tarwater settled down to pass the long winter. Several hours' work a day, chopping firewood for the steamboat companies, sufficed to keep him in food. For the rest of the time there was nothing to do but hibernate in his log cabin.

Warmth, rest, and plenty to eat, cured his hacking cough and put him in as good physical condition as was possible for his advanced years. But, even before Christmas, the lack of fresh vegetables caused scurvy to break out, and disappointed adventurer after disappointed adventurer took to his bunk in abject surrender to this culminating misfortune. Not so Tarwater. Even before the first symptoms appeared on him, he was putting into practice his one prescription, namely, exercise. From the junk of the old trading post he resurrected a number of rusty traps, and from one of the steamboat captains he borrowed a rifle.

Thus equipped, he ceased from wood-chopping, and began to make more than a mere living. Nor was he downhearted when the scurvy broke out on his own body. Ever he ran his trap-lines and sang his ancient chant. Nor could the pessimist shake his surety of the three hundred thousand of Alaskan gold he was going to shake out of the moss-roots.

"But this ain't gold-country," they told him.

"Gold is where you find it, son, as I should know who was mining before you was born, 'way back in Forty-Nine," was his reply. "What was Bonanza Creek but a moose-pasture? No miner'd look at it; yet they washed five-hundred-dollar pans and took out fifty million dollars. Eldorado was just as bad. For all you know, right under this here cabin, or right over the next hill, is millions just waiting for a lucky one like me to come and shake it out."

At the end of January came his disaster. Some powerful animal that he decided was a bob-cat, managing to get caught in one of his smaller traps, dragged it away. A heavy snow-fall put a stop midway to his pursuit, losing the trail for him and losing himself. There were but several hours of daylight each day between the twenty hours of intervening darkness, and his efforts in the gray light and continually falling snow succeeded only in losing him more thoroughly. Fortunately, when winter snow falls in the Northland the thermometer invariably rises; so, instead of the customary forty and fifty and even sixty degrees below zero, the temperature remained fifteen below. Also, he was warmly clad and had a full matchbox. Further to mitigate his predicament, on the fifth day he killed a wounded moose that weighed over half a ton. Making his camp beside it on a spruce-bottom, he was prepared to last out the winter, unless a searching party found him or his scurvy grew worse.

But at the end of two weeks there had been no sign of search, while his scurvy had undeniably grown worse. Against his fire, banked from outer cold by a shelter-wall of spruce-boughs, he crouched long hours in sleep and long hours in waking. But the waking hours grew less, becoming semi-waking or half-dreaming hours as the processes of hibernation worked their way with him. Slowly the sparkle point of consciousness and identity that was John Tarwater sank, deeper and deeper, into the profounds of his being that had been compounded ere man was man, and while he was becoming man, when he, first of all animals regarded himself with an introspective eye and laid the beginnings of morality in foundations of nightmare peopled by the monsters of his own ethic-thwarted desires.

Like a man in fever, waking to intervals of consciousness, so Old Tarwater awoke, cooked his moose-meat, and fed the fire; but more and more time he spent in his torpor, unaware of what was daydream and what was sleep-dream in the content of his unconsciousness. And here, in the unforgettable crypts of man's unwritten history, unthinkable and unrealizable, like passages of nightmare or impossible adventures of lunacy, he encountered the monsters created of man's first morality that ever since have vexed him into the spinning of fantasies to elude them or do battle with them.

In short, weighted by his seventy years, in the vast and silent loneliness of the North, Old Tarwater, as in the delirium of drug or anæsthetic, recovered, within himself, the infantile mind of the child-man of the early world. It was in the dusk of Death's fluttery wings that Tarwater thus crouched, and, like his remote forebear, the child-man, went to myth-making, and sun-heroizing, himself hero-maker and the hero in quest of the immemorial treasure difficult of attainment.

Either must he attain the treasure—for so ran the inexorable logic of the shadow-land of the unconscious—or sink into the all-devouring sea, the blackness eater of the light that swallowed to extinction the sun each night . . . the sun that arose ever in rebirth next morning in the east, and that had become to man man's first symbol of immortality through rebirth. All this, in the deeps of his unconsciousness (the shadowy western land of descending light), was the near dusk of Death down into which he slowly ebbed.

But how to escape this monster of the dark that from within him slowly swallowed him? Too deep-sunk was he to dream of escape or feel the prod of desire to escape. For him reality had ceased. Nor from within the darkened chamber of himself could reality recrudesce. His years were too heavy upon him, the debility of disease and the lethargy and torpor of the silence and the cold were too profound. Only from without could reality impact upon him and reawake within him an awareness of reality. Otherwise he would ooze down through the shadow-realm of the unconscious into the all-darkness of extinction.

But it came, the smash of reality from without, crashing upon his ear drums in a loud, explosive snort. For twenty days, in a temperature that had never risen above fifty below, no breath of wind had blown movement, no slightest sound had broken the silence. Like the smoker on the opium couch refocusing his eyes from the spacious walls of dream to the narrow confines of the mean little room, so Old Tarwater stared vague-eyed before him, across his dying fire, at a huge moose that stared at him in startlement, dragging a wounded leg, manifesting all signs of extreme exhaustion; it, too, had been straying blindly in the shadow-land, and had wakened to reality only just ere it stepped into Tarwater's fire.

He feebly slipped the large fur mitten lined with thicknesses of wool from his right hand. Upon trial he found the trigger finger too numb for movement. Carefully, slowly, through long minutes, he worked the bare hand inside his blankets, up under his fur *parka*, through the chest openings of his shirts, and into the slightly warm hollow of his left arm-pit. Long minutes passed ere the finger could move, when, with equal slowness of caution, he gathered his rifle to his shoulder and drew bead upon the great animal across the fire.

At the shot, of the two shadow-wanderers, the one reeled downward to the dark and the other reeled upward to the light, swaying drunkenly on his scurvy-ravaged legs, shivering with nervousness and cold, rubbing swimming eyes with shaking fingers, and staring at the real world all about him that had returned to him with such sickening suddenness. He shook himself together, and realized that for long, how long he did not know, he had bedded in the arms of Death. He spat, with definite intention, heard the spittle crackle in the frost, and judged it must be below and far below sixty below.

In truth, that day at Fork Yukon, the spirit thermometer registered seventy-five degrees below zero, which, since freezing-point is thirty-two above, was equivalent to one hundred and seven degrees of frost.

Slowly Tarwater's brain reasoned to action. Here, in the vast alone, dwelt Death. Here had come two wounded moose. With the clearing of the sky after the great cold came on, he had located his bearings, and he knew that both wounded moose had trailed to him from the east. Therefore, in the east, were men—whites or Indians he could not tell, but at any rate men who might stand by him in his need and help moor him to reality above the sea of dark.

He moved slowly, but he moved in reality, girding himself with rifle, ammunition, matches, and a pack of twenty pounds of moose-meat. Then, an Argus rejuvenated, albeit lame of both legs and tottery, he turned his back on the perilous west and limped into the sun-arising, re-birthing east. . . .

Days later—how many days later he was never to know—dreaming dreams and seeing visions, cackling his old gold-chant of Forty-Nine, like one drowning and swimming feebly to keep his consciousness above the engulfing dark, he came out upon the snow-slope to a canyon and saw below smoke rising and men who ceased from work to gaze at him. He tottered down the hill to them, still singing; and when he ceased from lack of breath they called him variously: Santa Claus, Old Christmas, Whiskers, the Last of the Mohicans, and Father Christmas. And when he stood among them he stood very still, without speech, while great tears welled out of his eyes. He cried silently, a long time, till, as if suddenly bethinking himself, he sat down in the snow with much creaking and crackling of his joints, and from this low vantage point toppled sidewise and fainted calmly and easily away.

In less than a week Old Tarwater was up and limping about the housework of the cabin, cooking and dish-washing for the five men of the creek. Genuine sour-doughs (pioneers) they were, tough and hard-bitten, who had been buried so deeply inside the Circle that they did not know there was a Klondike Strike. The news he brought them was their first word of it. They lived on an almost straight-meat diet of moose, caribou, and smoked salmon, eked out with wild berries and somewhat succulent wild roots they had stocked up with in the summer. They had forgotten the taste of coffee, made fire with a burning glass, carried live fire-sticks with them wherever they traveled, and in their pipes smoked dry leaves that bit the tongue and were pungent to the nostrils.

Three years before, they had prospected from the head-reaches of the Koyokuk northward and clear across to the mouth of the Mackenzie on the Arctic Ocean. Here, on the whaleships, they had beheld their last white men and equipped themselves with the last whiteman's grub, consisting principally of salt and smoking tobacco. Striking south and west on the long traverse to the junction of the Yukon and Porcupine at Fort Yukon, they had found gold on this creek and remained over to work the ground.

They hailed the advent of Tarwater with joy, never tired of listening to his tales of Forty-Nine, and rechristened him Old Hero. Also, with tea made from spruce needles, with concoctions brewed from the inner willow bark, and with sour and bitter roots and bulbs from the ground, they dosed his scurvy out of him, so that he ceased limping and began to lay on flesh over his bony framework. Further, they saw no reason at all why he should not gather a rich treasure of gold from the ground.

"Don't know about all of three hundred thousand," they told him one morning, at breakfast, ere they departed to their work, "but how'd a hundred thousand do, Old Hero? That's what we figure a claim is worth, the ground being badly spotted, and we've already staked your location notices."

"Well, boys," Old Tarwater answered, "and thanking you kindly, all I can say is that a hundred thousand will do nicely, and very nicely, for a starter. Of course, I ain't goin' to stop till I get the full three hundred thousand. That's what I come into the country for."

They laughed and applauded his ambition and reckoned they'd have to hunt a richer creek for him. And Old Hero reckoned that as the spring came on and he grew spryer, he'd have to get out and do a little snooping around himself.

"For all anybody knows," he said, pointing to a hillside across the creek bottom, "the moss under the snow there may be plumb rooted in nugget gold."

He said no more, but as the sun rose higher and the days grew longer and warmer, he gazed often across the creek at the definite bench-formation half-way up the hill. And, one day, when the thaw was in full swing, he crossed the stream and climbed to the bench. Exposed patches of ground had already thawed an inch deep. On one such patch he stooped, gathered a bunch of moss in his big gnarled hands, and ripped it out by the roots. The sun smoldered on dully glistening yellow. He shook the handful of moss, and coarse nuggets, like gravel, fell to the ground. It was the Golden Fleece ready for the shearing.

Not entirely unremembered in Alaskan annals is the summer stampede of 1898 from Fort Yukon to the bench diggings of Tarwater Hill. And when Tarwater sold his holdings to the Bowdie interests for a sheer half-million and faced for California, he rode a mule over a new-cut trail, with convenient road houses along the way, clear to the steamboat landing at Fort Yukon.

At the first meal on the ocean-going steamship out of St. Michaels, a waiter, grayish-haired, pain-ravaged of face, scurvy-twisted of body, served him. Old Tarwater was compelled to look him over twice in order to make certain he was Charles Crayton.

"Got it bad, eh, son?" Tarwater queried.

"Just my luck," the other complained, after recognition and greeting. "Only one of the party that the scurvy attacked. I've been through hell. The other three are all at work and healthy, getting grub-stake to prospect up White River this winter. Anson's earning twenty-five a day at carpentering, Liverpool getting twenty logging for the saw-mill, and Big Bill's getting forty a day as chief sawyer. I tried my best, and if it hadn't been for scurvy . . ."

"Sure, son, you done your best, which ain't much, you being naturally irritable and hard from too much business. Now I'll tell you what. You ain't fit to work crippled up this way. I'll pay your passage with the captain in kind remembrance of the voyage you gave me, and you can lay up and take it easy the rest of the trip. And what are your circumstances when you land at San Francisco?"

Charles Crayton shrugged his shoulders.

"Tell you what," Tarwater continued. "There's work on the ranch for you till you can start business again."

"I could manage your business for you—" Charles began eagerly.

"No, siree," Tarwater declared emphatically. "But there's always post-holes to dig, and cordwood to chop, and the climate's fine. . . ."

Tarwater arrived home a true prodigal grandfather for whom the fatted calf was killed and ready. But first, ere he sat down at table, he must stroll out and around. And sons and daughters of his flesh and of the law needs must go with him, fulsomely eating out of the gnarled old hand that had half a million to disburse. He led the way, and no opinion he slyly uttered was preposterous or impossible enough to draw dissent from his following. Pausing by the ruined water wheel which he had built from the standing timber, his face beamed as he gazed across the stretches of Tarwater Valley, and on and up the far heights to the summit of Tarwater Mountain—now all his again.

A thought came to him that made him avert his face and blow his nose in order to hide the twinkle in his eyes. Still attended by the entire family, he strolled on to the dilapidated barn. He picked up an age-weathered single-tree from the ground.

"William," he said. "Remember that little conversation we had just before I started to Klondike? Sure, William, you remember. You told me I was crazy. And I said my father'd have walloped the tar out of me with a single-tree if I'd spoke to him that way."

"Aw, but that was only foolin'," William temporized.

William was a grizzled man of forty-five, and his wife and grown sons stood in the group, curiously watching Grandfather Tarwater take off his coat and hand it to Mary to hold.

"William—come here," he commanded imperatively.

No matter how reluctantly, William came.

"Just a taste, William, son, of what my father give me often enough," Old Tarwater crooned, as he laid on his son's back and shoulders with the single-tree. "Observe, I ain't hitting you on the head. My father had a gosh-wollickin' temper and never drew the line at heads when he went after tar.—Don't jerk your elbows back that way! You're likely to get a crack on one by accident. And just tell me one thing, William, son: is there any notion in your head that I'm crazy?"

"No!" William yelped out in pain, as he danced about. "You ain't crazy, father! Of course you ain't crazy!"

"You said it," Old Tarwater remarked sententiously, tossing the single-tree aside and starting to struggle into his coat. "Now let's all go in and eat."

THE WHITE SILENCE

(Overland Monthly, February, 1899)

Originally titled "Northland Episode" and turned down by *Godey's* and *Lippincott's* magazines, "The White Silence" sold finally—for $5 (a cheap buy even by 1899 standards)—to *The Overland Monthly* on January 3, 1899.

London biographer Irving Stone *(Sailor on Horseback,* 1938) calls this story "one of our imperishable classics of the frozen country" but London himself, depressed over the state of his newly launched writing career, had grave doubts about it. Not long after its appearance, in a letter to Cloudesley Johns, a young Southern California postal employee who had written a fan letter on the appearance of Jack's "To the Man on the Trail" in the January *Overland,* London said: "I was sick at heart, felt that it was a most miserable performance, and was heartily ashamed that it had escaped the waste-paper basket."

(London later had to visit the offices of the then moribund *Overland* to demand the $12.50 owed him for the two stories and ended up with $5 from the pockets of the magazine's proprietors.)

Literary scholar Earle Labor *(Jack London,* 1974) speaks of the "instinctive mysticism" dominating London's northland fiction. It is a felicitous phrase for the kind of passage one finds, for example, in that most famous of all London's works, *The Call of the Wild* (1903), when John Thornton and his partners seek a lost mine in the "uncharted vastness" of the Yukon. At last, "In the fall of the year they penetrated a weird lake country, sad and silent, where wild fowl had been, but where now there was no life, nor sign of life—only the blowing of chill winds, the forming of ice in sheltered places, and the melancholy waves on lonely beaches."

And, perhaps nowhere in his short fiction is this "instinctive mysticism" more in evidence than in the striking images of this story: "Nature has many tricks wherewith she convinces man of his finity—the ceaseless flow of the tides, the fury of the storm, the shock of the earthquake—but the most tremendous, the most stupefying of all, is the passive phase of the White Silence. All movement ceases, the sky clears, the heavens are as brass . . . sole speck of life journeying across the ghostly wastes of a dead world . . ."

The Malemute Kid is London's youthful Leatherstocking, a born raconteur, a straight-thinker, a man who can act quickly and, when necessary, make the rough choices. The Kid has the imagination lacking in the tenderfoot of "To Build a Fire," knows what it means to live on "rabbit tracks and salmon belly," grasps the full import of facing two hundred miles of unbroken trail at sixty-five below zero with six days of food—knows, without knowing Darwin, the law of survival.

THE WHITE SILENCE

"CARMEN WON'T LAST more than a couple of days." Mason spat out a chunk of ice and surveyed the poor animal ruefully, then put her foot in his mouth and proceeded to bite out the ice which clustered cruelly between the toes.

"I never saw a dog with a highfalutin' name that ever was worth a rap," he said, as he concluded his task and shoved her aside. "They just fade away and die under the responsibility. Did ye ever see one go wrong with a sensible name like Cassiar, Siwash, or Husky? No, sir! Take a look at Shookum here, he's"—

Snap! The lean brute flashed up, the white teeth just missing Mason's throat.

"Ye will, will ye?" A shrewd clout behind the ear with the butt of the dogwhip stretched the animal in the snow, quivering softly, a yellow slaver dripping from its fangs.

"As I was saying, just look at Shookum, here—he's got the spirit. Bet ye he eats Carmen before the week's out."

"I'll bank another proposition against that," replied Malemute Kid, reversing the frozen bread placed before the fire to thaw. "We'll eat Shookum before the trip is over. What d' ye say, Ruth?"

The Indian woman settled the coffee with a piece of ice, glanced from Malemute Kid to her husband, then at the dogs, but vouchsafed no reply. It was such a palpable truism that none was necessary. Two hundred miles of unbroken trail in prospect, with a scant six days' grub for themselves and none for the dogs, could admit no other alternative. The two men and the woman grouped about the fire and began their meagre meal. The dogs lay in their harnesses, for it was a midday halt, and watched each mouthful enviously.

"No more lunches after to-day," said Malemute Kid. "And we've got to keep a close eye on the dogs—they're getting vicious. They'd just as soon pull a fellow down as not, if they get a chance."

"And I was president of an Epworth once, and taught in the Sunday school." Having irrelevantly delivered himself of this, Mason fell into a dreamy contemplation of his steaming moccasins, but was aroused by Ruth filling his cup. "Thank God, we've got slathers of tea! I've seen it growing, down in Tennessee. What wouldn't I give for a hot corn pone just now! Never mind, Ruth; you won't starve much longer, nor wear moccasins either."

The woman threw off her gloom at this, and in her eyes welled up a great love for her white lord—the first white man she had ever seen—the first man whom she had known to treat a woman as something better than a mere animal or beast of burden.

"Yes, Ruth," continued her husband, having recourse to the macaronic jargon in which it was alone possible for them to understand each other: "wait till we clean up and pull for the Outside. We'll take the White Man's canoe and go to the Salt Water. Yes, bad water, rough water—great mountains dance up and down all the time. And so big, so far, so far away—you travel ten sleep, twenty sleep, forty sleep" (he graphically enumerated the days on his fingers), "all the time water, bad water. Then you come to great village, plenty people, just the same mosquitoes next summer. Wigwams oh, so high—ten, twenty pines. Hi-yu skookum!"

He paused impotently, cast an appealing glance at Malemute Kid, then laboriously placed the twenty pines, end on end, by sign language. Malemute Kid smiled with cheery cynicism; but Ruth's eyes were wide with wonder, and with pleasure; for she half believed he was joking, and such condescension pleased her poor woman's heart.

"And then you step into a—a box, and pouf! up you go." He tossed his empty cup in the air by way of illustration, and as he deftly caught it, cried: "And biff! down you come. Oh, great medicine-men! You go Fort Yukon, I go Arctic City—twenty-five sleep—big string, all the time—I catch him string—I say, 'Hello, Ruth! How are ye?'—and you say, 'Is that my good husband?'—and I say 'Yes'—and you say, 'No can bake good bread, no more soda'—then I say, 'Look in cache, under flour; good-by.' You look and catch plenty soda. All the time you Fort Yukon, me Arctic City. Hi-yu medicine-man!"

Ruth smiled so ingenuously at the fairy story, that both men burst into laughter. A row among the dogs cut short the wonders of the Outside, and by the time the snarling combatants were separated, she had lashed the sleds and all was ready for the trail.

"Mush! Baldy! Hi! Mush on!" Mason worked his whip smartly, and as the dogs whined low in the traces, broke out the sled with the gee-pole. Ruth followed with the second team, leaving Malemute Kid, who had helped her start, to bring up the rear. Strong man, brute that he was, capable of felling an ox at a blow, he could not bear to beat the poor animals, but humored them as a dog-driver rarely does—nay, almost wept with them in their misery.

"Come, mush on there, you poor sorefooted brutes!" he murmured, after several ineffectual attempts to start the load. But his patience was at last rewarded, and though whimpering with pain, they hastened to join their fellows.

No more conversation; the toil of the trail will not permit such extravagance. And of all deadening labors, that of the Northland trail is the worst. Happy is the man who can weather a day's travel at the price of silence, and that on a beaten track.

And of all heart-breaking labors, that of breaking trail is the worst. At every step the great webbed shoe sinks till the snow is level with the knee. Then up, straight up, the deviation of a fraction of an inch being a certain precursor of disaster, the snowshoe must be lifted till the surface is cleared; then forward, down, and the other foot is raised perpendicularly for the matter of half a yard. He who tries this for the first time, if haply he avoids bringing his shoes in dangerous propinquity and measures not his length on the treacherous footing, will give up exhausted at the end of a hundred yards; he who can keep out of the way of the dogs for a whole day may well crawl into his sleeping-bag with a clear conscience and a pride which passeth all understanding; and he who travels twenty sleeps on the Long Trail is a man whom the gods may envy.

The afternoon wore on, and with the awe, born of the White Silence, the voiceless travelers bent to their work. Nature has many tricks wherewith she convinces man of his finity—the ceaseless flow of the tides, the fury of the storm, the shock of the earthquake, the long roll of heaven's artillery—but the most tremendous, the most stupefying of all, is the passive phase of the White Silence. All movement ceases, the sky clears, the heavens are as brass; the slightest whisper seems sacrilege, and man becomes timid, affrighted at the sound of his own voice. Sole speck of life journeying across the ghostly wastes of a dead world, he trembles at his audacity, realizes that his is a maggot's life, nothing more. Strange thoughts arise unsummoned, and the mystery of all things strives for utterance. And the fear of death, of God, of the universe, comes over him—the hope of the Resurrection and the Life, the yearning for immortality, the vain striving of the imprisoned essence—it is then, if ever, man walks alone with God.

So wore the day away. The river took a great bend, and Mason headed his team for the cut-off across the narrow neck of land. But the dogs balked at the high bank. Again and again, though Ruth and Malemute Kid were shoving on the sled, they slipped back. Then came the concerted effort. The miserable creatures, weak from hunger, exerted their last strength. Up—up—the sled poised on the top of the bank; but the leader swung the string of dogs behind him to the right, fouling Mason's snowshoes. The result was grievous. Mason was whipped off his feet; one of the dogs fell in the traces; and the sled toppled back, dragging everything to the bottom again.

Slash! the whip fell among the dogs savagely, especially upon the one which had fallen.

"Don't, Mason," entreated Malemute Kid; "the poor devil's on its last legs. Wait and we'll put my team on."

Mason deliberately withheld the whip till the last word had fallen, then out flashed the long lash, completely curling about the offending creature's body. Carmen—for it was Carmen—cowered in the snow, cried piteously, then rolled over on her side.

It was a tragic moment, a pitiful incident of the trail—a dying dog, two comrades in anger. Ruth glanced solicitously from man to man. But Malemute Kid restrained himself, though there was a world of reproach in his eyes, and bending over the dog, cut the traces. No word was spoken. The teams were double-spanned and the difficulty overcome; the sleds were under way again, the dying dog dragging herself along in the rear. As long as an animal can travel, it is not shot, and this last chance is accorded it—the crawling into camp, if it can, in the hope of a moose being killed.

Already penitent for his angry action, but too stubborn to make amends, Mason toiled on at the head of the cavalcade, little dreaming that danger hovered in the air. The timber clustered thick in the sheltered bottom, and through this they threaded their way. Fifty feet or more from the trail towered a lofty pine. For generations destiny had had this one end in view—perhaps the same had been decreed of Mason.

He stopped to fasten the loosened thong of his moccasin. The sleds came to a halt and the dogs lay down in the snow without a whimper. The stillness was weird; not a breath rustled the frost-encrusted forest; the cold and silence of outer space had chilled the heart and smote the trembling lips of nature. A sigh pulsed through the air—they did not seem to actually hear it, but rather felt it, like the premonition of movement in a motionless void. Then the great tree, burdened with its weight of years and snow, played its last part in the tragedy of life. He heard the warning crash and attempted to spring up, but almost erect, caught the blow squarely on the shoulder.

The sudden danger, the quick death—how often had Malemute Kid faced it! The pine needles were still quivering as he gave his commands and sprang into action. Nor did the Indian girl faint or raise her voice in idle wailing, as might many of her white sisters. At his order, she threw her weight on the end of a quickly extemporized handspike, easing the pressure and listening to her husband's groans, while Malemute Kid attacked the tree with his axe.

The steel rang merrily as it bit into the frozen trunk, each stroke being accompanied by a forced, audible respiration, the "Huh!" "Huh!" of the woodsman.

At last the Kid laid the pitiable thing that was once a man in the snow. But worse than his comrade's pain was the dumb anguish in the woman's face, the blended look of hopeful, hopeless query. Little was said; those of the Northland are early taught the futility of words and the inestimable value of deeds. With the temperature at sixty-five below zero, a man cannot lie many minutes in the snow and live. So the sled-lashings were cut, and the sufferer, rolled in furs, laid on a couch of boughs. Before him roared a fire, built of the very wood which wrought the mishap. Behind and partially over him was stretched the primitive fly—a piece of canvas, which caught the radiating heat and threw it back and down upon him—a trick which men may know who study physics at the fount.

And men who have shared their bed with death know when the call is sounded. Mason was terribly crushed. The most cursory examination revealed it. His right arm, leg, and back, were broken; his limbs were paralyzed from the hips; and the likelihood of internal injuries was large. An occasional moan was his only sign of life.

No hope; nothing to be done. The pitiless night crept slowly by—Ruth's portion, the despairing stoicism of her race, and Malemute Kid adding new lines to his face of bronze. In fact, Mason suffered least of all, for he spent his time in Eastern Tennessee, in the Great Smoky Mountains, living over the scenes of his childhood. And most pathetic was the melody of his long-forgotten Southern vernacular, as he raved of swimming-holes and coon-hunts and watermelon raids. It was as Greek to Ruth, but the Kid understood and felt—felt as only one can feel who has been shut out for years from all that civilization means.

Morning brought consciousness to the stricken man, and Malemute Kid bent closer to catch his whispers.

"You remember when we foregathered on the Tanana, four years come next ice-run? I didn't care so much for her then. It was more like she was pretty, and there was a smack of excitement about it, I think. But d' ye know, I've come to think a heap of her. She's been a good wife to me, always at my shoulder in the pinch. And when it comes to trading, you know there isn't her equal. D' ye recollect the time she shot the Moosehorn Rapids to pull you and me off that rock, the bullets whipping the water like hailstones?—and the time of the famine at Nuklukyeto?—or when she raced the ice-run to bring the news? Yes, she's been a good wife to me, better 'n that other one. Didn't know I'd been there? Never told you, eh? Well, I tried it once, down in the States. That's why I'm here. Been raised together, too. I came away to give her a chance for divorce. She got it.

"But that's got nothing to do with Ruth. I had thought of cleaning up and pulling for the Outside next year—her and I—but it's too late. Don't send her back to her people, Kid. It's beastly hard for a woman to go back. Think of it!—nearly four years on our bacon and beans and flour and dried fruit, and then to go back to her fish and cariboo. It's not good for her to have tried our ways, to come to know they're better 'n her people's, and then return to them. Take care of her, Kid—why don't you—but no, you always fought shy of them—and you never told me why you came to this country. Be kind to her, and send her back to the States as soon as you can. But fix it so as she can come back—liable to get homesick, you know.

"And the youngster—it's drawn us closer, Kid. I only hope it is a boy. Think of it!—flesh of my flesh, Kid. He mustn't stop in this country. And if it's a girl, why she can't. Sell my furs; they'll fetch at least five thousand, and I've got as much more with the company. And handle my interests with yours. I think that bench claim will show up. See that he gets a good schooling; and Kid, above all, don't let him come back. This country was not made for white men.

"I'm a gone man, Kid. Three or four sleeps at the best. You've got to go on. You must go on! Remember, it's my wife, it's my boy—O God! I hope it's a boy! You can't stay by me—and I charge you, a dying man, to pull on."

"Give me three days," pleaded Malemute Kid. "You may change for the better; something may turn up."

"No."

"Just three days."

"You must pull on."

"Two days."

"It's my wife and my boy, Kid. You would not ask it."

"One day."

"No, no! I charge"—

"Only one day. We can shave it through on the grub, and I might knock over a moose."

"No—all right; one day, but not a minute more. And, Kid, don't—don't leave me to face it alone. Just a shot, one pull on the trigger. You understand. Think of it! Think of it! Flesh of my flesh, and I'll never live to see him!

"Send Ruth here. I want to say good-by and tell her that she must think of the boy and not wait till I'm dead. She might refuse to go with you if I didn't. Good-by, old man; good-by.

"Kid! I say—a—sink a hole above the pup, next to the slide. I panned out forty cents on my shovel there.

"And, Kid!" he stooped lower to catch the last faint words, the dying man's surrender of his pride. "I'm sorry—for—you know—Carmen."

Leaving the girl crying softly over her man, Malemute Kid slipped into his *parka* and snowshoes, tucked his rifle under his arm, and crept away into the forest. He was no tyro in the stern sorrows of the Northland, but never had he faced so stiff a problem as this. In the abstract, it was a plain, mathematical proposition—three possible lives as against one doomed one. But now he hesitated. For five years, shoulder to shoulder, on the rivers and trails, in the camps and mines, facing death by field and flood and famine, had they knitted the bonds of their comradeship. So close was the tie, that he had often been conscious of a vague jealousy of Ruth, from the first time she had come between. And now it must be severed by his own hand.

Though he prayed for a moose, just one moose, all game seemed to have deserted the land, and nightfall found the exhausted man crawling into camp, light-handed, heavy-hearted. An uproar from the dogs and shrill cries from Ruth hastened him.

Bursting into the camp, he saw the girl in the midst of the snarling pack, laying about her with an axe. The dogs had broken the iron rule of their masters and were rushing the grub. He joined the issue with his rifle reversed, and the hoary game of natural selection was played out with all the ruthlessness of its primeval environment. Rifle and axe went up and down, hit or missed with monotonous regularity; lithe bodies flashed, with wild eyes and dripping fangs; and man and beast fought for supremacy to the bitterest conclusion. Then the beaten brutes crept to the edge of the firelight, licking their wounds, voicing their misery to the stars.

The whole stock of dried salmon had been devoured, and perhaps five pounds of flour remained to tide them over two hundred miles of wilderness. Ruth returned to her husband, while Malemute Kid cut up the warm body of one of the dogs, the skull of which had been crushed by the axe. Every portion was carefully put away, save the hide and offal, which were cast to his fellows of the moment before.

Morning brought fresh trouble. The animals were turning on each other. Carmen, who still clung to her slender thread of life, was downed by the pack. The lash fell among them unheeded. They cringed and cried under the blows, but refused to scatter till the last wretched bit had disappeared—bones, hide, hair, everything.

Malemute Kid went about his work, listening to Mason, who was back in Tennessee, delivering tangled discourses and wild exhortations to his brethren of other days.

Taking advantage of neighboring pines, he worked rapidly, and Ruth watched him make a cache similar to those sometimes used by hunters to preserve their meat from the wolverines and dogs. One after the other, he bent the tops of two small pines toward each other and nearly to the ground, making them fast with thongs of moosehide. Then he beat the dogs into submission and harnessed them to two of the sleds, loading the same with everything but the furs which enveloped Mason. These he wrapped and lashed tightly about him, fastening either end of the robes to the bent pines. A single stroke of his hunting-knife would release them and send the body high in the air.

Ruth had received her husband's last wishes and made no struggle. Poor girl, she had learned the lesson of obedience well. From a child, she had bowed, and seen all women bow, to the lords of creation, and it did not seem in the nature of things for woman to resist. The Kid permitted her one outburst of grief, as she kissed her husband—her own people had no such custom—then led her to the foremost sled and helped her into her snowshoes. Blindly, instinctively, she took the gee-pole and whip, and "mushed" the dogs out on the trail. Then he returned to Mason, who had fallen into a coma; and long after she was out of sight, crouched by the fire, waiting, hoping, praying for his comrade to die.

It is not pleasant to be alone with painful thoughts in the White Silence. The silence of gloom is merciful, shrouding one as with protection and breathing a thousand intangible sympathies; but the bright White Silence, clear and cold, under steely skies, is pitiless.

An hour passed—two hours—but the man would not die. At high noon, the sun, without raising its rim above the southern horizon, threw a suggestion of fire athwart the heavens, then quickly drew it back. Malemute Kid roused and dragged himself to his comrade's side. He cast one glance about him. The White Silence seemed to sneer, and a great fear came upon him. There was a sharp report; Mason swung into his aerial sepulchre; and Malemute Kid lashed the dogs into a wild gallop as he fled across the snow.

THE LAW OF LIFE

(McClure's Magazine, March, 1901)

In April, 1900, appeared Jack London's first book, a collection of
Northland stories titled *A Son of the Wolf*, published by the pres-
tigious house of Houghton Mifflin. With that single book, London
took his place with Edgar Allan Poe, Bret Harte, Stephen Crane,
and Ambrose Bierce as an important, unconventional American
storyteller. Up to the advent of *A Son of the Wolf*, Irving Stone
wrote in 1938, "the bulk of short stories had been written for maiden
ladies; Jack's stories were for every class of American except maiden
ladies."

"The Law of Life" has a direct relationship with that first story
collection. *A Son of the Wolf* appeared in April, 1900, and a month
later, with the sale of "The Law of Life," London began an asso-
ciation with S. S. McClure, whose magazine featured action stories
with a male slant. *McClure's* had published much of Rudyard Kipling's work in the mid- and late 1890s, including serializations of
Captains Courageous and *Stalky & Co.*, and so it was perhaps
inevitable that Jack London—called "the American Kipling" by his
early critics—would become a *McClure's* writer.

S. S. McClure, indeed, provided London a reliable source of
income in the early months of his professional career, sending the
young author $125 a month while he worked on his first novel, *A
Daughter of the Snows*, and publishing London's second story collection, *The God of His Fathers* (1901).

"The Law of Life" is London at his economical, 2,500-word best, and in writing it he had turned a corner from those days of self-torment when even a story as brilliant as "The White Silence" might be consigned to the trashcan. Now, he could write Cloudesley Johns a letter brimming with confidence, one even offering a bit of instruction to his tyro friend: "How do I approach the event?" he wrote Johns of dealing with Koskoosh's death. "What point of view do I take? Why, the old Indian's, of course. . . . Don't you see, nothing, even the moralizing and generalizing, is done, save through him, in expressions of experience." (Quoted in Franklin Walker, *Jack London & the Klondike*, 1966.)

In telling the story of old Koskoosh, says James McClintock in his analysis of London's short fiction (*White Logic*, 1975), London "gives his metaphor of the human situation . . . it is the poetry of this story that discloses the horror, the nightmare of existence."

One thing is certain: It was no story for a maiden lady in 1900 and it is strong meat even today.

THE LAW OF LIFE

OLD KOSKOOSH LISTENED greedily. Though his sight had long since faded, his hearing was still acute, and the slightest sound penetrated to the glimmering intelligence which yet abode behind the withered forehead, but which no longer gazed forth upon the things of the world. Ah! That was Sit-cum-to-ha, shrilly anathematizing the dogs as she cuffed and beat them into the harnesses. Sit-cum-to-ha was his daughter's daughter, but she was too busy to waste a thought upon her broken grandfather, sitting alone there in the snow, forlorn and helpless. Camp must be broken. The long trail waited while the short day refused to linger. Life called her, and the duties of life, not death. And he was very close to death now.

The thought made the old man panicky for the moment, and he stretched forth a palsied hand which wandered tremblingly over the small heap of dry wood beside him. Reassured that it was indeed there, his hand returned to the shelter of his mangy furs, and he again fell to listening. The sulky crackling of half-frozen hides told him that the chief's moose-skin lodge had been struck, and even then was being rammed and jammed into portable compass. The chief was his son, stalwart and strong, headman of the tribesman, and a mighty hunter. As the women toiled with the camp luggage, his voice rose, chiding them for their slowness. Old Koskoosh strained his ears. It was the last time he would hear that voice. There went Geehow's lodge! And Tusken's! Seven, eight, nine; only the shaman's could be still standing. There! They were at work upon it now. He could hear the shaman grunt as he piled it on the sled. A child whimpered, and a woman soothed it with soft, crooning gutturals. Little Koo-tee, the old man thought, a fretful child, and not overstrong. It would die soon, perhaps, and they would burn a hole through the frozen tundra and pile rocks above to keep the wolverines away. Well, what did it matter? A few years at best, and as many an empty belly as a full one. And in the end, Death waited, ever-hungry and hungriest of them all.

What was that? Oh, the men lashing the sleds and drawing tight the thongs. He listened, who would listen no more. The whiplashes snarled and bit among the dogs. Hear them whine! How they hated the work and the trail! They were off! Sled after sled churned slowly away into the silence. They were gone. They had passed out of his life, and he faced the last bitter hour alone. No. The snow crunched beneath a moccasin; a man stood beside him; upon his head a hand rested gently. His son was good to do this thing. He remembered other old men whose sons had not waited after the tribe. But his son had. He wandered away into the past, till the young man's voice brought him back.

"It is well with you?" he asked.

And the old man answered, "It is well."

"There be wood beside you," the younger man continued, "and the fire burns bright. The morning is gray, and the cold has broken. It will snow presently. Even now it is snowing."

"Aye, even now is it snowing."

"The tribesmen hurry. Their bales are heavy and their bellies flat with lack of feasting. The trail is long and they travel fast. I go now. It is well?"

"It is well. I am as a last year's leaf, clinging lightly to the stem. The first breath that blows, and I fall. My voice is become like an old woman's. My eyes no longer show me the way of my feet, and my feet are heavy, and I am tired. It is well."

He bowed his head in content till the last noise of the complaining snow had died away, and he knew his son was beyond recall. Then his hand crept out in haste to the wood. It alone stood between him and the eternity that yawned in upon him. At last the measure of his life was a handful of faggots. One by one they would go to feed the fire, and just so, step by step, death would creep upon him. When the last stick had surrendered up its heat, the frost would begin to gather strength. First his feet would yield, then his hands; and the numbness would travel, slowly, from the extremities to the body. His head would fall forward upon his knees, and he would rest. It was easy. All men must die.

He did not complain. It was the way of life, and it was just. He had been born close to the earth, close to the earth had he lived, and the law thereof was not new to him. It was the law of all flesh. Nature was not kindly to the flesh. She had no concern for that concrete thing called the individual. Her interest lay in the species, the race. This was the deepest abstraction old Koskoosh's barbaric mind was capable of, but he grasped it firmly. He saw it exemplified in all life. The rise of the sap, the bursting greenness of the willow bud, the fall of the yellow leaf—in this alone was told the whole history. But one task did Nature set the individual. Did he not perform it, he died. Did he perform it, it was all the same, he died. Nature did not care; there were plenty who were obedient, and it was only the obedience in this matter, not the obedient, which lived and lived always. The tribe of Koskoosh was very old. The old men he had known when a boy had known old men before them. Therefore it was true that the tribe lived, that it stood for the obedience of all its members, way down into the forgotten past, whose very resting places were unremembered. They did not count; they were episodes. They had passed away like clouds from a summer sky. He also was an episode and would pass away. Nature did not care. To life she set one task, gave one law. To perpetuate was the task of life, its law was death. A maiden was a good creature to look upon, full-breasted and strong, with spring to her step and light in her eyes. But her task was yet before her. The light in her eyes brightened, her step quickened, she was now bold with the young men, now timid, and she gave them of her own unrest. And she grew fairer and yet fairer to look upon till some hunter, able no longer to withhold himself, took her to his lodge to cook and toil for him and to become the mother of his children. And with the coming of her offspring her looks left her. Her limbs dragged and shuffled, her eyes dimmed and bleared, and only the little children found joy against the withered cheek of the old squaw by the fire. Her task was done. But a little while, on the first pinch of famine or the first long trail, and she would be left, even as he had been left, in the snow, with a little pile of wood. Such was the law.

He placed a stick carefully upon the fire and resumed his meditations. It was the same everywhere, with all things. The mosquitoes vanished with the first frost. The little tree squirrel crawled away to die. When age settled upon the rabbit it became slow and heavy and could no longer outfoot its enemies. Even the big baldface grew clumsy and blind and quarrelsome, in the end to be dragged down by a handful of yelping huskies. He remembered how he had abandoned his own father on an upper reach of the Klondike one winter, the winter before the missionary came with his talk books and his box of medicines. Many a time had Koskoosh smacked his lips over the recollection of that box, though now his mouth refused to moisten. The "painkiller" had been especially good. But the missionary was a bother after all, for he brought no meat into the camp, and he ate heartily, and the hunters grumbled. But he chilled his lungs on the divide by the Mayo, and the dogs afterward nosed the stones away and fought over his bones.

Koskoosh placed another stick on the fire and harked back deeper into the past. There was the time of the great famine, when the old men crouched empty-bellied to the fire, and let fall from their lips dim traditions of the ancient day when the Yukon ran wide open for three winters, and then lay frozen for three summers. He had lost his mother in that famine. In the summer the salmon run had failed, and the tribe looked forward to the winter and the coming of the caribou. Then the winter came, but with it there were no caribou. Never had the like been known, not even in the lives of the old men. But the caribou did not come, and it was the seventh year, and the rabbits had not replenished, and the dogs were naught but bundles of bones. And through the long darkness the children wailed and died, and the women, and the old men; and not one in ten of the tribe lived to meet the sun when it came back in the spring. That *was* a famine!

But he had seen times of plenty, too, when the meat spoiled on their hands, and the dogs were fat and worthless with overeating—times when they let the game go unkilled, and the women were fertile, and the lodges were cluttered with sprawling men-children and women-children. Then it was the men became high-stomached, and revived ancient quarrels, and crossed the divides to the south to kill the Pellys, and to the west that they might sit by the dead fires of the Tananas. He remembered, when a boy, during a time of plenty, when he saw a moose pulled down by the wolves. Zing-ha lay with him in the snow and watched—Zing-ha, who later became the craftiest of hunters, and who, in the end, fell through an air hole on the Yukon. They found him, a month afterward, just as he had crawled halfway out and frozen stiff to the ice.

But the moose. Zing-ha and he had gone out that day to play at hunting after the manner of their fathers. On the bed of the creek they struck the fresh track of a moose, and with it the tracks of many wolves. "An old one," Zing-ha, who was quicker at reading the sign, said, "an old one who cannot keep up with the herd. The wolves have cut him out from his brothers, and they will never leave him." And it was so. It was their way. By day and by night, never resting, snarling on his heels, snapping at his nose, they would stay by him to the end. How Zing-ha and he felt the blood lust quicken! The finish would be a sight to see!

Eager-footed, they took the trail, and even he, Koskoosh, slow of sight and an unversed tracker, could have followed it blind, it was so wide. Hot were they on the heels of the chase, reading the grim tragedy, fresh-written, at every step. Now they came to where the moose had made a stand. Thrice the length of a grown man's body, in every direction, had the snow been stamped about and uptossed. In the midst were the deep impressions of the splayhoofed game, and all about, everywhere, were the lighter footmarks of the wolves. Some, while their brothers harried the kill, had lain to one side and rested. The full-stretched impress of their bodies in the snow was as perfect as though made the moment before. One wolf had been caught in a wild lunge of the maddened victim and trampled to death. A few bones, well picked, bore witness.

Again, they ceased the uplift of their snowshoes at a second stand. Here the great animal had fought desperately. Twice had he been dragged down, as the snow attested, and twice had he shaken his assailants clear and gained footing once more. He had done his task long since, but none the less was life dear to him. Zing-ha said it was a strange thing, a moose once down to get free again; but this one certainly had. The shaman would see signs and wonders in this when they told him.

And yet again, they come to where the moose had made to mount the bank and gain the timber. But his foes had laid on from behind, till he reared and fell back upon them, crushing two deep into the snow. It was plain the kill was at hand, for their brothers had left them untouched. Two more stands were hurried past, brief in time length and very close together. The trail was red now, and the clean stride of the great beast had grown short and slovenly. Then they heard the first sounds of the battle—not the full-throated chorus of the chase, but the short, snappy bark which spoke of close quarters and teeth to flesh. Crawling up the wind, Zing-ha bellied it through the snow, and with him crept he, Koskoosh, who was to be chief of the tribesmen in the years to come. Together they shoved aside the underbranches of a young spruce and peered forth. It was the end they saw.

The picture, like all of youth's impressions, was still strong with him, and his dim eyes watched the end played out as vividly as in that far-off time. Koskoosh marveled at this, for in the days which followed, when he was a leader of men and a head of councilors, he had done great deeds and made his name a curse in the mouths of the Pellys, to say naught of the strange white man he had killed, knife to knife, in open fight.

For long he pondered on the days of his youth, till the fire died down and the frost bit deeper. He replenished it with two sticks this time, and gauged his grip on life by what remained. If Sit-cum-to-ha had only remembered her grandfather, and gathered a larger armful, his hours would have been longer. It would have been easy. But she was ever a careless child, and honored not her ancestors from the time the Beaver, son of the son of Zing-ha, first cast eyes upon her. Well, what mattered it? Had he not done likewise in his own quick youth? For a while he listened to the silence. Perhaps the heart of his son might soften, and he would come back with the dogs to take his old father on with the tribe to where the caribou ran thick and the fat hung heavy upon them.

He strained his ears, his restless brain for the moment stilled. Not a stir, nothing. He alone took breath in the midst of the great silence. It was very lonely. Hark! What was that? A chill passed over his body. The familiar, long-drawn howl broke the void, and it was close at hand. Then on his darkened eyes was projected the vision of the moose—the old bull moose—the torn flanks and bloody sides, the riddled mane, and the great branching horns, down low and tossing to the last. He saw the flashing forms of gray, the gleaming eyes, the lolling tongues, the slavered fangs. And he saw the inexorable circle close in till it became a dark point in the midst of the stamped snow.

A cold muzzle thrust against his cheek, and at its touch his soul leaped back to the present. His hand shot into the fire and dragged out a burning faggot. Overcome for the nonce by his hereditary fear of man, the brute retreated, raising a prolonged call to his brothers; and greedily they answered, till a ring of crouching, jaw-slobbered gray was stretched round about. The old man listened to the drawing in of this circle. He waved his brand wildly, and sniffs turned to snarls; but the panting brutes refused to scatter. Now one wormed his chest forward, dragging his haunches after, now a second, now a third; but never a one drew back. Why should he cling to life? he asked, and dropped the blazing stick into the snow. It sizzled and went out. The circle grunted uneasily but held its own. Again he saw the last stand of the old bull moose, and Koskoosh dropped his head wearily upon his knees. What did it matter after all? Was it not the law of life?

ALASKA

LOST FACE

(New York *Herald,* December 13, 1908)

Jack London's wife, Charmian, has recorded (in her *Voyaging in Wild Seas,* 1909) that this gruesome piece of business was written during the *Snark* voyage—just as was "To Build a Fire"—and that she typed it at Pago Pago, American Samoa, in May, 1908.

London biographer Andrew Sinclair (*Jack*, 1977) claims the *Snark* journey to Hawaii and the South Seas (1907-1909) ruined Jack's physical health and made inroads into his mental stability as well. There can be little doubt of the physical debility London endured, occasioned by contracting malaria, yaws, skin eruptions, and various other ailments, during the long voyage. But it appears to be taking it a step too far to say that the stories he wrote, "memorable in their grim irony," during and after the venture, evidenced some kind of mental disorder. Sinclair claims that London, following the *Snark's* return to San Francisco, "could no longer distinguish between the sublime and the sadistic, the tragic and sentimental, the heroic and the cruel, the myth and the posture."

The truth may be that London *never* saw much difference between the sublime and sadistic, tragic and sentimental, heroic and cruel, myth and posture. His stories reveal a magnificent ability to juggle and juxtapose such notions. "To Build a Fire" is heroic and cruel, "In a Far Country" is sublimely tragic; "Like Argus of the Ancient Times" has elements of sentimentality, heroism, tragedy and myth; "The Apostate" is certainly both tragic and sentimental, heroic and cruel.

"Lost Face" has a little bit of all Sinclair's contrasting elements. Subienkow, the Pole who awaits torture and death at the hands of the Nulato Indians, is a dreamer, a poet, and an artist. He is also a barbaric freebooter and fur thief, come now to harvest the blood he has helped sow.

Maxwell Geismar (*Rebels and Ancestors: The American Novel, 1890-1915*, 1963) writes of "Lost Face"—indeed, all the stories, including "To Build a Fire," in the collection by that name which London published in 1910, as having as their central mood an "inhuman, but almost mechanical, misery." And James McClintock, in his *White Logic* (1975), uses the phrase "motiveless malignancy" to characterize this tale and its companions in *Lost Face*.

But let the reader judge . . .

LOST FACE

IT WAS THE end. Subienkow had travelled a long trail of bitterness and horror, homing like a dove for the capitals of Europe, and here, farther away than ever, in Russian America, the trail ceased. He sat in the snow, arms tied behind him, waiting the torture. He stared curiously before him at a huge Cossack, prone in the snow, moaning in his pain. The men had finished handling the giant and turned him over to the women. That they exceeded the fiendishness of the men, the man's cries attested.

Subienkow looked on, and shuddered. He was not afraid to die. He had carried his life too long in his hands, on that weary trail from Warsaw to Nulato, to shudder at mere dying. But he objected to the torture. It offended his soul. And this offence, in turn, was not due to the mere pain he must endure, but to the sorry spectacle the pain would make of him. He knew that he would pray, and beg, and entreat, even as Big Ivan and the others that had gone before. This would not be nice. To pass out bravely and cleanly, with a smile and a jest—ah! that would have been the way. But to lose control, to have his soul upset by the pangs of the flesh, to screech and gibber like an ape, to become the veriest beast—ah, that was what was so terrible.

There had been no chance to escape. From the beginning, when he dreamed the fiery dream of Poland's independence, he had become a puppet in the hands of Fate. From the beginning, at Warsaw, at St. Petersburg, in the Siberian mines, in Kamtchatka, on the crazy boats of the fur-thieves, Fate had been driving him to this end. Without doubt, in the foundations of the world was graved this end for him—for him, who was so fine and sensitive, whose nerves scarcely sheltered under his skin, who was a dreamer, and a poet, and an artist. Before he was dreamed of, it had been determined that the quivering bundle of sensitiveness that constituted him should be doomed to live in raw and howling savagery, and to die in this far land of night, in this dark place beyond the last boundaries of the world.

He sighed. So that thing before him was Big Ivan—Big Ivan the giant, the man without nerves, the man of iron, the Cossack turned freebooter of the seas, who was as phlegmatic as an ox, with a nervous system so low that what was pain to ordinary men was scarcely a tickle to him. Well, well, trust these Nulato Indians to find Big Ivan's nerves and trace them to the roots of his quivering soul. They were certainly doing it. It was inconceivable that a man could suffer so much and yet live. Big Ivan was paying for his low order of nerves. Already he had lasted twice as long as any of the others.

Subienkow felt that he could not stand the Cossack's sufferings much longer. Why didn't Ivan die? He would go mad if that screaming did not cease. But when it did cease, his turn would come. And there was Yakaga awaiting him, too, grinning at him even now in anticipation—Yakaga, whom only last week he had kicked out of the fort, and upon whose face he had laid the lash of his dog-whip. Yakaga would attend to him. Doubtlessly Yakaga was saving for him more refined tortures, more exquisite nerve-racking. Ah! that must have been a good one, from the way Ivan screamed. The squaws bending over him stepped back with laughter and clapping of hands. Subienkow saw the monstrous thing that had been perpetrated, and began to laugh hysterically. The Indians looked at him in wonderment that he should laugh. But Subienkow could not stop.

This would never do. He controlled himself, the spasmodic twitchings slowly dying away. He strove to think of other things, and began reading back in his own life. He remembered his mother and his father, and the little spotted pony, and the French tutor who had taught him dancing and sneaked him an old worn copy of Voltaire. Once more he saw Paris, and dreary London, and gay Vienna, and Rome. And once more he saw that wild group of youths who had dreamed, even as he, the dream of an independent Poland with a king of Poland on the throne at Warsaw. Ah, there it was that the long trail began. Well, he had lasted longest. One by one, beginning with the two executed at St. Petersburg, he took up the count of the passing of those brave spirits. Here one had been beaten to death by a jailer, and there, on that blood-stained highway of the exiles, where they had marched for endless months, beaten and maltreated by their Cossack guards, another had dropped by the way. Always it had been savagery—brutal, bestial savagery. They had died—of fever, in the mines, under the knout. The last two had died after the escape, in the battle with the Cossacks, and he alone had won to Kamtchatka with the stolen papers and the money of a traveller he had left lying in the snow.

It had been nothing but savagery. All the years, with his heart in studios, and theatres, and courts, he had been hemmed in by savagery. He had purchased his life with blood. Everybody had killed. He had killed that traveller for his passports. He had proved that he was a man of parts by duelling with two Russian officers on a single day. He had had to prove himself in order to win to a place among the fur-thieves. He had had to win to that place. Behind him lay the thousand-years-long road across all Siberia and Russia. He could not escape that way. The only way was ahead, across the dark and icy sea of Behring to Alaska. The way had led from savagery to deeper savagery. On the scurvy-rotten ships of the fur-thieves, out of food and out of water, buffeted by the interminable storms of that stormy sea, men had become animals. Thrice he had sailed east from Kamtchatka. And thrice, after all manner of hardship and suffering, the survivors had come back to Kamtchatka. There had been no outlet for escape, and he could not go back the way he had come, for the mines and the knout awaited him.

Again, the fourth and last time, he had sailed east. He had been with those who first found the fabled Seal Islands; but he had not returned with them to share the wealth of furs in the mad orgies of Kamtchatka. He had sworn never to go back. He knew that to win to those dear capitals of Europe he must go on. So he had changed ships and remained in the dark new land. His comrades were Slavonian hunters and Russian adventurers, Mongols and Tartars and Siberian aborigines; and through the savages of the new world they had cut a path of blood. They had massacred whole villages that refused to furnish the fur-tribute; and they, in turn, had been massacred by ships' companies. He, with one Finn, had been the sole survivors of such a company. They had spent a winter of solitude and starvation on a lonely Aleutian isle, and their rescue in the spring by another fur-ship had been one chance in a thousand.

But always the terrible savagery had hemmed him in. Passing from ship to ship, and ever refusing to return, he had come to the ship that explored south. All down the Alaska coast they had encountered nothing but hosts of savages. Every anchorage among the beetling islands or under the frowning cliffs of the mainland had meant a battle or a storm. Either the gales blew, threatening destruction, or the war canoes came off, manned by howling natives with the war-paint on their faces, who came to learn the bloody virtues of the sea-rovers' gunpowder. South, south they had coasted, clear to the myth-land of California. Here, it was said, were Spanish adventurers who had fought their way up from Mexico. He had had hopes of those Spanish adventurers. Escaping to them, the rest would have been easy—a year or two, what did it matter more or less—and he would win to Mexico, then a ship, and Europe would be his. But they had met no Spaniards. Only had they encountered the same impregnable wall of savagery. The denizens of the confines of the world, painted for war, had driven them back from the shores. At last, when one boat was cut off and every man killed, the commander had abandoned the quest and sailed back to the north.

The years had passed. He had served under Tebenkoff when Michaelovski Redoubt was built. He had spent two years in the Kuskokwim country. Two summers, in the month of June, he had managed to be at the head of Kotzebue Sound. Here, at this time, the tribes assembled for barter; here were to be found spotted deerskins from Siberia, ivory from the Diomedes, walrus skins from the shores of the Arctic, strange stone lamps, passing in trade from tribe to tribe, no one knew whence, and, once, a hunting-knife of

English make; and here, Subienkow knew, was the school in which
to learn geography. For he met Eskimos from Norton Sound, from
King Island and St. Lawrence Island, from Cape Prince of Wales,
and Point Barrow. Such places had other names, and their distances
were measured in days.

It was a vast region these trading savages came from, and a vaster
region from which, by repeated trade, their stone lamps and that
steel knife had come. Subienkow bullied, and cajoled, and bribed.
Every far-journeyer or strange tribesman was brought before him.
Perils unaccountable and unthinkable were mentioned, as well as
wild beasts, hostile tribes, impenetrable forests, and mighty mountain ranges; but always from beyond came the rumor and the tale
of white-skinned men, blue of eye and fair of hair, who fought like
devils and who sought always for furs. They were to the east—far,
far to the east. No one had seen them. It was the word that had
been passed along.

It was a hard school. One could not learn geography very well
through the medium of strange dialects, from dark minds that min-
gled fact and fable and that measured distances by "sleeps" that
varied according to the difficulty of the going. But at last came the
whisper that gave Subienkow courage. In the east lay a great river
where were these blue-eyed men. The river was called the Yukon.
South of Michaelovski Redoubt emptied another great river which
the Russians knew as the Kwikpak. These two rivers were one, ran
the whisper.

Subienkow returned to Michaelovski. For a year he urged an
expedition up the Kwikpak. Then arose Malakoff, the Russian half-
breed, to lead the wildest and most ferocious of the hell's broth of
mongrel adventurers who had crossed from Kamtchatka. Subienkow
was his lieutenant. They threaded the mazes of the great delta of
the Kwikpak, picked up the first low hills on the northern bank,
and for half a thousand miles, in skin canoes loaded to the gunwales
with trade-goods and ammunition, fought their way against the five-
knot current of a river that ran from two to ten miles wide in a
channel many fathoms deep. Malakoff decided to build the fort at
Nulato. Subienkow urged to go farther. But he quickly reconciled
himself to Nulato. The long winter was coming on. It would be
better to wait. Early the following summer, when the ice was gone,

he would disappear up the Kwikpak and work his way to the Hudson Bay Company's posts. Malakoff had never heard the whisper that the Kwikpak was the Yukon, and Subienkow did not tell him.

Came the building of the fort. It was enforced labor. The tiered walls of logs arose to the sighs and groans of the Nulato Indians. The lash was laid upon their backs, and it was the iron hand of the freebooters of the sea that laid on the lash. There were Indians that ran away, and when they were caught they were brought back and spread-eagled before the fort, where they and their tribe learned the efficacy of the knout. Two died under it; others were injured for life; and the rest took the lesson to heart and ran away no more. The snow was flying ere the fort was finished, and then it was the time for furs. A heavy tribute was laid upon the tribe. Blows and lashings continued, and that the tribute should be paid, the women and children were held as hostages and treated with the barbarity that only the fur-thieves knew.

Well, it had been a sowing of blood, and now was come the harvest. The fort was gone. In the light of its burning, half the fur-thieves had been cut down. The other half had passed under the torture. Only Subienkow remained, or Subienkow and Big Ivan, if that whimpering, moaning thing in the snow could be called Big Ivan. Subienkow caught Yakaga grinning at him. There was no gain-saying Yakaga. The mark of the lash was still on his face. After all, Subienkow could not blame him, but he disliked the thought of what Yakaga would do to him. He thought of appealing to Makamuk, the head-chief; but his judgment told him that such appeal was useless. Then, too, he thought of bursting his bonds and dying fighting. Such an end would be quick. But he could not break his bonds. Caribou thongs were stronger than he. Still devising, another thought came to him. He signed for Makamuk, and that an interpreter who knew the coast dialect should be brought.

"Oh, Makamuk," he said, "I am not minded to die. I am a great man, and it were foolishness for me to die. In truth, I shall not die. I am not like these other carrion."

He looked at the moaning thing that had once been Big Ivan, and stirred it contemptuously with his toe.

"I am too wise to die. Behold, I have a great medicine. I alone know this medicine. Since I am not going to die, I shall exchange this medicine with you."

"What is this medicine?" Makamuk demanded.

"It is a strange medicine."

Subienkow debated with himself for a moment, as if loath to part with the secret.

"I will tell you. A little bit of this medicine rubbed on the skin makes the skin hard like rock, hard like iron, so that no cutting weapon can cut it. The strongest blow of a cutting weapon is a vain thing against it. A bone knife becomes like a piece of mud; and it will turn the edge of the iron knives we have brought among you. What will you give me for the secret of the medicine?"

"I will give you your life," Makamuk made answer through the interpreter.

Subienkow laughed scornfully.

"And you shall be a slave in my house until you die."

The Pole laughed more scornfully.

"Untie my hands and feet and let us talk," he said.

The chief made the sign; and when he was loosed Subienkow rolled a cigarette and lighted it.

"This is foolish talk," said Makamuk. "There is no such medicine. It cannot be. A cutting edge is stronger than any medicine."

The chief was incredulous, and yet he wavered. He had seen too many deviltries of fur-thieves that worked. He could not wholly doubt.

"I will give you your life; but you shall not be a slave," he announced.

"More than that."

Subienkow played his game as coolly as if he were bartering for a foxskin.

"It is a very great medicine. It has saved my life many times. I want a sled and dogs, and six of your hunters to travel with me down the river and give me safety to one day's sleep from Michaelovski Redoubt."

"You must live here, and teach us all of your deviltries," was the reply.

Subienkow shrugged his shoulders and remained silent. He blew cigarette smoke out on the icy air, and curiously regarded what remained of the big Cossack.

"That scar!" Makamuk said suddenly, pointing to the Pole's neck, where a livid mark advertised the slash of a knife in a Kamtchatkan brawl. "The medicine is not good. The cutting edge was stronger than the medicine."

"It was a strong man that drove the stroke." (Subienkow considered.) "Stronger than you, stronger than your strongest hunter, stronger than he."

Again, with the toe of his moccasin, he touched the Cossack—a grisly spectacle, no longer conscious—yet in whose dismembered body the pain-racked life clung and was loath to go.

"Also, the medicine was weak. For at that place there were no berries of a certain kind, of which I see you have plenty in this country. The medicine here will be strong."

"I will let you go down river," said Makamuk; "and the sled and the dogs and the six hunters to give you safety shall be yours."

"You are slow," was the cool rejoinder. "You have committed an offence against my medicine in that you did not at once accept my terms. Behold, I now demand more. I want one hundred beaver skins." (Makamuk sneered.) "I want one hundred pounds of dried fish." (Makamuk nodded, for fish were plentiful and cheap.) "I want two sleds—one for me and one for my furs and fish. And my rifle must be returned to me. If you do not like the price, in a little while the price will grow."

Yakaga whispered to the chief.

"But how can I know your medicine is true medicine?" Makamuk asked.

"It is very easy. First, I shall go into the woods—"

Again Yakaga whispered to Makamuk, who made a suspicious dissent.

"You can send twenty hunters with me," Subienkow went on. "You see, I must get the berries and the roots with which to make the medicine. Then, when you have brought the two sleds and loaded on them the fish and the beaver skins and the rifle, and when you have told off the six hunters who will go with me—then, when all is ready, I will rub the medicine on my neck, so, and lay my neck there on that log. Then can your strongest hunter take the axe and strike three times on my neck. You yourself can strike the three times."

Makamuk stood with gaping mouth, drinking in this latest and most wonderful magic of the fur-thieves.

"But first," the Pole added hastily, "between each blow I must put on fresh medicine. The axe is heavy and sharp, and I want no mistakes."

"All that you have asked shall be yours," Makamuk cried in a rush of acceptance. "Proceed to make your medicine."

Subienkow concealed his elation. He was playing a desperate game, and there must be no slips. He spoke arrogantly.

"You have been slow. My medicine is offended. To make the offence clean you must give me your daughter."

He pointed to the girl, an unwholesome creature, with a cast in one eye and a bristling wolf-tooth. Makamuk was angry, but the Pole remained imperturbable, rolling and lighting another cigarette.

"Make haste," he threatened. "If you are not quick, I shall demand yet more."

In the silence that followed, the dreary northland scene faded from before him, and he saw once more his native land, and France, and, once, as he glanced at the wolf-toothed girl, he remembered another girl, a singer and a dancer, whom he had known when first as a youth he came to Paris.

"What do you want with the girl?" Makamuk asked.

"To go down the river with me." Subienkow glanced her over critically. "She will make a good wife, and it is an honor worthy of my medicine to be married to your blood."

Again he remembered the singer and dancer and hummed aloud a song she had taught him. He lived the old life over, but in a detached, impersonal sort of way, looking at the memory-pictures of his own life as if they were pictures in a book of anybody's life. The chief's voice, abruptly breaking the silence, startled him.

"It shall be done," said Makamuk. "The girl shall go down the river with you. But be it understood that I myself strike the three blows with the axe on your neck."

"But each time I shall put on the medicine," Subienkow answered, with a show of ill-concealed anxiety.

"You shall put the medicine on between each blow. Here are the hunters who shall see you do not escape. Go into the forest and gather your medicine."

Makamuk had been convinced of the worth of the medicine by the Pole's rapacity. Surely nothing less than the greatest of medicines could enable a man in the shadow of death to stand up and drive an old-woman's bargain.

"Besides," whispered Yakaga, when the Pole, with his guard, had disappeared among the spruce trees, "when you have learned the medicine you can easily destroy him."

"But how can I destroy him?" Makamuk argued. "His medicine will not let me destroy him."

"There will be some part where he has not rubbed the medicine," was Yakaga's reply. "We will destroy him through that part. It may be his ears. Very well; we will thrust a spear in one ear and out the other. Or it may be his eyes. Surely the medicine will be much too strong to rub on his eyes."

The chief nodded. "You are wise, Yakaga. If he possesses no other devil-things, we will then destroy him."

Subienkow did not waste time in gathering the ingredients for his medicine. He selected whatsoever came to hand such as spruce needles, the inner bark of the willow, a strip of birch bark, and a quantity of moss-berries, which he made the hunters dig up for him from beneath the snow. A few frozen roots completed his supply, and he led the way back to camp.

Makamuk and Yakaga crouched beside him, noting the quantities and kinds of the ingredients he dropped into the pot of boiling water.

You must be careful that the moss-berries go in first," he explained.

"And—oh, yes, one other thing—the finger of a man. Here, Yakaga, let me cut off your finger."

But Yakaga put his hands behind him and scowled.

"Just a small finger," Subienkow pleaded.

"Yakaga, give him your finger," Makamuk commanded.

"There be plenty of fingers lying around," Yakaga grunted, indicating the human wreckage in the snow of the score of persons who had been tortured to death.

"It must be the finger of a live man," the Pole objected.

"Then shall you have the finger of a live man," Yakaga strode over to the Cossack and sliced off a finger.

"He is not yet dead," he announced, flinging the bloody trophy in the snow at the Pole's feet. "Also, it is a good finger, because it is large."

Subienkow dropped it into the fire under the pot and began to sing. It was a French lovesong that with great solemnity he sang into the brew.

"Without these words I utter into it, the medicine is worthless," he explained. "The words are the chiefest strength of it. Behold, it is ready."

"Name the words slowly, that I may know them," Makamuk commanded.

"Not until after the test. When the axe flies back three times from my neck, then will I give you the secret of the words."

"But if the medicine is not good medicine?" Makamuk queried anxiously.

Subienkow turned upon him wrathfully.

"My medicine is always good. However, if it is not good, then do by me as you have done to the others. Cut me up a bit at a time, even as you have cut him up." He pointed to the Cossack. "The medicine is now cool. Thus, I rub it on my neck, saying this further medicine."

With great gravity he slowly intoned a line of the "Marseillaise," at the same time rubbing the villainous brew thoroughly into his neck.

An outcry interrupted his play-acting. The giant Cossack, with a last resurgence of his tremendous vitality, had arisen to his knees. Laughter and cries of surprise and applause arose from the Nulatos, as Big Ivan began flinging himself about in the snow with mighty spasms.

Subienkow was made sick by the sight, but he mastered his qualms and made believe to be angry.

"This will not do," he said. "Finish him, and then we will make the test. Here, you, Yakaga, see that his noise ceases."

While this was being done, Subienkow turned to Makamuk.

"And remember, you are to strike hard. This is not baby-work. Here, take the axe and strike the log, so that I can see you strike like a man."

Makamuk obeyed, striking twice, precisely and with vigor, cutting out a large chip.

"It is well." Subienkow looked about him at the circle of savage faces that somehow seemed to symbolize the wall of savagery that had hemmed him about ever since the Czar's police had first arrested him in Warsaw. "Take your axe, Makamuk, and stand so. I shall lie down. When I raise my hand, strike, and strike with all your might. And be careful that no one stands behind you. The medicine is good, and the axe may bounce off my neck and right out of your hands."

He looked at the two sleds, with the dogs in harness, loaded with furs and fish. His rifle lay on top of the beaver skins. The six hunters who were to act as his guard stood by the sleds."

"Where is the girl?" the Pole demanded. "Bring her up to the sleds before the test goes on."

When this had been carried out, Subienkow lay down in the snow, resting his head on the log like a tired child about to sleep. He had lived so many dreary years that he was indeed tired.

"I laugh at you and your strength, O Makamuk," he said. "Strike, and strike hard."

He lifted his hand. Makamuk swung the axe, a broadaxe for the squaring of logs. The bright steel flashed through the frosty air, poised for a perceptible instant above Makamuk's head, then descended upon Subienkow's bare neck. Clear through flesh and bone it cut its way, biting deeply into the log beneath. The amazed savages saw the head bounce a yard away from the blood-spouting trunk.

There was a great bewilderment and silence, while slowly it began to dawn in their minds that there had been no medicine. The fur-thief had outwitted them. Alone, of all their prisoners, he had escaped the torture. That had been the stake for which he played. A great roar of laughter went up. Makamuk bowed his head in shame. The fur-thief had fooled him. He had lost face before all his people. Still they continued to roar out their laughter. Makamuk turned, and with bowed head stalked away. He knew that thenceforth he would be no longer known as Makamuk. He would be Lost Face; the record of his shame would be with him until he died; and whenever the tribes gathered in the spring for the salmon, or in the summer for the trading, the story would pass back and forth across the camp-fires of how the fur-thief died peaceably, at a single stroke, by the hand of Lost Face.

"Who was Lost Face?" he could hear, in anticipation, some insolent young buck demand. "Oh, Lost Face," would be the answer, "he who once was Makamuk in the days before he cut off the fur-thief's head."

THE
CANADIAN
BARRENS

LOVE OF LIFE

(*McClure's Magazine*, December, 1905)

London's daughter Joan, in her *Jack London and His Times* (1939), recounts the story that in January, 1924, while the Russian revolutionary leader Vladimir Ilyich Ulyanov, known as Lenin, lay on his deathbed, his wife Krupskaya read to him this harrowing story. "The tale greatly pleased Ilyich," she later wrote. "Next day he asked me to read more of Jack London. But London's strong pieces of work are mixed with extraordinarily weak ones. The next tale happened to be quite another type—saturated with bourgeois morals . . . Ilyich smiled and dismissed it with a wave of the hand."

Whatever the case for his eloquent deathbed criticism, Lenin may have seen a familiar reflection in the ordeal and triumph of the nameless man lost in a "tremendous and terrible desolation" that is the substance of "Love of Life."

The story has a controversial history. It is loosely based on the real-life experience of one Charles Bunn, member of a small Canadian exploration party looking for mineral deposits in the Canadian Northwest in 1900. Bunn, abandoned by his companion, wandered lost for eight days until stumbling into an Indian camp where he recovered and was eventually rescued.

Bunn's story was written up by two journalists, Augustus Bridle and J. A. MacDonald, as "Lost in the Land of the Midnight Sun" and published, ironically, in *McClure's* in 1901.

When "Love of Life" appeared in the December, 1905, *McClure's*, London was quickly accused of plagiarism, a charge he dismissed out of hand, saying in a letter to *The Editor* that his story was a good example of "turning journalism into literature." (Good accounts of the plagiarism controversy can be found in Franklin Walker's *Jack London & the Klondike,* 1966, and in *Letters from Jack London,* edited by Irving Shepard and King Hendricks, 1965.)

In truth, other than the inspiration it gave him, there is little resemblance between London's magnificent story and the rather mundane reportage that preceded it.

LOVE OF LIFE

> This out of all will remain—
>   They have lived and have tossed:
> So much of the game will be gain,
>   Though the gold of the dice has been lost.

THEY LIMPED PAINFULLY down the bank, and once the foremost of the two men staggered among the rough-strewn rocks. They were tired and weak, and their faces had the drawn expression of patience which comes of hardship long endured. They were heavily burdened with blanket packs which were strapped to their shoulders. Head-straps, passing across the forehead, helped support these packs. Each man carried a rifle. They walked in a stooped posture, the shoulders well forward, the head still farther forward, the eyes bent upon the ground.

"I wish we had just about two of them cartridges that's layin' in that cache of ourn," said the second man.

His voice was utterly and drearily expressionless. He spoke without enthusiasm; and the first man, limping into the milky stream that foamed over the rocks, vouchsafed no reply.

The other man followed at his heels. They did not remove their foot-gear, though the water was icy cold—so cold that their ankles ached and their feet went numb. In places the water dashed against their knees, and both men staggered for footing.

The man who followed slipped on a smooth boulder, nearly fell, but recovered himself with a violent effort, at the same time uttering a sharp exclamation of pain. He seemed faint and dizzy and put out his free hand while he reeled, as though seeking support against the air. When he had steadied himself he stepped forward, but reeled again and nearly fell. Then he stood still and looked at the other man, who had never turned his head.

The man stood still for fully a minute, as though debating with himself. Then he called out:

"I say, Bill, I've sprained my ankle."

Bill staggered on through the milky water. He did not look around. The man watched him go, and though his face was expressionless as ever, his eyes were like the eyes of a wounded deer.

The other man limped up the farther bank and continued straight on without looking back. The man in the stream watched him. His lips trembled a little, so that the rough thatch of brown hair which covered them was visibly agitated. His tongue even strayed out to moisten them.

"Bill!" he cried out.

It was the pleading cry of a strong man in distress, but Bill's head did not turn. The man watched him go, limping grotesquely and lurching forward with stammering gait up the slow slope toward the soft sky-line of the low-lying hill. He watched him go till he passed over the crest and disappeared. Then he turned his gaze and slowly took in the circle of the world that remained to him now that Bill was gone.

Near the horizon the sun was smouldering dimly, almost obscured by formless mists and vapors, which gave an impression of mass and density without outline or tangibility. The man pulled out his watch, the while resting his weight on one leg. It was four o'clock, and as the season was near the last of July or first of August—he did not know the precise date within a week or two—he knew that the sun roughly marked the northwest. He looked to the south and knew that somewhere beyond those bleak hills lay the Great Bear Lake; also, he knew that in that direction the Arctic Circle cut its forbidding way across the Canadian Barrens. This stream in which he stood was a feeder to the Coppermine River, which in turn flowed north and emptied into Coronation Gulf and the Arctic Ocean. He had never been there, but he had seen it, once, on a Hudson Bay Company chart.

Again his gaze completed the circle of the world about him. It was not a heartening spectacle. Everywhere was soft sky-line. The hills were all low-lying. There were no trees, no shrubs, no grasses—naught but a tremendous and terrible desolation that sent fear swiftly dawning into his eyes.

"Bill!" he whispered, once and twice; "Bill!"

He cowered in the midst of the milky water, as though the vastness were pressing in upon him with overwhelming force, brutally crushing him with its complacent awfulness. He began to shake as with an ague-fit, till the gun fell from his hand with a splash. This served to rouse him. He fought with his fear and pulled himself together, groping in the water and recovering the weapon. He hitched his pack farther over on his left shoulder, so as to take a portion of its weight from off the injured ankle. Then he proceeded, slowly and carefully, wincing with pain, to the bank.

He did not stop. With a desperation that was madness, unmindful of the pain, he hurried up the slope to the crest of the hill over which his comrade had disappeared—more grotesque and comical by far than that limping, jerking comrade. But at the crest he saw a shallow valley, empty of life. He fought with his fear again, overcame it, hitched the pack still farther over on his left shoulder, and lurched on down the slope.

The bottom of the valley was soggy with water, which the thick moss held, spongelike, close to the surface. This water squirted out from under his feet at every step, and each time he lifted a foot the action culminated in a sucking sound as the wet moss reluctantly released its grip. He picked his way from muskeg to muskeg, and followed the other man's footsteps along and across the rocky ledges which thrust like islets through the sea of moss.

Though alone, he was not lost. Farther on he knew he could come to where dead spruce and fir, very small and weazened, bordered the shore of a little lake, the *titchin-nichilie*, in the tongue of the country, the "land of little sticks." And into that lake flowed a small stream, the water of which was not milky. There was rush-grass on that stream—this he remembered well—but no timber, and he would follow it till its first trickle ceased at a divide. He would cross this divide to the first trickle of another stream, flowing to the west, which he would follow until it emptied into the river Dease, and here he would find a cache under an upturned canoe and piled over with many rocks. And in this cache would be ammunition for his empty gun, fish-hooks and lines, a small net—all the utilities for the killing and snaring of food. Also, he would find flour—not much—a piece of bacon, and some beans.

Bill would be waiting for him there, and they would paddle away south down the Dease to the Great Bear Lake. And south across the lake they would go, ever south, till they gained the Mackenzie. And south, still south, they would go, while the winter raced vainly after them, and the ice formed in the eddies, and the days grew chill and crisp, south to some warm Hudson Bay Company post, where timber grew tall and generous and there was grub without end.

These were the thoughts of the man as he strove onward. But hard as he strove with his body, he strove equally hard with his mind, trying to think that Bill had not deserted him, that Bill would surely wait for him at the cache. He was compelled to think this thought, or else there would not be any use to strive, and he would have lain down and died. And as the dim ball of the sun sank slowly into the northwest he covered every inch—and many times—of his and Bill's flight south before the downcoming winter. And he conned the grub of the cache and the grub of the Hudson Bay Company post over and over again. He had not eaten for two days; for a far longer time he had not had all he wanted to eat. Often he stopped and picked pale muskeg berries, put them into his mouth, and chewed and swallowed them. A muskeg berry is a bit of seed enclosed in a bit of water. In the mouth the water melts away and the seed chews sharp and bitter. The man knew there was no nourishment in the berries, but he chewed them patiently with a hope greater than knowledge and defying experience.

At nine o'clock he stubbed his toe on a rocky ledge, and from sheer weariness and weakness staggered and fell. He lay for some time, without movement, on his side. Then he slipped out of the pack-straps and clumsily dragged himself into a sitting posture. It was not yet dark, and in the lingering twilight he groped about among the rocks for shreds of dry moss. When he had gathered a heap he built a fire—a smouldering, smudgy fire—and put a tin pot of water on to boil.

He unwrapped his pack and the first thing he did was to count his matches. There were sixty-seven. He counted them three times to make sure. He divided them into several portions, wrapping them in oil paper, disposing of one bunch in his empty tobacco pouch, of another bunch in the inside band of his battered hat, of a third bunch under his shirt on the chest. This accomplished, a panic came upon him, and he unwrapped them all and counted them again. There were still sixty-seven.

He dried his wet foot-gear by the fire. The moccasins were in soggy shreds. The blanket socks were worn through in places, and his feet were raw and bleeding. His ankle was throbbing, and he gave it an examination. It had swollen to the size of his knee. He tore a long strip from one of his two blankets and bound the ankle tightly. He tore other strips and bound them about his feet to serve for both moccasins and socks. Then he drank the pot of water, steaming hot, wound his watch, and crawled between his blankets.

He slept like a dead man. The brief darkness around midnight came and went. The sun arose in the northeast—at least the day dawned in that quarter, for the sun was hidden by gray clouds.

At six o'clock he awoke, quietly lying on his back. He gazed straight up into the gray sky and knew that he was hungry. As he rolled over on his elbow he was startled by a loud snort, and saw a bull caribou regarding him with alert curiosity. The animal was not more than fifty feet away, and instantly into the man's mind leaped the vision and the savor of a caribou steak sizzling and frying over a fire. Mechanically he reached for the empty gun, drew a bead, and pulled the trigger. The bull snorted and leaped away, his hoofs rattling and clattering as he fled across the ledges.

The man cursed and flung the empty gun from him. He groaned aloud as he started to drag himself to his feet. It was a slow and arduous task. His joints were like rusty hinges. They worked harshly in their sockets, with much friction, and each bending or unbending was accomplished only through a sheer exertion of will. When he finally gained his feet, another minute or so was consumed in straightening up, so that he could stand erect as a man should stand.

He crawled up a small knoll and surveyed the prospect. There were no trees, no bushes, nothing but a gray sea of moss scarcely diversified by gray rocks, gray lakelets, and gray streamlets. The sky was gray. There was no sun nor hint of sun. He had no idea of north, and he had forgotten the way he had come to this spot the night before. But he was not lost. He knew that. Soon he would come to the land of the little sticks. He felt that it lay off to the left somewhere, not far—possibly just over the next low hill.

He went back to put his pack into shape for travelling. He assured himself of the existence of his three separate parcels of matches, though he did not stop to count them. But he did linger, debating, over a squat moose-hide sack. It was not large. He could hide it under his two hands. He knew that it weighed fifteen pounds—as much as all the rest of the pack—and it worried him. He finally set it to one side and proceeded to roll the pack. He paused to gaze at the squat moose-hide sack. He picked it up hastily with a defiant glance about him, as though the desolation were trying to rob him of it; and when he rose to his feet to stagger on into the day, it was included in the pack on his back.

He bore away to the left, stopping now and again to eat muskeg berries. His ankle had stiffened, his limp was more pronounced, but the pain of it was as nothing compared with the pain of his stomach. The hunger pangs were sharp. They gnawed and gnawed until he could not keep his mind steady on the course he must pursue to gain the land of little sticks. The muskeg berries did not allay this gnawing, while they made his tongue and the roof of his mouth sore with their irritating bite.

He came upon a valley where rock ptarmigan rose on whirring wings from the ledges and muskegs. Ker—ker—ker was the cry they made. He threw stones at them, but could not hit them. He placed his pack on the ground and stalked them as a cat stalks a sparrow. The sharp rocks cut through his pants' legs till his knees left a trail of blood; but the hurt was lost in the hurt of his hunger. He squirmed over the wet moss, saturating his clothes and chilling his body; but he was not aware of it, so great was his fever for food. And always the ptarmigan rose, whirring, before him, till their ker—ker—ker became a mock to him, and he cursed them and cried aloud at them with their own cry.

Once he crawled upon one that must have been asleep. He did not see it till it shot up in his face from its rocky nook. He made a clutch as startled as was the rise of the ptarmigan, and there remained in his hand three tail-feathers. As he watched its flight he hated it, as though it had done him some terrible wrong. Then he returned and shouldered his pack.

As the day wore along he came into valleys or swales where game was more plentiful. A band of caribou passed by, twenty and odd animals, tantalizingly within rifle range. He felt a wild desire to run after them, a certitude that he could run them down. A black fox came toward him, carrying a ptarmigan in his mouth. The man shouted. It was a fearful cry, but the fox, leaping away in fright, did not drop the ptarmigan.

Late in the afternoon he followed a stream, milky with lime, which ran through sparse patches of rush-grass. Grasping these rushes firmly near the root, he pulled up what resembled a young opinion-sprout no larger than a shingle-nail. It was tender, and his teeth sank into it with a crunch that promised deliciously of food. But its fibers were tough. It was composed of stringy filaments saturated with water, like the berries, and devoid of nourishment. He threw off his pack and went into the rush-grass on hands and knees, crunching and munching, like some bovine creature.

He was very weary and often wished to rest—to lie down and sleep; but he was continually driven on—not so much by his desire to gain the land of little sticks as by his hunger. He searched little ponds for frogs and dug up the earth with his nails for worms, though he knew in spite that neither frogs nor worms existed so far north.

He looked into every pool of water vainly, until, as the long twilight came on, he discovered a solitary fish, the size of a minnow, in such a pool. He plunged his arm in up to the shoulder, but it eluded him. He reached for it with both hands and stirred up the milky mud at the bottom. In his excitement he fell in, wetting himself to the waist. Then the water was too muddy to admit of his seeing the fish, and he was compelled to wait until the sediment had settled.

The pursuit was renewed, till the water was again muddied. But he could not wait. He unstrapped the tin bucket and began to bale the pool. He baled wildly at first, splashing himself and flinging the water so short a distance that it ran back into the pool. He worked more carefully, striving to be cool, though his heart was pounding against his chest and his hands were trembling. At the end of half an hour the pool was nearly dry. Not a cupful of water remained. And there was no fish. He found a hidden crevice among the stones through which it had escaped to the adjoining and larger pool—a pool which he could not empty in a night and a day. Had he known of the crevice, he could have closed it with a rock at the beginning and the fish would have been his.

Thus he thought, and crumpled up and sank down upon the wet earth. At first he cried softly to himself, then he cried loudly to the pitiless desolation that ringed him around; and for a long time after he was shaken by great dry sobs.

He built a fire and warmed himself by drinking quarts of hot water, and made camp on a rocky ledge in the same fashion he had the night before. The last thing he did was to see that his matches were dry and to wind his watch. The blankets were wet and clammy. His ankle pulsed with pain. But he knew only that he was hungry, and through his restless sleep he dreamed of feasts and banquets and of food served and spread in all imaginable ways.

He awoke chilled and sick. There was no sun. The gray of earth and sky had become deeper, more profound. A raw wind was blowing, and the first flurries of snow were whitening the hilltops. The air about him thickened and grew white while he made a fire and boiled more water. It was wet snow, half rain, and the flakes were large and soggy. At first they melted as soon as they came in contact with the earth, but ever more fell, covering the ground, putting out the fire, spoiling his supply of moss-fuel.

This was a signal for him to strap on his pack and stumble onward, he knew not where. He was not concerned with the land of little sticks, nor with Bill and the cache under the upturned canoe by the river Dease. He was mastered by the verb "to eat." He was hunger-mad. He took no heed of the course he pursued, so long as that course led him through the swale bottoms. He felt his way through the wet snow to the watery muskeg berries, and went by feel as he pulled up the rush-grass by the roots. But it was tasteless stuff and did not satisfy. He found a weed that tasted sour and he ate all he could find of it, which was not much, for it was a creeping growth, easily hidden under the several inches of snow.

He had no fire that night, nor hot water, and crawled under his blanket to sleep the broken hunger-sleep. The snow turned into a cold rain. He awakened many times to feel it falling on his upturned face. Day came—a gray day and no sun. It had ceased raining. The keenness of his hunger had departed. Sensibility, as far as concerned the yearning for food, had been exhausted. There was a dull, heavy ache in his stomach, but it did not bother him so much. He was more rational, and once more he was chiefly interested in the land of little sticks and the cache by the river Dease.

He ripped the remnant of one of his blankets into strips and bound his bleeding feet. Also, he recinched the injured ankle and prepared himself for a day of travel. When he came to his pack, he paused long over the squat moose-hide sack, but in the end it went with him.

The snow had melted under the rain, and only the hilltops showed white. The sun came out, and he succeeded in locating the points of the compass, though he knew now that he was lost. Perhaps, in his previous days' wanderings, he had edged away too far to the left. He now bore off to the right to counteract the possible deviation from his true course.

Though the hunger pangs were no longer so exquisite, he realized that he was weak. He was compelled to pause for frequent rests, when he attacked the muskeg berries and rush-grass patches. His tongue felt dry and large, as though covered with a fine hairy growth, and it tasted bitter in his mouth. His heart gave him a great deal of trouble. When he had travelled a few minutes it would begin a remorseless thump, thump, thump, and then leap up and away in a painful flutter of beats that choked him and made him go faint and dizzy.

In the middle of the day he found two minnows in a large pool. It was impossible to bale it, but he was calmer now and managed to catch them in his tin bucket. They were no longer than his little finger, but he was not particularly hungry. The dull ache in his stomach had been growing duller and fainter. It seemed almost that his stomach was dozing. He ate the fish raw, masticating with painstaking care, for the eating was an act of pure reason. While he had no desire to eat, he knew that he must eat to live.

In the evening he caught three more minnows, eating two and saving the third for breakfast. The sun had dried stray shreds of moss, and he was able to warm himself with hot water. He had not covered more than ten miles that day; and the next day, travelling whenever his heart permitted him, he covered no more than five miles. But his stomach did not give him the slightest uneasiness. It had gone to sleep. He was in a strange country, too, and the caribou were growing more plentiful, also the wolves. Often their yelps drifted across the desolation, and once he saw three of them slinking away before his path.

Another night; and in the morning, being more rational, he untied the leather string that fastened the squat moose-hide sack. From its open mouth poured a yellow stream of coarse gold-dust and nuggets. He roughly divided the gold in halves, caching one half on a prominent ledge, wrapped in a piece of blanket, and returning the other half to the sack. He also began to use strips of the one remaining blanket for his feet. He still clung to his gun, for there were cartridges in that cache by the river Dease.

This was a day of fog, and this day hunger awoke in him again. He was very weak and was afflicted with a giddiness which at times blinded him. It was no uncommon thing now for him to stumble and fall; and stumbling once, he fell squarely into a ptarmigan nest. There were four newly hatched chicks, a day old—little specks of pulsating life no more than a mouthful; and he ate them ravenously, thrusting them alive in his mouth and crunching them like egg-shells between his teeth. The mother ptarmigan beat about him with great outcry. He used his gun as a club with which to knock her over, but she dodged out of reach. He threw stones at her and with one chance shot broke a wing. Then she fluttered away, running, trailing the broken wing, with him in pursuit.

The little chicks had no more than whetted his appetite. He hopped and bobbed clumsily along on his injured ankle, throwing stones and screaming hoarsely at times; at other times hopping and bobbing silently along, picking himself up grimly and patiently when he fell, or rubbing his eyes with his hand when the giddiness threatened to overpower him.

The chase led him across swampy ground in the bottom of the valley, and he came upon footprints in the soggy moss. They were not his own—he could see that. They must be Bill's. But he could not stop, for the mother ptarmigan was running on. He would catch her first, then he would return and investigate.

He exhausted the mother ptarmigan; but he exhausted himself. She lay panting on her side. He lay panting on his side, a dozen feet away, unable to crawl to her. And as he recovered she recovered, fluttering out of reach as his hungry hand went out to her. The chase was resumed. Night settled down and she escaped. He stumbled from weakness and pitched head foremost on his face, cutting his cheek, his pack upon his back. He did not move for a long while; then he rolled over on his side, wound his watch, and lay there until morning.

Another day of fog. Half of his last blanket had gone into foot-wrappings. He failed to pick up Bill's trail. It did not matter. His hunger was driving him too compellingly—only—only he wondered if Bill, too, were lost. By midday the irk of his pack became too oppressive. Again he divided the gold, this time merely spilling half of it on the ground. In the afternoon he threw the rest of it away, there remaining to him only the half-blanket, the tin bucket, and the rifle.

An hallucination began to trouble him. He felt confident that one cartridge remained to him. It was in the chamber of the rifle and he had overlooked it. On the other hand, he knew all the time that the chamber was empty. But the hallucination persisted. He fought it off for hours, then threw his rifle open and was confronted with emptiness. The disappointment was as bitter as though he had really expected to find the cartridge.

He plodded on for half an hour, when the hallucination arose again. Again he fought it, and still it persisted, till for very relief he opened his rifle to unconvince himself. At times his mind wandered farther afield, and he plodded on, a mere automaton, strange conceits and whimsicalities gnawing at his brain like worms. But these excursions out of the real were of brief duration, for ever the pangs of the hunger-bite called him back. He was jerked back abruptly once from such an excursion by a sight that caused him nearly to faint. He reeled and swayed, doddering like a drunken man to keep from falling. Before him stood a horse. A horse! He could not believe his eyes. A thick mist was in them, intershot with sparkling points of light. He rubbed his eyes savagely to clear his vision, and beheld, not a horse, but a great brown bear. The animal was studying him with bellicose curiosity.

The man had brought his gun halfway to his shoulder before he realized. He lowered it and drew his hunting-knife from its beaded sheath at his hip. Before him was meat and life. He ran his thumb along the edge of his knife. It was sharp. The point was sharp. He would fling himself upon the bear and kill it. But his heart began its warning thump, thump, thump. Then followed the wild upward leap and tattoo of flutters, the pressing as of an iron band about his forehead, the creeping of the dizziness into his brain.

His desperate courage was evicted by a great surge of fear. In his weakness, what if the animal attacked him? He drew himself up to his most imposing stature, gripping the knife and staring hard at the bear. The bear advanced clumsily a couple of steps, reared up, and gave vent to a tentative growl. If the man ran, he would run after him; but the man did not run. He was animated now with the courage of fear. He, too, growled, savagely, terribly, voicing the fear that is to life germane and that lies twisted about life's deepest roots.

The bear edged away to one side, growling menacingly, himself appalled by this mysterious creature that appeared upright and un-afraid. But the man did not move. He stood like a statue till the danger was past, when he yielded to a fit of trembling and sank down into the wet moss.

He pulled himself together and went on, afraid now in a new way. It was not the fear that he should die passively from lack of food, but that he should be destroyed violently before starvation had exhausted the last particle of the endeavor in him that made toward surviving. There were the wolves. Back and forth across the desolation drifted their howls, weaving the very air into a fabric of menace that was so tangible that he found himself, arms in the air, pressing it back from him as it might be the walls of a wind-blown tent.

Now and again the wolves, in packs of two and three, crossed his path. But they sheered clear of him. They were not in sufficient numbers, and besides they were hunting the caribou, which did not battle, while this strange creature that walked erect might scratch and bite.

In the late afternoon he came upon scattered bones where the wolves had made a kill. The débris had been a caribou calf an hour before, squawking and running and very much alive. He contemplated the bones, clean-picked and polished, pink with the cell-life in them which had not yet died. Could it possibly be that he might be that ere the day was done! Such was life, eh? A vain and fleeting thing. It was only life that pained. There was no hurt in death. To die was to sleep. It meant cessation, rest. Then why was he not content to die?

But he did not moralize long. He was squatting in the moss, a bone in his mouth, sucking at the shreds of life that still dyed it faintly pink. The sweet meaty taste, thin and elusive almost as a memory, maddened him. He closed his jaws on the bones and crunched. Sometimes it was the bone that broke, sometimes his teeth. Then he crushed the bones between rocks, pounded them to a pulp, and swallowed them. He pounded his fingers, too, in his haste, and yet found a moment in which to feel surprise at the fact that his fingers did not hurt much when caught under the descending rock.

Came frightful days of snow and rain. He did not know when he made camp, when he broke camp. He travelled in the night as much as in the day. He rested wherever he fell, crawled on whenever the dying life in him flickered up and burned less dimly. He, as a man, no longer strove. It was the life in him, unwilling to die, that drove him on. He did not suffer. His nerves had become blunted, numb, while his mind was filled with weird visions and delicious dreams.

But ever he sucked and chewed on the crushed bones of the caribou calf, the least remnants of which he had gathered up and carried with him. He crossed no more hills or divides, but automatically followed a large stream which flowed through a wide and shallow valley. He did not see this stream nor this valley. He saw nothing save visions. Soul and body walked or crawled side by side, yet apart, so slender was the thread that bound them.

He awoke in his right mind, lying on his back on a rocky ledge. The sun was shining bright and warm. Afar off he heard the squawking of caribou calves. He was aware of vague memories of rain and wind and snow, but whether he had been beaten by the storm for two days or two weeks he did not know.

For some time he lay without movement, the genial sunshine pouring upon him and saturating his miserable body with its warmth.

A fine day, he thought. Perhaps he could manage to locate himself. By a painful effort he rolled over on his side. Below him flowed a wide and sluggish river. Its unfamiliarity puzzled him. Slowly he followed it with his eyes, winding in wide sweeps among the bleak, bare hills, bleaker and barer and lower-lying than any hills he had yet encountered. Slowly, deliberately, without excitement or more than the most casual interest, he followed the course of the strange stream toward the sky-line and saw it emptying into a bright and shining sea. He was still unexcited. Most unusual, he thought, a vision or a mirage—more likely a vision, a trick of his disordered mind. He was confirmed in this by sight of a ship lying at anchor in the midst of the shining sea. He closed his eyes for a while, then opened them. Strange how the vision persisted! Yet not strange. He knew there were no seas or ships in the heart of the barren lands, just as he had known there was no cartridge in the empty rifle.

He heard a snuffle behind him—a half-choking gasp or cough. Very slowly, because of his exceeding weakness and stiffness, he rolled over on his other side. He could see nothing near at hand, but he waited patiently. Again came the snuffle and cough, and outlined between two jagged rocks not a score of feet away he made out the gray head of a wolf. The sharp ears were not pricked so sharply as he had seen them on other wolves; the eyes were bleared and bloodshot, the head seemed to droop limply and forlornly. The animal blinked continually in the sunshine. It seemed sick. As he looked it snuffled and coughed again.

This, at least, was real, he thought, and turned on the other side so that he might see the reality of the world which had been veiled from him before by the vision. But the sea still shone in the distance and the ship was plainly discernible. Was it reality, after all? He closed his eyes for a long while and thought, and then it came to him. He had been making north by east, away from the Dease Divide and into the Coppermine Valley. This wide and sluggish river was the Coppermine. That shining sea was the Arctic Ocean. That ship was a whaler, strayed east, far east, from the mouth of the Mackenzie, and it was lying at anchor in Coronation Gulf. He remembered the Hudson Bay Company chart he had seen long ago, and it was all clear and reasonable to him.

He sat up and turned his attention to immediate affairs. He had worn through the blanket-wrappings, and his feet were shapeless lumps of raw meat. His last blanket was gone. Rifle and knife were both missing. He had lost his hat somewhere, with the bunch of matches in the band, but the matches against his chest were safe and dry inside the tobacco pouch and oil paper. He looked at his watch. It marked eleven o'clock and was still running. Evidently he had kept it wound.

He was calm and collected. Though extremely weak, he had no sensation of pain. He was not hungry. The thought of food was not even pleasant to him, and whatever he did was done by his reason alone. He ripped off his pants' legs to the knees and bound them about his feet. Somehow he had succeeded in retaining the tin bucket. He would have some hot water before he began what he foresaw was to be a terrible journey to the ship.

His movements were slow. He shook as with a palsy. When he started to collect dry moss, he found he could not rise to his feet. He tried again and again, then contented himself with crawling about on hands and knees. Once he crawled near to the sick wolf. The animal dragged itself reluctantly out of his way, licking its chops with a tongue which seemed hardly to have the strength to curl. The man noticed that the tongue was not the customary healthy red. It was a yellowish brown and seemed coated with a rough and half-dry mucus.

After he had drunk a quart of hot water the man found he was able to stand, and even to walk as well as a dying man might be supposed to walk. Every minute or so he was compelled to rest. His steps were feeble and uncertain, just as the wolf's that trailed him were feeble and uncertain; and that night, when the shining sea was blotted out by blackness, he knew he was nearer to it by no more than four miles.

Throughout the night he heard the cough of the sick wolf, and now and then the squawking of the caribou calves. There was life all around him, but it was strong life, very much alive and well, and he knew the sick wolf clung to the sick man's trail in the hope that the man would die first. In the morning, on opening his eyes, he beheld it regarding him with a wistful and hungry stare. It stood crouched, with tail between its legs, like a miserable and woe-be-gone dog. It shivered in the chill morning wind, and grinned dispiritedly when the man spoke to it in a voice that achieved no more than a hoarse whisper.

The sun rose brightly, and all morning the man tottered and fell toward the ship on the shining sea. The weather was perfect. It was the brief Indian Summer of the high latitudes. It might last a week. Tomorrow or next day it might be gone.

In the afternoon the man came upon a trail. It was of another man, who did not walk, but who dragged himself on all fours. The man thought it might be Bill, but he thought in a dull, uninterested way. He had no curiosity. In fact, sensation and emotion had left him. He was no longer susceptible to pain. Stomach and nerves had gone to sleep. Yet the life that was in him drove him on. He was very weary, but it refused to die. It was because it refused to die that he still ate muskeg berries and minnows, drank his hot water, and kept a wary eye on the sick wolf.

He followed the trail of the other man who dragged himself along, and soon came to the end of it—a few fresh-picked bones where the soggy moss was marked by the foot-pads of many wolves. He saw a squat moose-hide sack, mate to his own, which had been torn by sharp teeth. He picked it up, though its weight was almost too much for his feeble fingers. Bill had carried it to the last. Ha! ha! He would have the laugh on Bill. He would survive and carry it to the ship in the shining sea. His mirth was hoarse and ghastly, like a raven's croak, and the sick wolf joined him, howling lugubriously. The man ceased suddenly. How could he have the laugh on Bill if that were Bill; if those bones, so pinky-white and clean, were Bill?

He turned away. Well, Bill had deserted him; but he would not take the gold, nor would he suck Bill's bones. Bill would have, though, had it been the other way around, he mused as he staggered on.

He came to a pool of water. Stooping over in quest of minnows, he jerked his head back as though he had been stung. He had caught sight of his reflected face. So horrible was it that sensibility awoke long enough to be shocked. There were three minnows in the pool, which was too large to drain; and after several ineffectual attempts to catch them in the tin bucket he forbore. He was afraid, because of his great weakness, that he might fall in and drown. It was for this reason that he did not trust himself to the river astride one of the many drift-logs which lined its sand-spits.

That day he decreased the distance between him and the ship by three miles; the next day by two—for he was crawling now as Bill had crawled; and the end of the fifth day found the ship still seven miles away and him unable to make even a mile a day. Still the Indian Summer held on, and he continued to crawl and faint, turn and turn about; and ever the sick wolf coughed and wheezed at his heels. His knees had become raw meat like his feet, and though he padded them with the shirt from his back it was a red track he left behind him on the moss and stones. Once, glancing back, he saw the wolf licking hungrily his bleeding trail, and he saw sharply what his own end might be—unless—unless he could get the wolf. Then began as grim a tragedy of existence as was ever played—a sick man that crawled, a sick wolf that limped, two creatures dragging their dying carcasses across the desolation and hunting each other's lives.

Had it been a well wolf, it would not have mattered so much to the man; but the thought of going to feed the maw of that loathsome and all but dead thing was repugnant to him. He was finicky. His mind had begun to wander again, and to be perplexed by hallucinations, while his lucid intervals grew rare and shorter.

He was awakened once from a faint by a wheeze close in his ear. The wolf leaped lamely back, losing its footing and falling in its weakness. It was ludicrous, but he was not amused. Nor was he even afraid. He was too far gone for that. But his mind was for the moment clear, and he lay and considered. The ship was no more than four miles away. He could see it quite distinctly when he rubbed the mists out of his eyes, and he could see the white sail of a small boat cutting the water of the shining sea. But he could never crawl those four miles. He knew that, and was very calm in the knowledge. He knew that he could not crawl half a mile. And yet he wanted to live. It was unreasonable that he should die after all he had undergone. Fate asked too much of him. And, dying, he declined to die. It was stark madness, perhaps, but in the very grip of Death he defied Death and refused to die.

He closed his eyes and composed himself with infinite precaution. He steeled himself to keep above the suffocating languor that lapped like a rising tide through all the wells of his being. It was very like a sea, this deadly languor, that rose and rose and drowned his consciousness bit by bit. Sometimes he was all but submerged, swimming through oblivion with a faltering stroke; and again, by some strange alchemy of soul, he would find another shred of will and strike out more strongly.

Without movement he lay on his back, and he could hear, slowly drawing near and nearer, the wheezing intake and output of the sick wolf's breath. It drew closer, ever closer, through an infinitude of time, and he did not move. It was at his ear. The harsh dry tongue grated like sandpaper against his cheek. His hands shot out—or at least he willed them to shoot out. The fingers were curved like talons, but they closed on empty air. Swiftness and certitude require strength, and the man had not this strength.

The patience of the wolf was terrible. The man's patience was no less terrible. For half a day he lay motionless, fighting off unconsciousness and waiting for the thing that was to feed upon him and upon which he wished to feed. Sometimes the languid sea rose over him and he dreamed long dreams; but ever through it all, waking and dreaming, he waited for the wheezing breath and the harsh caress of the tongue.

He did not hear the breath, and he slipped slowly from some dream to the feel of the tongue along his hand. He waited. The fangs pressed softly; the pressure increased; the wolf was exerting its last strength in an effort to sink teeth in the food for which it had waited so long. But the man had waited long, and the lacerated hand closed on the jaw. Slowly, while the wolf struggled feebly and the hand clutched feebly, the other hand crept across to a grip. Five minutes later the whole weight of the man's body was on top of the wolf. The hands had not sufficient strength to choke the wolf, but the face of the man was pressed close to the throat of the wolf and the mouth of the man was full of hair. At the end of half an hour the man was aware of a warm trickle in his throat. It was not pleasant. It was like molten lead being forced into his stomach, and it was forced by his will alone. Later the man rolled over on his back and slept.

There were some members of a scientific expedition on the whale-ship *Bedford*. From the deck they remarked a strange object on the shore. It was moving down the beach toward the water. They were unable to classify it, and, being scientific men, they climbed into the whale-boat alongside and went ashore to see. And they saw something that was alive but which could hardly be called a man.

It was blind, unconscious. It squirmed along the ground like some monstrous worm. Most of its efforts were ineffectual, but it was persistent, and it writhed and twisted and went ahead perhaps a score of feet an hour.

Three weeks afterward the man lay in a bunk on the whale-ship *Bedford,* and with tears streaming down his wasted cheeks told who he was and what he had undergone. He also babbled incoherently of his mother, of sunny Southern California, and a home among the orange groves and flowers.

The days were not many after that when he sat at table with the scientific men and ship's officers. He gloated over the spectacle of so much food, watching it anxiously as it went into the mouths of others. With the disappearance of each mouthful an expression of deep regret came into his eyes. He was quite sane, yet he hated those men at mealtime. He was haunted by a fear that the food would not last. He inquired of the cook, the cabinboy, the captain, concerning the food stores. They reassured him countless times; but he could not believe them, and pried cunningly about the lazarette to see with his own eyes.

It was noticed that the man was getting fat. He grew stouter with each day. The scientific men shook their heads and theorized. They limited the man at his meals, but still his girth increased and he swelled prodigiously under his shirt.

The sailors grinned. They knew. And when the scientific men set a watch on the man, they knew too. They saw him slouch for'ard after breakfast, and, like a mendicant, with outstretched palm, accost a sailor. The sailor grinned and passed him a fragment of sea biscuit. He clutched it avariciously, looked at it as a miser looks at gold, and thrust it into his shirt bosom. Similar were the donations from other grinning sailors.

The scientific men were discreet. They let him alone. But they privily examined his bunk. It was lined with hardtack; the mattress was stuffed with hardtack; every nook and cranny was filled with hardtack. Yet he was sane. He was taking precautions against another possible famine—that was all. He would recover from it, the scientific men said; and he did, ere the *Bedford's* anchor rumbled down in San Francisco Bay.

CALIFORNIA

ALL GOLD CANYON

(*The Century Magazine,* November, 1905)

Just as Jack London readers admire his Klondike "sourdoughs"—the Malemute Kid, Mason, Bettles, Sloper, Elam Harnish (known as "Burning Daylight" in the novel by that name), the whole company of them—Bill, the "pocket" hunting prospector in "All Gold Canyon" is a captivating creation. He is operating in the California Sierras with his burro and two packhorses. We do not know much about him except that he is genial, good-humored and mobile-faced—"Ideas chased across his face like wind-flaws across the surface of a lake"—has merry blue eyes and a habit, born of his lonely profession, of soliloquy.

We admire his humor and his perseverance. His work as a placer miner is back-breaking, he counts the specks of gold in his pan, he talks to the hillside he is mining as if it could talk back, and when he finds the pocket, we can't help but share his unalloyed joy and triumph.

This is a deceptively quiet story set among the cottonwoods, manzanitas, and mariposa lilies of a drowsy, sweetly aired place untrammeled by men. But violence lurks there, not only in the form of human intruders, but the violence left in the virgin wilderness.

Andrew Sinclair, in his *Jack: A Biography of Jack London* (1977), gives a curious interpretation of "All Gold Canyon." He notes that the story was published after London's divorce and remarriage and after London's purchase of the land that would become his great ranch at Glen Ellen, north of San Francisco. Sinclair likens the prospector Bill's invasion of the canyon to that of a slug—"He fouled beauty with his monstrous trail"—and that only when he left with his booty in gold did the peace of the place return to heal the torn and scarred hillsides. So too, Sinclair says, did Jack London, in establishing his "Beauty Ranch," intend returning to the earth "to heal the scars left by the forty-niners and the bonanza farmers."

London seldom acknowledged, and may have found ludicrous, such heavy messages in his life and work. He aspired to tell a good story. "All Gold Canyon" is an example of how well he succeeded in this ambition.

ALL GOLD CANYON

IT WAS THE green heart of the canyon, where the walls swerved back from the rigid plan and relieved their harshness of line by making a little sheltered nook and filling it to the brim with sweetness and roundness and softness. Here all things rested. Even the narrow stream ceased its turbulent down-rush long enough to form a quiet pool. Knee-deep in the water, with drooping head and half-shut eyes, drowsed a red-coated, many-antlered buck.

On one side, beginning at the very lip of the pool, was a tiny meadow, a cool, resilient surface of green that extended to the base of the frowning wall. Beyond the pool a gentle slope of earth ran up and up to meet the opposing wall. Fine grass covered the slope—grass that was spangled with flowers, with here and there patches of color, orange and purple and golden. Below, the canyon was shut in. There was no view. The walls leaned together abruptly and the canyon ended in a chaos of rocks, moss-covered and hidden by a green screen of vines and creepers and boughs of trees. Up the canyon rose far hills and peaks, the big foothills, pine-covered and remote. And far beyond, like clouds upon the border of the sky, towered minarets of white, where the Sierra's eternal snows flashed austerely the blazes of the sun.

There was no dust in the canyon. The leaves and flowers were clean and virginal. The grass was young velvet. Over the pool three cottonwoods sent their snowy fluffs fluttering down the quiet air.

On the slope the blossoms of the winewooded manzanita filled the air with springtime odors, while the leaves, wise with experience, were already beginning their vertical twist against the coming aridity of summer. In the open spaces on the slope, beyond the farthest shadow-reach of the manzanita, poised the mariposa lilies, like so many flights of jewelled moths suddenly arrested and on the verge of trembling into flight again. Here and there that woods harlequin, the madrone, permitting itself to be caught in the act of changing its pea-green trunk to madder-red, breathed its fragrance into the air from great clusters of waxen bells. Creamy white were these bells, shaped like lilies-of-the-valley, with the sweetness of perfume that is of the springtime.

There was not a sigh of wind. The air was drowsy with its weight of perfume. It was a sweetness that would have been cloying had the air been heavy and humid. But the air was sharp and thin. It was as starlight transmuted into atmosphere, shot through and warmed by sunshine, and flower-drenched with sweetness.

An occasional butterfly drifted in and out through the patches of light and shade. And from all about rose the low and sleepy hum of mountain bees—feasting Sybarites that jostled one another good-naturedly at the board, nor found time for rough discourtesy. So quietly did the little stream drip and ripple its way through the canyon that it spoke only in faint and occasional gurgles. The voice of the stream was as a drowsy whisper, ever interrupted by dozings and silences, ever lifted again in the awakenings.

The motion of all things was a drifting in the heart of the canyon. Sunshine and butterflies drifted in and out among the trees. The hum of the bees and the whisper of the stream were a drifting of sound. And the drifting sound and drifting color seemed to weave together in the making of a delicate and intangible fabric which was the spirit of the place. It was a spirit of peace that was not of death, but of smooth-pulsing life, of quietude that was not silence, of movement that was not action, of repose that was quick with existence without being violent with struggle and travail. The spirit of the place was the spirit of the peace of the living, somnolent with the easement and content of prosperity, and undisturbed by rumors of far wars.

The red-coated, many-antlered buck acknowledged the lordship of the spirit of the place and dozed knee-deep in the cool, shaded pool. There seemed no flies to vex him and he was lanquid with rest. Sometimes his ears moved when the stream awoke and whispered; but they moved lazily, with foreknowledge that it was merely the stream grown garrulous at discovery that it had slept.

But there came a time when the buck's ears lifted and tensed with swift eagerness for sound. His head was turned down the canyon. His sensitive, quivering nostrils scented the air. His eyes could not pierce the green screen through which the stream rippled away, but to his ears came the voice of a man. It was a steady, monotonous, singsong voice. Once the buck heard the harsh clash of metal upon rock. At the sound he snorted with a sudden start that jerked him through the air from water to meadow, and his feet sank into the young velvet, while he pricked his ears and again scented the air. Then he stole across the tiny meadow, pausing once and again to listen, and faded away out of the canyon like a wraith, soft-footed and without sound.

The clash of steel-shod soles against the rocks began to be heard, and the man's voice grew louder. It was raised in a sort of chant and became distinct with nearness, so that the words could be heard:

> Tu'n around an' tu'n yo' face
> Untoe them sweet hills of grace
>   (D' pow'rs of sin yo' am scornin'!).
> Look about an' look aroun',
> Fling yo' sin-pack on d' groun'
>   (Yo' will meet wid d' Lord in d' mornin'!).

A sound of scrambling accompanied the song, and the spirit of the place fled away on the heels of the red-coated buck. The green screen was burst asunder, and a man peered out at the meadow and the pool and the sloping side-hill. He was a deliberate sort of man. He took in the scene with one embracing glance, then ran his eyes over the details to verify the general impression. Then, and not until then, did he open his mouth in vivid and solemn approval:

"Smoke of life an' snakes of purgatory! Will you just look at that! Wood an' water an' grass an' a side-hill! A pocket-hunter's delight an' a cayuse's paradise! Cool green for tired eyes! Pink pills for pale people ain't in it. A secret pasture for prospectors and a resting-place for tired burros, by damn!"

He was a sandy-complexioned man in whose face geniality and humor seemed the salient characteristics. It was a mobile face, quick-changing to inward mood and thought. Thinking was in him a visible process. Ideas chased across his face like wind-flaws across the surface of a lake. His hair, sparse and unkempt of growth, was as indeterminate and colorless as his complexion. It would seem that all the color of his frame had gone into his eyes, for they were startlingly blue. Also, they were laughing and merry eyes, within them much of the naïveté and wonder of the child; and yet, in an unassertive way, they contained much of calm self-reliance and strength of purpose founded upon self-experience and experience of the world.

From out the screen of vines and creepers he flung ahead of him a miner's pick and shovel and gold-pan. Then he crawled out himself into the open. He was clad in faded overalls and black cotton shirt, with hobnailed brogans on his feet, and on his head a hat whose shapelessness and stains advertised the rough usage of wind and rain and sun and camp-smoke. He stood erect, seeing wide-eyed the secrecy of the scene and sensuously inhaling the warm, sweet breath of the canyon-garden through nostrils that dilated and quivered with delight. His eyes narrowed to laughing slits of blue, his face wreathed itself in joy, and his mouth curled in a smile as he cried aloud:

"Jumping dandelions and happy hollyhocks, but that smells good to me! Talk about your attar o' roses an' cologne factories! They ain't in it!"

He had the habit of soliloquy. His quick-changing facial expressions might tell every thought and mood, but the tongue, perforce, ran hard after, repeating, like a second Boswell.

The man lay down on the lip of the pool and drank long and deep of its water. "Tastes good to me," he murmured, lifting his head and gazing across the pool at the side-hill, while he wiped his mouth with the back of his hand. The side-hill attracted his attention. Still lying on his stomach, he studied the hill formation long and carefully. It was a practised eye that travelled up the slope to the crumbling canyon-wall and back and down again to the edge of the pool. He scrambled to his feet and favored the side-hill with a second survey.

"Looks good to me," he concluded, picking up his pick and shovel and gold-pan.

He crossed the stream below the pool, stepping agilely from stone to stone. Where the side-hill touched the water he dug up a shovelful of dirt and put it into the gold-pan. He squatted down, holding the pan in his two hands, and partly immersing it in the stream. Then he imparted to the pan a deft circular motion that sent the water sluicing in and out through the dirt and gravel. The larger and the lighter particles worked to the surface, and these, by a skilful dipping movement of the pan, he spilled out and over the edge. Occasionally, to expedite matters, he rested the pan and with his fingers raked out the large pebbles and pieces of rock.

The contents of the pan diminished rapidly until only fine dirt and the smallest bits of gravel remained. At this stage he began to work very deliberately and carefully. It was fine washing, and he washed fine and finer, with a keen scrutiny and delicate and fastidious touch. At last the pan seemed empty of everything but water; but with a quick semicircular flirt that sent the water flying over the shallow rim into the stream, he disclosed a layer of black sand on the bottom of the pan. So thin was this layer that it was like a streak of paint. He examined it closely. In the midst of it was a tiny golden speck. He dribbled a little water in over the depressed edge of the pan. With a quick flirt he sent the water sluicing across the bottom, turning the grains of black sand over and over. A second tiny golden speck rewarded his effort.

The washing had now become very fine—fine beyond all need of ordinary placer-mining. He worked the black sand, a small portion at a time, up the shallow rim of the pan. Each small portion he examined sharply, so that his eyes saw every grain of it before he allowed it to slide over the edge and away. Jealously, bit by bit, he let the black sand slip away. A golden speck, no larger than a pinpoint, appeared on the rim, and by his manipulation of the water it returned to the bottom of the pan. And in such fashion another speck was disclosed, and another. Great was his care of them. Like a shepherd he herded his flock of golden specks so that not one should be lost. At last, of the pan of dirt nothing remained but his golden herd. He counted it, and then, after all his labor, sent it flying out of the pan with one final swirl of water.

But his blue eyes were shining with desire as he rose to his feet. "Seven," he muttered aloud, asserting the sum of the specks for which he had toiled so hard and which he had so wantonly thrown away. "Seven," he repeated, with the emphasis of one trying to impress a number on his memory.

He stood still a long while, surveying the hillside. In his eyes was a curiosity, new-aroused and burning. There was an exultance about his bearing and a keenness like that of a hunting animal catching the fresh scent of game.

He moved down the stream a few steps and took a second panful of dirt.

Again came the careful washing, the jealous herding of the golden specks, and the wantonness with which he sent them flying into the stream when he had counted their number.

"Five," he muttered, and repeated, "five."

He could not forbear another survey of the hill before filling the pan farther down the stream. His golden herds diminished. "Four, three, two, two, one," were his memory tabulations as he moved down the stream. When but one speck of gold rewarded his washings, he stopped and built a fire of dry twigs. Into this he thrust the goldpan and burned it till it was blue-black. He held up the pan and examined it critically. Then he nodded approbation. Against such a color-background he could defy the tiniest yellow speck to elude him

Still moving down the stream, he panned again. A single speck was his reward. A third pan contained no gold at all. Not satisfied with this, he panned three times again, taking his shovels of dirt within a foot of one another. Each pan proved empty of gold, and the fact, instead of discouraging him, seemed to give him satisfaction. His elation increased with each barren washing, until he arose, exclaiming jubilantly:

"If it ain't the real thing, may God knock off my head with sour apples!"

Returning to where he had started operations, he began to pan up the stream. At first his golden herds increased—increased prodigiously. "Fourteen, eighteen, twenty-one, twenty-six," ran his memory tabulations. Just above the pool he struck his richest pan—thirty-five colors.

"Almost enough to save," he remarked regretfully as he allowed the water to sweep them away.

The sun climbed to the top of the sky. The man worked on. Pan by pan, he went up the stream, the tally of results steadily decreasing.

"It's just booful, the way it peters out," he exulted when a shovelful of dirt contained no more than a single speck of gold.

And when no specks at all were found in several pans, he straightened up and favored the hillside with a confident glance.

"Ah, ha! Mr. Pocket!" he cried out, as though to an auditor hidden somewhere above him beneath the surface of the slope. "Ah, ha! Mr. Pocket! I'm a-comin', I'm a comin', an' I'm shorely gwine to get yer! You heah me, Mr. Pocket? I'm gwine to get yer as shore as punkins ain't cauliflowers!"

He turned and flung a measuring glance at the sun poised above him in the azure of the cloudless sky. Then he went down the canyon, following the line of shovel-holes he had made in filling the pans. He crossed the stream below the pool and disappeared through the green screen. There was little opportunity for the spirit of the place to return with its quietude and repose, for the man's voice, raised in ragtime song, still dominated the canyon with possession.

After a time, with a greater clashing of steel-shod feet on rock, he returned. The green screen was tremendously agitated. It surged back and forth in the throes of a struggle. There was a loud grating and clanging of metal. The man's voice leaped to a higher pitch and was sharp with imperativeness. A large body plunged and panted. There was a snapping and ripping and rending, and amid a shower of falling leaves a horse burst through the screen. On its back was a pack, and from this trailed broken vines and torn creepers. The animal gazed with astonished eyes at the scene into which it had been precipitated, then dropped its head to the grass and began contentedly to graze. A second horse scrambled into view, slipping once more on the mossy rocks and regaining equilibrium when its hoofs sank into the yielding surface of the meadow. It was riderless, though on its back was a high-horned Mexican saddle, scarred and discolored by long usage.

The man brought up the rear. He threw off pack and saddle, with an eye to camp location, and gave the animals their freedom to graze. He unpacked his food and got out frying-pan and coffeepot. He gathered an armful of dry wood, and with a few stones made a place for his fire.

"My!" he said, "but I've got an appetite. I could scoff iron-filings an' horseshoe nails an' thank you kindly, ma'am, for a second helpin'."

He straightened up, and while he reached for matches in the pocket of his overalls, his eyes travelled across the pool to the side-hill. His fingers had clutched the match-box, but they relaxed their hold and the hand came out empty. The man wavered perceptibly. He looked at his preparations for cooking and he looked at the hill.

"Guess I'll take another whack at her," he concluded, starting to cross the stream.

"They ain't no sense in it, I know," he mumbled apologetically. "But keepin' grub back an hour ain't goin' to hurt none, I reckon."

A few feet back from his first line of test-pans he started a second line. The sun dropped down the western sky, the shadows lengthened, but the man worked on. He began a third line of test-pans. He was cross-cutting the hillside, line by line, as he ascended. The centre of each line produced the richest pans, while the ends came where no colors showed in the pan. And as he ascended the hillside the lines grew perceptibly shorter. The regularity with which their length diminished served to indicate that somewhere up the slope the last line would be so short as to have scarcely length at all, and that beyond could come only a point. The design was growing into an inverted "V." The converging sides of this "V" marked the boundaries of the gold-bearing dirt.

The apex of the "V" was evidently the man's goal. Often he ran his eye along the converging sides and on up the hill, trying to divine the apex, the point where the gold-bearing dirt must cease. Here resided "Mr. Pocket"—for so the man familiarly addressed the imaginary point above him on the slope, crying out:

"Come down out o' that, Mr. Pocket! Be right smart an' agreeable, an' come down!"

"All right," he would add later, in a voice resigned to determination. "All right, Mr. Pocket. It's plain to me I got to come right up an' snatch you out bald-headed. An' I'll do it! I'll do it!" he would threaten still later.

Each pan he carried down to the water to wash, and as he went higher up the hill the pans grew richer, until he began to save the gold in an empty baking-powder can which he carried carelessly in his hip-pocket. So engrossed was he in his toil that he did not notice the long twilight of oncoming night. It was not until he tried vainly to see the gold colors in the bottom of the pan that he realized the passage of time. He straightened up abruptly. An expression of whimsical wonderment and awe overspread his face as he drawled:

"Gosh darn my buttons! if I didn't plumb forget dinner!"

He stumbled across the stream in the darkness and lighted his long-delayed fire. Flapjacks and bacon and warmed-over beans constituted his supper. Then he smoked a pipe by the smouldering coals, listening to the night noises and watching the moonlight stream through the canyon. After that he unrolled his bed, took off his heavy shoes, and pulled the blankets up to his chin. His face showed white in the moonlight, like the face of a corpse. But it was a corpse that knew its resurrection, for the man rose suddenly on one elbow and gazed across at the hillside.

"Good night, Mr. Pocket" he called sleepily. "Good night."

He slept through the early gray of morning until the direct rays of the sun smote his closed eyelids, when he awoke with a start and looked about him until he had established the continuity of his existence and identified his present self with the days previously lived.

To dress, he had merely to buckle on his shoes. He glanced at his fireplace and at his hillside, wavered, but fought down the temptation and started the fire.

"Keep yer shirt on, Bill; keep yer shirt on," he admonished himself. "What's the good of rushin'? No use in gettin' all het up an' sweaty. Mr. Pocket'll wait for you. He ain't a-runnin' away before you can get your breakfast. Now, what you want, Bill, is something fresh in yer bill o' fare. So it's up to you to go an' get it."

He cut a short pole at the water's edge and drew from one of his pockets a bit of line and a draggled fly that had once been a royal coachman.

"Mebbe they'll bite in the early morning," he muttered, as he made his first cast into the pool. And a moment later he was gleefully crying: "What'd I tell you, eh? What'd I tell you?"

He had no reel, nor any inclination to waste time, and by main strength and swiftly, he drew out of the water a flashing ten-inch trout. Three more, caught in rapid succession, furnished his breakfast. When he came to the stepping-stones on his way to his hillside, he was struck by a sudden thought, and paused.

"I'd better take a hike down-stream a ways," he said. "There's no tellin' what cuss may be snoopin' around."

But he crossed over on the stones, and with a "I really oughter take that hike," the need of the precaution passed out of his mind and he fell to work.

At nightfall he straightened up. The small of his back was stiff from stooping toil, and as he put his hand behind him to soothe the protesting muscles, he said:

"Now what d'ye think of that, by damn? I clean forgot my dinner again! If I don't watch out, I'll sure be degeneratin' into a two-meal-a-day crank."

"Pockets is the damnedest things I ever see for makin' a man absent-minded," he communed that night, as he crawled into his blankets. Nor did he forget to call up the hillside, "Good night, Mr. Pocket! Good night!"

Rising with the sun, and snatching a hasty breakfast, he was early at work. A fever seemed to be growing in him, nor did the increasing richness of the test-pans allay this fever. There was a flush in his cheek other than that made by the heat of the sun, and he was oblivious to fatigue and the passage of time. When he filled a pan with dirt, he ran down the hill to wash it; nor could he forbear running up the hill again, panting and stumbling profanely, to refill the pan.

He was now a hundred yards from the water, and the inverted "V" was assuming definite proportions. The width of the pay-dirt steadily decreased, and the man extended in his mind's eye the sides of the "V" to their meeting-place far up the hill. This was his goal, the apex of the "V," and he panned many times to locate it.

"Just about two yards above that manzanita bush an' a yard to the right," he finally concluded.

Then the temptation seized him. "As plain as the nose on your face," he said, as he abandoned his laborious cross-cutting and climbed to the indicated apex. He filled a pan and carried it down the hill to wash. It contained no trace of gold. He dug deep, and he dug shallow, filling and washing a dozen pans, and was unrewarded even by the tiniest golden speck. He was enraged at having yielded to the temptation, and cursed himself blasphemously and pridelessly. Then he went down the hill and took up the cross-cutting.

"Slow an' certain, Bill; slow an' certain," he crooned. "Short-cuts to fortune ain't in your line, an' it's about time you know it. Get wise, Bill; get wise. Slow an' certain's the only hand you can play; so go to it, an' keep to it, too."

As the cross-cuts decreased, showing that the sides of the "V" were converging, the depth of the "V" increased. The gold-trace was dipping into the hill. It was only at thirty inches beneath the surface that he could get colors in his pan. The dirt he found at twenty-five inches from the surface and at thirty-five inches, yielded barren pans. At the base of the "V," by the water's edge, he had found the gold colors at the grass roots. The higher he went up the hill, the deeper the gold dipped. To dig a hole three feet deep in order to get one test-pan was a task of no mean magnitude; while between the man and the apex intervened an untold number of such holes to be dug. "An' there's no tellin' how much deeper it'll pitch," he sighed, in a moment's pause, while his fingers soothed his aching back.

Feverish with desire, with aching back and stiffening muscles, with pick and shovel gouging and mauling the soft brown earth, the man toiled up the hill. Before him was the smooth slope, spangled with flowers and made sweet with their breath. Behind him was devastation. It looked like some terrible eruption breaking out on the smooth skin of the hill. His slow progress was like that of a slug, befouling beauty with a monstrous trail.

Though the dipping gold-trace increased the man's work, he found consolation in the increasing richness of the pans. Twenty cents, thirty cents, fifty cents, sixty cents, were the values of the gold found in the pans, and at nightfall he washed his banner pan, which gave him a dollar's worth of gold-dust from a shovelful of dirt.

"I'll just bet it's my luck to have some inquisitive cuss come buttin' in here on my pasture," he mumbled sleepily that night as he pulled the blankets up to his chin.

Suddenly he sat upright. "Bill!" he called sharply. "Now, listen to me, Bill; d'ye hear! It's up to you, tomorrow mornin', to mosey round an' see what you can see. Understand? Tomorrow morning, an' don't you forget it!"

He yawned and glanced across at his side-hill. "Good night, Mr. Pocket," he called.

In the morning he stole a march on the sun, for he had finished breakfast when its first rays caught him, and he was climbing the wall of the canyon where it crumbled away and gave footing. From the outlook at the top he found himself in the midst of loneliness. As far as he could see, chain after chain of mountains heaved themselves into his vision. To the east of his eyes, leaping the miles between range and range and between many ranges, brought up at last against the white-peaked Sierras—the main crest, where the backbone of the Western world reared itself against the sky. To the north and south he could see more distinctly the cross-systems that broke through the main trend of the sea of mountains. To the west the ranges fell away, one behind the other, diminishing and fading into the gentle foothills that, in turn, descended into the great valley which he could not see.

And in all that mighty sweep of earth he saw no sign of man nor of the handiwork of man—save only the torn bosom of the hillside at his feet. The man looked long and carefully. Once, far down his own canyon, he thought he saw in the air a faint hint of smoke. He looked again and decided that it was the purple haze of the hills made dark by a convolution of the canyon wall at its back.

"Hey, you, Mr. Pocket!" he called down into the canyon. "Stand out from under! I'm a-comin', Mr. Pocket! I'm a-comin'!"

The heavy brogans on the man's feet made him appear clumsy-footed, but he swung down from the giddy height as lightly and airily as a mountain goat. A rock, turning under his foot on the edge of the precipice, did not disconcert him. He seemed to know the precise time required for the turn to culminate in disaster, and in the meantime he utilized the false footing itself for the momentary earth-contact necessary to carry him on into safety. Where the earth sloped so steeply it was impossible to stand for a second upright, the man did not hesitate. His foot pressed the impossible surface for but a fraction of the fatal second and gave him the bound that carried him onward. Again, where even the fraction of a second's footing was out of the question, he would swing his body past by a moment's hand-grip on a jutting knob of rock, a crevice, or a precariously rooted shrub. At last, with a wild leap and yell, he exchanged the face of the wall for an earth-slide and finished the descent in the midst of several tons of sliding earth and gravel.

His first pan of the morning washed out over two dollars in coarse gold. It was from the centre of the "V." To either side the diminution in the values of the pans was swift. His lines of crosscutting holes were growing very short. The converging sides of the inverted "V" were only a few yards apart. Their meeting-point was only a few yards above him. But the pay-streak was dipping deeper and deeper into the earth. By early afternoon he was sinking the test-holes five feet before the pans could show the gold-trace.

For that matter, the gold-trace had become something more than a trace; it was a placer mine in itself, and the man resolved to come back after he had found the pocket and work over the ground. But the increasing richness of the pans began to worry him. By late afternoon the worth of the pans had grown to three and four dollars. The man scratched his head perplexedly and looked a few feet up the hill at the manzanita bush that marked approximately the apex of the "V." He nodded his head and said oracularly:

"It's one o' two things," Bill; one o' two things. Either Mr. Pocket's spilled himself all out an' down the hill, or else Mr. Pocket's that damned rich you maybe won't be able to carry him all away with you. And that'd be hell, wouldn't it, now?" He chuckled at contemplation of so pleasing a dilemma.

Nightfall found him by the edge of the stream, his eyes wrestling with the gathering darkness over the washing of a five-dollar pan.

"Wisht I had an electric light to go on working," he said.

He found sleep difficult that night. Many times he composed himself and closed his eyes for slumber to overtake him; but his blood pounded with too strong desire, and as many times his eyes opened and he murmured wearily, "Wisht it was sun-up."

Sleep came to him in the end, but his eyes were open with the first paling of the stars, and the gray of dawn caught him with breakfast finished and climbing the hillside in the direction of the secret abiding-place of Mr. Pocket.

The first cross-cut the man made, there was space for only three holes, so narrow had become the pay-streak and so close was he to the fountainhead of the golden stream he had been following for four days.

"Be ca'm, Bill; be ca'm," he admonished himself, as he broke ground for the final hole where the sides of the "V" had at last come together in a point.

"I've got the almighty cinch on you, Mr. Pocket, an' you can't lose me," he said many times as he sank the hole deeper and deeper.

Four feet, five feet, six feet, he dug his way down into the earth. The digging grew harder. His pick grated on broken rock. He examined the rock. "Rotten quartz," was his conclusion as, with the shovel, he cleared the bottom of the hole of loose dirt. He attacked the crumbling quartz with the pick, bursting the disintegrating rock asunder with every stroke.

He thrust his shovel into the loose mass. His eye caught a gleam of yellow. He dropped the shovel and squatted suddenly on his heels. As a farmer rubs the clinging earth from fresh-dug potatoes, so the man, a piece of rotten quartz held in both hands, rubbed the dirt away.

"Sufferin' Sardanopolis!" he cried. "Lumps an' chunks of it! Lumps an' chunks of it!"

It was only half rock he held in his hand. The other half was virgin gold. He dropped it into his pan and examined another piece. Little yellow was to be seen, but with his strong fingers he crumbled the rotten quartz away till both hands were filled with glowing yellow. He rubbed the dirt away from fragment after fragment, tossing them into the gold-pan. It was a treasure-hole. So much had the quartz rotted away that there was less of it than there was of gold. Now and again he found a piece to which no rock clung—a piece that was all gold. A chunk, where the pick had laid open the heart of the gold, glittered like a handful of yellow jewels, and he cocked his head at it and slowly turned it around and over to observe the rich play of the light upon it.

"Talk about yer Too Much Gold diggin's!" the man snorted contemptuously. "Why, this diggin' 'd make it look like thirty cents. This diggin' is All Gold. An' right here an' now I name this yere canyon 'All Gold Canyon,' b'gosh!"

Still squatting on his heels, he continued examining the fragments and tossing them into the pan. Suddenly there came to him a premonition of danger. It seemed a shadow had fallen upon him. But there was no shadow. His heart had given a great jump up into his throat and was choking him. Then his blood slowly chilled and he felt the sweat of his shirt cold against his flesh.

He did not spring up nor look around. He did not move. He was considering the nature of the premonition he had received, trying to locate the source of the mysterious force that had warned him, striving to sense the imperative presence of the unseen thing that threatened him. There is an aura of things hostile, made manifest by messengers too refined for the senses to know; and this aura he felt, but knew not how he felt it. His was the feeling as when a cloud passes over the sun. It seemed that between him and life had passed something dark and smothering and menacing; a gloom, as it were, that swallowed up life and made for death—his death.

Every force of his being impelled him to spring up and confront the unseen danger, but his soul dominated the panic, and he remained squatting on his heels, in his hands a chunk of gold. He did not dare to look around, but he knew by now that there was something behind him and above him. He made believe to be interested in the gold in his hand. He examined it critically, turned it over and over, and rubbed the dirt from it. And all the time he knew that something behind him was looking at the gold over his shoulder.

Still feigning interest in the chunk of gold in his hand, he listened intently and he heard the breathing of the thing behind him. His eyes searched the ground in front of him for a weapon, but they saw only the uprooted gold, worthless to him now in his extremity. There was his pick, a handy weapon on occasion; but this was not such an occasion. The man realized his predicament. He was in a narrow hole that was seven feet deep. His head did not come to the surface of the ground. He was in a trap.

He remained squatting on his heels. He was quite cool and collected; but his mind, considering every factor, showed him only his helplessness. He continued rubbing the dirt from the quartz fragments and throwing the gold into the pan. There was nothing else for him to do. Yet he knew that he would have to rise up, sooner or later, and face the danger that breathed at his back. The minutes passed, and with the passage of each minute he knew that by so much he was nearer the time when he must stand up, or else—and his wet shirt went cold against his flesh again at the thought—or else he might receive death as he stooped there over his treasure.

Still he squatted on his heels, rubbing dirt from gold and debating in just what manner he should rise up. He might rise up with a rush and claw his way out of the hole to meet whatever threatened on the even footing above ground. Or he might rise up slowly and carelessly, and feign casually to discover the thing that breathed on his back. His instinct and every fighting fibre of his body favored the mad, clawing rush to the surface. His intellect, and the craft thereof, favored the slow and cautious meeting with the thing that menaced and which he could not see. And while he debated, a loud, crashing noise burst on his ear. At the same instant he received a stunning blow on the left side of the back, and from the point of impact felt a rush of flame through his flesh. He sprang up in the air, but halfway to his feet collapsed. His body crumpled in like a leaf withered in sudden heat, and he came down, his chest across his pan of gold, his face in the dirt and rock, his legs tangled and twisted because of the restricted space at the bottom of the hole. His legs twitched convulsively several times. His body was shaken as with a mighty ague. There was a slow expansion of the lungs, accompanied by a deep sigh. Then the air was slowly, very slowly, exhaled, and his body as slowly flattened itself down into inertness.

Above, revolver in hand, a man was peering down over the edge of the hole. He peered for a long time at the prone and motionless body beneath him. After a while the stranger sat down on the edge of the hole so that he could see into it, and rested the revolver on his knee. Reaching his hand into a pocket, he drew out a wisp of brown paper. Into this he dropped a few crumbs of tobacco. The combination became a cigarette, brown and squat, with the ends turned in. Not once did he take his eyes from the body at the bottom of the hole. He lighted the cigarette and drew its smoke into his lungs with a caressing intake of the breath. He smoked slowly. Once the cigarette went out and he relighted it. And all the while he studied the body beneath him.

In the end he tossed the cigarette stub away and rose to his feet. He moved to the edge of the hole. Spanning it, a hand resting on each edge, and with the revolver still in the right hand, he muscled his body down into the hole. While his feet were yet a yard from the bottom he released his hands and dropped down.

At the instant his feet struck bottom he saw the pocket-miner's arm leap out, and his own legs knew a swift, jerking grip that overthrew him. In the nature of the jump his revolver-hand was above his head. Swiftly as the grip had flashed about his legs, just as swiftly he brought the revolver down. He was still in the air, his fall in process of completion, when he pulled the trigger. The explosion was deafening in the confined space. The smoke filled the hole so that he could see nothing. He struck the bottom on his back, and like a cat's the pocket-miner's body was on top of him. Even as the miner's body passed on top, the stranger crooked in his right arm to fire; and even in that instant the miner, with a quick thrust of elbow, struck his wrist. The muzzle was thrown up and the bullet thudded into the dirt of the side of the hole.

The next instant the stranger felt the miner's hand grip his wrist. The struggle was now for the revolver. Each man strove to turn it against the other's body. The stranger, lying on his back, was beginning to see dimly. But suddenly he was blinded by a handful of dirt deliberately flung into his eyes by his antagonist. In that moment of shock his grip on the revolver was broken. In the next moment he felt a smashing darkness descend upon his brain, and in the midst of the darkness even the darkness ceased.

But the pocket-miner fired again and again, until the revolver was empty. Then he tossed it from him and, breathing heavily, sat down on the dead man's legs.

The miner was sobbing and struggling for breath. "Measly skunk!" he panted; "a-campin' on my trail an' lettin' me do the work, an' then shootin' me in the back!"

He was half crying from anger and exhaustion. He peered at the face of the dead man. It was sprinkled with loose dirt and gravel, and it was difficult to distinguish the features.

"Never laid eyes on him before," the miner concluded his scrutiny. "Just a common an' ordinary thief, damn him! An' he shot me in the back! He shot me in the back!"

He opened his shirt and felt himself, front and back, on his left side.

"Went clean through, and no harm done!" he cried jubilantly. "I'll bet he aimed all right all right; but he drew the gun over when he pulled the trigger—the cuss! But I fixed 'm! Oh, I fixed 'm!"

His fingers were investigating the bullet-hole in his side, and a shade of regret passed over his face. "It's goin' to be stiffer'n hell," he said. "An' it's up to me to get mended an' get out o' here."

He crawled out of the hole and went down the hill to his camp. Half an hour later he returned, leading his pack-horse. His open shirt disclosed the rude bandages with which he had dressed his wound. He was slow and awkward with his left-hand movements, but that did not prevent his using the arm.

The bight of the pack-rope under the dead man's shoulders enabled him to heave the body out of the hole. Then he set to work gathering up his gold. He worked steadily for several hours, pausing often to rest his stiffening shoulder and to exclaim:

"He shot me in the back, the measly skunk! He shot me in the back!"

When his treasure was quite cleaned up and wrapped securely into a number of blanket-covered parcels, he made an estimate of its value.

"Four hundred pounds, or I'm a Hottentot," he concluded. "Say two hundred in quartz an' dirt—that leaves two hundred pounds of gold. Bill! Wake up! Two hundred pounds of gold! Forty thousand dollars! An' it's yourn—all yourn!"

He scratched his head delightedly and his fingers blundered into an unfamiliar groove. They quested along it for several inches. It was a crease through his scalp where the second bullet had ploughed.

He walked angrily over to the dead man.

"You would, would you?" he bullied. "You would, eh? Well, I fixed you good an' plenty, an' I'll give you decent burial, too. That's more'n you'd have done for me."

He dragged the body to the edge of the hole and toppled it in. It struck the bottom with a dull crash, on its side, the face twisted up to the light. The miner peered down at it.

"An' you shot me in the back!" he said accusingly.

With pick and shovel he filled the hole. Then he loaded the gold on his horse. It was too great a load for the animal, and when he had gained his camp he transferred part of it to his saddle-horse. Even so, he was compelled to abandon a portion of his outfit—pick and shovel and gold-pan, extra food and cooking utensils, and divers odds and ends.

The sun was at the zenith when the man forced the horses at the screen of vines and creepers. To climb the huge bolders the animals were compelled to uprear and struggle blindly through the tangled mass of vegetation. Once the saddle-horse fell heavily and the man removed the pack to get the animal on its feet. After it started on its way again the man thrust his head out from among the leaves and peered up at the hillside.

"The measly skunk!" he said, and disappeared.

There was a ripping and tearing of vines and boughs. The trees surged back and forth, marking the passage of the animals through the midst of them. There was a clashing of steel-shod hoofs on stone, and now and again an oath or a sharp cry of command. Then the voice of the man was raised in song:

> Tu'n around an' tu'n yo' face
> Untoe them sweet hills of grace
>   (D' pow'rs of sin yo' am scornin'!).
> Look about an' look aroun',
> Fling yo' sin-pack on d' groun'
>   (Yo' will meet wid d' Lord in d' mornin'!).

The song grew faint and fainter, and through the silence crept back the spirit of the place. The stream once more drowsed and whispered; the hum of the mountain bees rose sleepily. Down through the perfume-weighted air fluttered the snowy fluffs of the cottonwoods. The butterflies drifted in and out among the trees, and over all blazed the quiet sunshine. Only remained the hoof-marks in the meadow and the torn hillside to mark the boisterous trail of the life that had broken the peace of the place and passed on.

WHITE AND YELLOW

(The Youth's Companion, February 16, 1905)

At the age of sixteen, Jack London, with $300 of borrowed money, bought a sloop, the *Razzle-Dazzle*, and launched a brief, dangerous but lucrative career as an oyster pirate on San Francisco Bay. He and his one-man crew, a like-minded young ruffian named Spider Healy, ran the small vessel with its single mast, jib, and mainsail, into privately owned oyster beds along the bay, raided the beds and sold the oysters to the highest bidder. So daring and skillful did young Jack become at this felonious work, and so charismatic and two-fisted a drinker was he at Johnny Heinold's First and Last Chance Saloon on Webster Street in Oakland, he became known as the "Prince of the Oyster Pirates."

He was anything but stupid and he knew that every oyster raid was a crime punishable by a term in state prison, complete with stripes and lockstep. So, when a California Fish Patrol agent named Charley Le Grant offered him a job as a deputy in the patrol, young Jack accepted. He worked out of the old town of Benicia, on the Carquinez Straits, and his experiences on both sides of the law gave verisimilitude to the stories he wrote for *The Youth's Companion*, later collected in the book *Tales of the Fish Patrol* (1905). "Some of these tales," says Russ Kingman in his authoritative *A Pictorial Life of Jack London* (1979), "are based on Jack's own experience and some on those of his fellow deputies, but all are real."

In "White and Yellow" London tells of the wildest of the fisherfolk on the bay, the Chinese shrimpers off Point Pinole in San Pablo Bay.

It is worth remembering that this teenaged baywaterman, the year after he quit the Fish Patrol, served seven months on the sealing schooner *Sophia Sutherland* in the Bering Sea and North Pacific. And when he returned, a deepwater sailor at the age of seventeen, he wrote his "Story of a Typhoon Off the Coast of Japan," published in the *San Francisco Call* on November 12, 1893. It was Jack London's first published work and it won the newspaper's prize of $25 for the "Best Descriptive Article."

WHITE AND YELLOW

SAN FRANCISCO BAY is so large that often its storms are more disastrous to ocean-going craft than is the ocean itself in its violent moments. The waters of the bay contain all manner of fish, wherefore its surface is ploughed by the keels of all manner of fishing boats manned by all manner of fishermen. To protect the fish from this motley floating population many wise laws have been passed, and there is a fish patrol to see that these laws are enforced. Exciting times are the lot of the fish patrol: in its history more than one dead patrolman has marked defeat, and more often dead fishermen across their illegal nets have marked success.

Wildest among the fisher-folk may be accounted the Chinese shrimp-catchers. It is the habit of the shrimp to crawl along the bottom in vast armies till it reaches fresh water, when it turns about and crawls back again to the salt. And where the tide ebbs and flows, the Chinese sink great bag-nets to the bottom, with gaping mouths, into which the shrimp crawls and from which it is transferred to the boiling-pot. This in itself would not be bad, were it not for the small mesh of the nets, so small that the tiniest fishes, little new-hatched things not a quarter of an inch long, cannot pass through. The beautiful beaches of Points Pedro and Pablo, where are the shrimp-catchers' villages, are made fearful by the stench from myriads of decaying fish, and against this wasteful destruction it has ever been the duty of the fish patrol to act.

When I was a youngster of sixteen, a good sloop-sailor and all-around baywaterman, my sloop, the *Reindeer*, was chartered by the

Fish Commission, and I became for the time being a deputy patrolman. After a deal of work among the Greek fishermen of the Upper Bay and rivers, where knives flashed at the beginning of trouble and men permitted themselves to be made prisoners only after a revolver was thrust in their faces, we hailed with delight an expedition to the Lower Bay against the Chinese shrimp-catchers.

There were six of us, in two boats, and to avoid suspicion we ran down after dark and dropped anchor under a projecting bluff of land known as Point Pinole. As the east paled with the first light of dawn we got under way again, and hauled close on the land breeze as we slanted across the bay toward Point Pedro. The morning mists curled and clung to the water so that we could see nothing, but we busied ourselves driving the chill from our bodies with hot coffee. Also we had to devote ourselves to the miserable task of bailing, for in some incomprehensible way the *Reindeer* had sprung a generous leak. Half the night had been spent in overhauling the ballast and exploring the seams, but the labor had been without avail. The water still poured in, and perforce we doubled up in the cockpit and tossed it out again.

After coffee, three of the men withdrew to the other boat, a Columbia River salmon boat, leaving three of us in the *Reindeer*. Then the two craft proceeded in company till the sun showed over the eastern skyline. Its fiery rays dispelled the clinging vapors, and there, before our eyes, like a picture, lay the shrimp fleet, spread out in a great half-moon, the tips of the crescent fully three miles apart, and each junk moored fast to the buoy of a shrimp-net. But there was no stir, no sign of life.

The situation dawned upon us. While waiting for slack water, in which to lift their heavy nets from the bed of the bay, the Chinese had all gone to sleep below. We were elated, and our plan of battle was swiftly formed.

"Throw each of your two men on to a junk" whispered Le Grant to me from the salmon boat. "And you make fast to a third yourself. We'll do the same, and there's no reason in the world why we shouldn't capture six junks at the least."

Then we separated. I put the *Reindeer* about on the other tack, ran up under the lee of a junk, shivered the mainsail into the wind and lost headway, and forged past the stern of the junk so slowly and so near that one of the patrolmen stepped lightly aboard. Then I kept off, filled the mainsail, and bore away for a second junk.

Up to this time there had been no noise, but from the first junk captured by the salmon boat an uproar now broke forth. There was shrill Oriental yelling, a pistol shot, and more yelling.

"It's all up. They're warning the others," said George, the remaining patrolman, as he stood beside me in the cockpit.

By this time we were in the thick of the fleet, and the alarm was spreading with incredible swiftness. The decks were beginning to swarm with half-awakened and half-naked Chinese. Cries and yells of warning and anger were flying over the quiet water, and somewhere a conch shell was being blown with great success. To the right of us I saw the captain of a junk chop away his mooring line with an axe and spring to help his crew at the hoisting of the huge, outlandish lug-sail. But to the left the first heads were popping up from below on another junk, and I rounded up the *Reindeer* alongside long enough for George to spring aboard.

The whole fleet was now under way. In addition to the sails they had gotten out long sweeps, and the bay was being ploughed in every direction by the fleeing junks. I was now alone in the *Reindeer*, seeking feverishly to capture a third prize. The first junk I took after was a clean miss, for it trimmed its sheets and shot away surprisingly into the wind. By fully half a point it outpointed the *Reindeer*, and I began to feel respect for the clumsy craft. Realizing the hopelessness of the pursuit, I filled away, threw out the main-sheet, and drove down before the wind upon the junks to leeward, where I had them at a disadvantage.

The one I had selected wavered indecisively before me, and, as I swung wide to make the boarding gentle, filled suddenly and darted away, the swart Mongols shouting a wild rhythm as they bent to the sweeps. But I had been ready for this. I luffed suddenly. Putting the tiller hard down, and holding it down with my body, I brought the main-sheet in, hand over hand, on the run, so as to retain all possible striking force. The two starboard sweeps of the junk were crumpled up, and then the two boats came together with a crash. The *Reindeer's* bowsprit, like a monstrous hand, reached over and ripped out the junk's chunky mast and towering sail.

This was met by a curdling yell of rage. A big Chinaman, remarkably evil-looking, with his head swathed in a yellow silk handkerchief and face badly pock-marked, planted a pike-pole on the *Reindeer's* bow and began to shove the entangled boats apart. Pausing long enough to let go the jib halyards, and just as the *Reindeer* cleared and began to drift astern, I leaped aboard the junk with a line and made fast. He of the yellow handkerchief and pock-marked face came toward me threateningly, but I put my hand into my hip pocket, and he hesitated. I was unarmed, but the Chinese have learned to be fastidiously careful of American hip pockets, and it was upon this that I depended to keep him and his savage crew at a distance.

I ordered him to drop the anchor at the junk's bow, to which he replied, "No sabbe." The crew responded in like fashion, and though I made my meaning plain by signs, they refused to understand. Realizing the inexpediency of discussing the matter, I went forward myself, overran the line, and let the anchor go.

"Now get aboard, four of you," I said in a loud voice, indicating with my fingers that four of them were to go with me and the fifth was to remain by the junk. The Yellow Handkerchief hesitated; but I repeated the order fiercely (much more fiercely than I felt), at the same time sending my hand to my hip. Again the Yellow Handkerchief was overawed, and with surly looks he led three of his men aboard the *Reindeer*. I cast off at once, and, leaving the jib down, steered a course for George's junk. Here it was easier, for there were two of us, and George had a pistol to fall back on if it came to the worst. And here, as with my junk, four Chinese were transferred to the sloop and one left behind to take care of things.

Four more were added to our passenger list from the third junk. By this time the salmon boat had collected its twelve prisoners and came alongside, badly overloaded. To make matters worse, as it was a small boat, the patrolmen were so jammed in with their prisoners that they would have little chance in case of trouble.

"You'll have to help us out," said Le Grant.

I looked over my prisoners, who had crowded into the cabin and on top of it. "I can take three," I answered.

"Make it four," he suggested, "and I'll take Bill with me." (Bill was the third patrolman.) "We haven't elbow room here, and in case of a scuffle one white to every two of them will be just about the right proportion."

The exchange was made, and the salmon boat got up its spritsail and headed down the bay toward the marshes off San Rafael. I ran up the jib and followed with the *Reindeer*. San Rafael, where we were to turn our catch over to the authorities, communicated with the bay by way of a long and tortuous slough, or marshland creek, which could be navigated only when the tide was in. Slack water had come, and, as the ebb was commencing, there was need for hurry if we cared to escape waiting half a day for the next tide.

But the land breeze had begun to die away with the rising sun, and now came only in failing puffs. The salmon boat got out its oars and soon left us far astern. Some of the Chinese stood in the forward part of the cockpit, near the cabin doors, and once, as I leaned over the cockpit rail to flatten down the jib-sheet a bit, I felt some one brush against my hip pocket. I made no sign, but out of the corner of my eye I saw that the Yellow Handkerchief had discovered the emptiness of the pocket which had hitherto overawed him.

To make matters serious, during all the excitement of boarding the junks the *Reindeer* had not been bailed, and the water was beginning to slush over the cockpit floor. The shrimp-catchers pointed at it and looked to me questioningly.

"Yes," I said. "Bime by, allee same dlown, velly quick, you no bail now. Sabbe?"

No, they did not "sabbe," or at least they shook their heads to that effect, though they chattered most comprehendingly to one another in their own lingo. I pulled up three or four of the bottom boards, got a couple of buckets from a locker, and by unmistakable sign-language invited them to fall to. But they laughed, and some crowded into the cabin and some climbed up on top.

Their laughter was not good laughter. There was a hint of menace in it, a maliciousness which their black looks verifed. The Yellow Handkerchief, since his discovery of my empty pocket, had become more insolent in his bearing, and he wormed about among the other prisoners talking to them with great earnestness.

Swallowing my chagrin, I stepped down into the cockpit and began throwing out the water. But hardly had I begun, when the boom swung overhead, the mainsail filled with a jerk, and the *Reindeer* heeled over. The day wind was springing up. George was the veriest of landlubbers, so I was forced to give over bailing and take the tiller. The wind was blowing directly off Point Pedro and the high mountains behind, and because of this was squally and uncertain, half the time bellying the canvas out, and the other half flapping it idly.

George was about the most all-around helpless man I had ever met. Among his other disabilities, he was a consumptive, and I knew that if he attempted to bail, it might bring on a hemorrhage. Yet the rising water warned me that something must be done. Again I ordered the shrimp-catchers to lend a hand with the buckets. They laughed defiantly, and those inside the cabin, the water up to their ankles, shouted back and forth with those on top.

"You'd better get out your gun and make them bail," I said to George.

But he shook his head and showed all too plainly that he was afraid. The Chinese could see the funk he was in as well as I could, and their insolence became insufferable. Those in the cabin broke into the food lockers, and those above scrambled down and joined them in a feast on our crackers and canned goods.

"What do we care?" George said weakly.

I was fuming with helpless anger. "If they get out of hand, it will be too late to care. The best thing you can do is to get them in check right now."

The water was rising higher and higher, and the gusts, forerunners of a steady breeze, were growing stiffer and stiffer. And between the gusts, the prisoners, having gotten away with a week's grub, took to crowding first to one side and then to the other till the *Reindeer* rocked like a cockleshell. Yellow Handkerchief approached me, and, pointing out his village on the Point Pedro beach, gave me to understand that if I turned the *Reindeer* in that direction and put them ashore, they, in turn, would go to bailing. By now the water in the cabin was up to the bunks, and the bedclothes were sopping. It was a foot deep on the cockpit floor. Nevertheless I refused, and I could see by George's face that he was disappointed.

"If you don't show some nerve, they'll rush us and throw us overboard," I said to him. "Better give me your revolver, if you want to be safe."

"The safest thing to do, " he chattered cravenly, "is to put them ashore. I, for one, don't want to be drowned for the sake of a handful of dirty Chinamen."

"And I, for another, don't care to give in to a handful of dirty Chinamen to escape drowning," I answered hotly.

"You'll sink the *Reindeer* under us all at this rate," he whined. "And what good that'll do I can't see."

"Every man to his taste," I retorted.

He made no reply, but I could see he was trembling pitifully. Between the threatening Chinese and the rising water he was beside himself with fright; and, more than the Chinese and the water, I feared him and what his fright might impel him to do. I could see him casting longing glances at the small skiff towing astern, so in the next calm I hauled the skiff alongside. As I did so his eyes brightened with hope; but before he could guess my intention, I stove the frail bottom through with a hand-axe, and the skiff filled to its gunwales.

"It's sink or float together," I said. "And if you'll give me your revolver, I'll have the *Reindeer* bailed out in a jiffy."

"They're too many for us," he whimpered. "We can't fight them all."

I turned my back on him in disgust. The salmon boat had long since passed from sight behind a little archipelago known as the Marin Islands, so no help could be looked for from that quarter. Yellow Handkerchief came up to me in a familiar manner, the water in the cockpit slushing against his legs. I did not like his looks. I felt that beneath that pleasant smile he was trying to put on his face there was an ill purpose. I ordered him back, and so sharply that he obeyed.

"Now keep your distance," I commanded, "and don't you come closer!"

"What' fo'?" he demanded indignantly. "I t'ink-um talkee talkee heap good."

"Talkee talkee," I answered bitterly, for I knew now that he had understood all that passed between George and me. "What for talkee talkee? You no sabbe talkee talkee."

He grinned in a sickly fashion. "Yep, I sabbe velly much. I honest Chinaman."

"All right," I answered, "You sabbe talkee talkee, then you bail water plenty plenty. After that we talkee talkee."

He shook his head, at the same time pointing over his shoulder to his comrades. "No can do. Velly bad Chinamen, heap velly bad. I t'ink-um—"

"Stand back!" I shouted, for I had noticed his hand disappear beneath his blouse and his body prepare for a spring.

Disconcerted, he went back into the cabin, to hold a council, apparently, from the way the jabbering broke forth. The *Reindeer* was very deep in the water, and her movements had grown quite loggy. In a rough sea she would have inevitably swamped; but the wind, when it did blow, was off the land, and scarcely a ripple disturbed the surface of the bay.

"I think you'd better head for the beach," George said abruptly, in a manner that told me his fear had forced him to make up his mind to some course of action.

"I think not," I answered shortly.

"I command you," he said in a bullying tone.

"I was commanded to bring these prisoners into San Rafael," was my reply.

Our voices were raised, and the sound of the altercation brought the Chinese out of the cabin.

"Now will you head for the beach?"

This from George, and I found myself looking into the muzzle of his revolver—of the revolver he dared to use on me, but was too cowardly to use on the prisoners.

My brain seemed smitten with a dazzling brightness. The whole situation, in all its bearings, was focussed sharply before me—the shame of losing the prisoners, the worthlessness and cowardice of George, the meeting with Le Grant and the other patrolmen and the lame explanation; and then there was the fight I had fought so hard, victory wrenched from me just as I thought I had it within my grasp. And out of the tail of my eye I could see the Chinese crowding together by the cabin doors and leering triumphantly. It would never do.

I threw my hand up and my head down. The first act elevated the muzzle, and the second removed my head from the path of the bullet which went whistling past. One hand closed on George's wrist, the other on the revolver. Yellow Handkerchief and his gang sprang toward me. It was now or never. Putting all my strength into a sudden effort, I swung George's body forward to meet them. Then

I pulled back with equal suddenness, ripping the revolver out of his fingers and jerking him off his feet. He fell against Yellow Handkerchief's knees, who stumbled over him, and the pair wallowed in the bailing hole where the cockpit floor was torn open. The next instant I was covering them with my revolver, and the wild shrimp-catchers were cowering and cringing away.

But I swiftly discovered that there was all the difference in the world between shooting men who are attacking and men who are doing nothing more than simply refusing to obey. For obey they would not when I ordered them into the bailing hole. I threatened them with the revolver, but they sat stolidly in the flooded cabin and on the roof and would not move.

Fifteen minutes passed, the *Reindeer* sinking deeper and deeper, her mainsail flapping in the calm. But from off the Point Pedro shore I saw a dark line form on the water and travel toward us. It was the steady breeze I had been expecting so long. I called to the Chinese and pointed it out. They hailed it with exclamation. Then I pointed to the sail and to the water in the *Reindeer*, and indicated by signs that when the wind reached the sail, what of the water aboard we would capsize. But they jeered defiantly, for they knew it was in my power to luff the helm and let go the main-sheet, so as to spill the wind and escape damage.

But my mind was made up. I hauled in the main-sheet a foot or two, took a turn with it, and bracing my feet, put my back against the tiller. This left me one hand for the sheet and one for the revolver. The dark line drew nearer, and I could see them looking from me to it and back again with an apprehension they could not successfully conceal. My brain and will and endurance were pitted against theirs, and the problem was which could stand the strain of imminent death the longer and not give in.

Then the wind struck us. The mainsheet tautened with a brisk rattling of the blocks, the boom uplifted, the sail bellied out, and the *Reindeer* heeled over—over, and over, till the lee-rail went under, the deck went under, the cabin windows went under, and the bay began to pour in over the cockpit rail. So violently had she heeled over, that the men in the cabin had been thrown on top of one another into the lee bunk, where they squirmed and twisted and were washed about, those underneath being perilously near to drowning.

The wind freshed a bit, and the *Reindeer* went over farther than ever. For the moment I thought she was gone, and I knew that another puff like that and she surely would go. While I pressed her under and debated whether I should give up or not, the Chinese cried for mercy. I think it was the sweetest sound I have ever heard. And then, and not until then, did I luff up and ease out the mainsheet. The *Reindeer* righted very slowly, and when she was on an even keel was so much awash that I doubted if she could be saved.

But the Chinese scrambled madly into the cockpit and fell to bailing with buckets, pots, pans, and everything they could lay hands on. It was a beautiful sight to see that water flying over the side! And when the *Reindeer* was high and proud on the water once more, we dashed away with the breeze on our quarter, and at the last possible moment crossed the mud flats and entered the slough.

The spirit of the Chinese was broken, and so docile did they become that ere we made San Rafael they were out with the towrope, Yellow Handkerchief at the head of the line. As for George, it was his last trip with the fish patrol. He did not care for that sort of thing, he explained, and he thought a clerkship ashore was good enough for him. And we thought so, too.

THE APOSTATE

(*Woman's Home Companion*, September, 1906)

The best one-sentence assessment of this story is that of the noted Jack London scholar Earle Labor, who, in his *Jack London* (1974) states: " 'The Apostate' was emotionally, if not literally, autobiographical."

Young Jack knew what it meant to be a "work-beast": when he was fourteen, he worked twelve to eighteen hours a day, and once for thirty-six hours straight, at ten cents an hour wage, in an Oakland cannery. He dutifully gave his pay to his mother. He sold newspapers, sat pins in a bowling alley, shoveled coal. It is small wonder, when he was sixteen and "Prince of the Oyster Pirates" on San Francisco Bay, he was regarded as "a boy in years but a man amongst men."

Johnny, the bobbin boy of "The Apostate," is most certainly the emotional, not literal, Jack London, but there is nothing exaggerated about Johnny's plight. In the first decade of this century there were an estimated 1.5 million U.S. workers under the age of sixteen with an average work-day of thirteen hours and an average hourly wage of ten cents. Sweatshop workers, children and adults alike, suffered from a high rate of tuberculosis and other lung ailments, then virtually irreversible. Wretched working and living conditions rendered old, in physical and mental health, children still in their teens. There were children whose entire life experience consisted of the daily grind of the inside of the mine, mill or factory where they worked as automatons from dawn to dusk.

Thus, when Johnny, the apostate, speaks of being tired even of *moving*, when his most inordinate hunger is for *rest*, Jack London writes both from experience and historical fact.

The story carries an impact even today, but one cannot help but wonder about the genteel readers of the *Woman's Home Companion* in 1906 and their reaction to it.

Certainly "The Apostate" accomplished more than its author may have intended. Widely distributed as a propaganda tract, the story is credited as a major weapon in the fight against child labor in the United States.

THE APOSTATE

> Now I wake me up to work;
> I pray the Lord I may not shirk.
> If I should die before the night,
> I pray the Lord my work's all right.
> AMEN.

IF YOU DON'T git up, Johnny, I won't give you a bite to eat!"

The threat had no effect on the boy. He clung stubbornly to sleep, fighting for its oblivion as the dreamer fights for his dream. The body's hands loosely clenched themselves, and he made feeble, spasmodic blows at the air. These blows were intended for his mother, but she betrayed practised familiarity in avoiding them as she shook him roughly by the shoulder.

"Lemme 'lone!"

It was a cry that began, muffled, in the deeps of sleep, that swiftly rushed upward, like a wail, into passionate belligerence, and that died away and sank down into an inarticulate whine. It was a bestial cry, as of a soul in torment, filled with infinite protest and pain.

But she did not mind. She was a sad-eyed, tired-faced woman, and she had grown used to this task, which she repeated every day of her life. She got a grip on the bedclothes and tried to strip them down; but the boy, ceasing his punching, clung to them desperately. In a huddle, at the foot of the bed, he still remained covered. Then she tried dragging the bedding to the floor. The boy opposed her. She braced herself. Hers was the superior weight, and the boy and bedding gave, the former instinctively following the latter in order to shelter against the chill of the room that bit into his body.

As he toppled on the edge of the bed it seemed that he must fall head-first to the floor. But consciousness fluttered up in him. He righted himself and for a moment perilously balanced. Then he struck the floor on his feet. On the instant his mother seized him by the shoulders and shook him. Again his fists struck out, this time with more force and directness. At the same time his eyes opened. She released him. He was awake.

"All right," he mumbled.

She caught up the lamp and hurried out, leaving him in darkness.

"You'll be docked," she warned back to him.

He did not mind the darkness. When he had got into his clothes, he went out into the kitchen. His tread was very heavy for so thin and light a boy. His legs dragged with their own weight, which seemed unreasonable because they were such skinny legs. He drew a broken-bottomed chair to the table.

"Johnny!" his mother called sharply.

He arose as sharply from the chair, and, without a word, went to the sink. It was a greasy, filthy sink. A smell came up from the outlet. He took no notice of it. That a sink should smell was to him part of the natural order, just as it was a part of the natural order that the soap should be grimy with dish-water and hard to lather. Nor did he try very hard to make it lather. Several splashes of the cold water from the running faucet completed the function. He did not wash his teeth. For that matter he had never seen a toothbrush, nor did he know that there existed beings in the world who were guilty of so great a foolishness as tooth washing.

"You might wash yourself wunst a day without bein' told," his mother complained.

She was holding a broken lid on the pot as she poured two cups of coffee. He made no remark, for this was a standing quarrel between them, and the one thing upon which his mother was hard as adamant. "Wunst" a day it was compulsory that he should wash his face. He dried himself on a greasy towel, damp and dirty and ragged, that left his face covered with shreds of lint.

"I wish we didn't live so far away," she said, as he sat down. "I try to do the best I can. You know that. But a dollar on the rent is such a savin', an' we've more room here. You know that."

He scarcely followed her. He had heard it all before, many times. The range of her thought was limited, and she was ever harking back to the hardship worked upon them by living so far from the mills.

"A dollar means more grub," he remarked sententiously. "I'd sooner do the walkin' an' git the grub."

He ate hurriedly, half chewing the bread and washing the unmasticated chunks down with coffee. The hot and muddy liquid went by the name of coffee. Johnny thought it was coffee—and excellent coffee. That was one of the few of life's illusions that remained to him. He had never drunk real coffee in his life.

In addition to the bread, there was a small piece of cold pork. His mother refilled his cup with coffee. As he was finishing the bread, he began to watch if more was forthcoming. She intercepted his questioning glance.

"Now, don't be hoggish, Johnny," was her comment. "You've had your share. Your brothers an' sisters are smaller'n you."

He did not answer the rebuke. He was not much of a talker. Also, he ceased his hungry glancing for more. He was uncomplaining, with a patience that was as terrible as the school in which it had been learned. He finished his coffee, wiped his mouth on the back of his hand, and started to rise.

"Wait a second," she said hastily. "I guess the loaf kin stand you another slice—a thin un."

There was legerdemain in her actions. With all the seeming of cutting a slice from the loaf for him, she put loaf and slice back in the bread box and conveyed to him one of her own two slices. She believed she had deceived him, but he had noted her sleight-of-hand. Nevertheless, he took the bread shamelessly. He had a philosophy that his mother, what of her chronic sickliness, was not much of an eater anyway.

She saw that he was chewing the bread dry, and reached over and emptied her coffee cup into his.

"Don't set good somehow on my stomach this morning," she explained.

A distant whistle, prolonged and shrieking, brought both of them to their feet. She glanced at the tin alarm-clock on the shelf. The hands stood at half-past five. The rest of the factory world was just arousing from sleep. She drew a shawl about her shoulders, and on her head a dingy hat, shapeless and ancient.

"We've got to run," she said, turning the wick of the lamp and blowing down the chimney.

They groped their way out and down the stairs. It was clear and cold, and Johnny shivered at the first contact with the outside air. The stars had not yet begun to pale in the sky, and the city lay in blackness. Both Johnny and his mother shuffled their feet as they walked. There was no ambition in the leg muscles to swing the feet clear of the ground.

After fifteen silent minutes, his mother turned off to the right.

"Don't be late," was her final warning from out of the dark that was swallowing her up.

He made no response, steadily keeping on his way. In the factory quarter, doors were opening everywhere, and he was soon one of a multitude that passed onward through the dark. As he entered the factory gate the whistle blew again. He glanced at the east. Across a ragged sky-line of housetops a pale light was beginning to creep. This much he saw of the day as he turned his back upon it and joined his work gang.

He took his place in one of many long rows of machines. Before him, above a bin filled with small bobbins, were large bobbins revolving rapidly. Upon these he wound the jute-twine of the small bobbins. The work was simple. All that was required was celerity. The small bobbins were emptied so rapidly, and there were so many large bobbins that did the emptying, that there were no idle moments.

He worked mechanically. When a small bobbin ran out, he used his left hand for a brake, stopping the large bobbin and at the same time, with thumb and forefinger, catching the flying end of twine. Also, at the same time, with his right hand, he caught up the loose twine-end of a small bobbin. These various acts with both hands were performed simultaneously and swiftly. Then there would come a flash of his hands as he looped the weaver's knot and released the bobbin. There was nothing difficult about weaver's knots. He once boasted he could tie them in his sleep. And for that matter, he sometimes did, toiling centuries long in a single night at tying an endless succession of weaver's knots.

Some of the boys shirked, wasted time and machinery by not replacing the small bobbins when they ran out. And there was an overseer to prevent this. He caught Johnny's neighbor at the trick, and boxed his ears.

"Look at Johnny there—why ain't you like him?" the overseer wrathfully demanded.

Johnny's bobbins were running full blast, but he did not thrill at the indirect praise. There had been a time . . . but that was long ago, very long ago. His apathetic face was expressionless as he listened to himself being held up as a shining example. He was the perfect worker. He knew that. He had been told so, often. It was a commonplace, and besides it didn't seem to mean anything to him any more. From the perfect worker he had evolved into the perfect machine. When his work went wrong, it was with him as with the machine, due to faulty material. It would have been as possible for a perfect nail-die to cut imperfect nails as for him to make a mistake.

And small wonder. There had never been a time when he had not been in intimate relationship with machines. Machinery had almost been bred into him, and at any rate he had been brought up on it. Twelve years before, there had been a small flutter of excitement in the loom room of this very mill. Johnny's mother had fainted. They stretched her out on the floor in the midst of the shrieking machines. A couple of elderly women were called from their looms. The foreman assisted. And in a few minutes there was one more soul in the loom room than had entered by the doors. It was Johnny, born with the pounding, crashing roar of the looms in his ears, drawing with his first breath the warm, moist air that was thick with flying lint. He had coughed that first day in order to rid his lungs of the lint; and for the same reason he had coughed ever since.

The boy alongside Johnny whimpered and sniffed. The boy's face was convulsed with hatred for the overseer who kept a threatening eye on him from a distance; but every bobbin was running full. The boy yelled terrible oaths into the whirling bobbins before him; but the sound did not carry half a dozen feet, the roaring of the room holding it in and containing it like a wall.

Of all this Johnny took no notice. He had a way of accepting things. Besides, things grow monotonous by repetition, and this particular happening he had witnessed many times. It seemed to him as useless to oppose the overseer as to defy the will of a machine. Machines were made to go in certain ways and to perform certain tasks. It was the same with the overseer.

But at eleven o'clock there was excitement in the room. In an apparently occult way the excitement instantly permeated everywhere. The one-legged boy who worked on the other side of Johnny bobbed swiftly across the floor to a bin truck that stood empty. Into this he dived out of sight, crutch and all. The superintendent of the mill was coming along, accompanied by a young man. He was well dressed and wore a starched shirt—a gentleman, in Johnny's classification of men, and also, "the Inspector."

He looked sharply at the boys as he passed along. Sometimes he stopped and asked questions. When he did so, he was compelled to shout at the top of his lungs, at which moments his face was ludicrously contorted with the strain of making himself heard. His quick eye noted the empty machine alongside of Johnny's, but he said nothing. Johnny also caught his eye, and he stopped abruptly. He caught Johnny by the arm to draw him back a step from the machine; but with an exclamation of surprise he released the arm.

"Pretty skinny," the superintendent laughed anxiously."

"Pipe stems," was the answer. "Look at those legs. The boy's got the rickets—incipient, but he's got them. If epilepsy doesn't get him in the end, it will be because tuberculosis gets him first."

Johnny listened, but did not understand. Furthermore he was not interested in future ills. There was an immediate and more serious ill that threatened him in the form of the inspector.

"Now, my boy, I want you to tell me the truth," the inspector said, or shouted, bending close to the boy's ear to make him hear. "How old are you?"

"Fourteen," Johnny lied, and he lied with the full force of his lungs. So loudly did he lie that it started him off in a dry, hacking cough that lifted the lint which had been settling in his lungs all morning.

"Looks sixteen at least," said the superintendent.

"Or sixty," snapped the inspector.

"He's always looked that way."

"How long?" asked the inspector, quickly.

"For years. Never gets a bit older."

"Or younger, I dare say. I suppose he's worked here all those years?"

"Off and on—but that was before the new law was passed," the superintendent hastened to add.

"Machine idle?" the inspector asked, pointing at the unoccupied machine beside Johnny's in which the part-filled bobbins were flying like mad.

"Looks that way." The superintendent motioned the overseer to him and shouted in his ear and pointed at the machine. "Machine's idle," he reported back to the inspector.

They passed on, and Johnny returned to his work, relieved in that the ill had been averted. But the one-legged boy was not so fortunate. The sharp-eyed inspector haled him out at arm's length from the bin truck. His lips were quivering, and his face had all the expression of one upon whom was fallen profound and irremediable disaster. The overseer looked astounded, as though for the first time he had laid eyes on the boy, while the superintendent's face expressed shock and displeasure.

"I know him," the inspector said. "He's twelve years old. I've had him discharged from three factories inside the year. This makes the fourth."

He turned to the one-legged boy. "You promised me, word and honor, that you'd go to school."

The one-legged boy burst into tears. "Please, Mr. Inspector, two babies died on us, and we're awful poor."

"What makes you cough that way?" the inspector demanded, as though charging him with crime.

And as in denial of guilt, the one-legged boy replied: "It ain't nothin'. I jes' caught a cold last week, Mr. Inspector, that's all."

In the end the one-legged boy went out of the room with the inspector, the latter accompanied by the anxious and protesting superintendent. After that monotony settled down again. The long morning and the longer afternoon wore away and the whistle blew for quitting time. Darkness had already fallen when Johnny passed out through the factory gate. In the interval the sun had made a golden ladder of the sky, flooded the world with its gracious warmth, and dropped down and disappeared in the west behind a ragged sky-line of housetops.

Supper was the family meal of the day—the one meal at which Johnny encountered his younger brothers and sisters. It partook of the nature of an encounter, to him, for he was very old, while they were distressingly young. He had no patience with their excessive and amazing juvenility. He did not understand it. His own childhood was too far behind him. He was like an old and irritable man, annoyed by the turbulence of their young spirits that was to him arrant silliness. He glowered silently over his food, finding compensation in the thought that they would soon have to go to work. That would take the edge off of them and make them sedate and dignified—like him. Thus it was, after the fashion of the human, that Johnny made of himself a yardstick with which to measure the universe.

During the meal, his mother explained in various ways and with infinite repetition that she was trying to do the best she could; so that it was with relief, the scant meal ended, that Johnny shoved back his chair and arose. He debated for a moment between bed and the front door, and finally went out the latter. He did not go far. He sat down on the stoop, his knees drawn up and his narrow shoulders drooping forward, his elbows on his knees and the palms of his hands supporting his chin.

As he sat there, he did no thinking. He was just resting. So far as his mind was concerned, it was asleep. His brothers and sisters came out, and with other children played noisily about him. An electric globe on the corner lighted their frolics. He was peevish and irritable, that they knew; but the spirit of adventure lured them into teasing him. They joined hands before him, and, keeping time with their bodies, chanted in his face weird and uncomplimentary doggerel. At first he snarled curses at them—curses he had learned from the lips of various foremen. Finding this futile, and remembering his dignity, he relapsed into dogged silence.

His brother Will, next to him in age, having just passed his tenth birthday, was the ringleader. Johnny did not possess particularly kindly feelings toward him. His life had early been embittered by continual giving over and giving way to Will. He had a definite feeling that Will was greatly in his debt and was ungrateful about it. In his own playtime, far back in the dim past, he had been robbed of a large part of that playtime by being compelled to take care of Will. Will was a baby then, and then, as now, their mother had spent her days in the mills. To Johnny had fallen the part of little father and little mother as well.

Will seemed to show the benefit of the giving over and the giving away. He was well-built, fairly rugged, as tall as his elder brother and even heavier. It was as though the life-blood of the one had been diverted into the other's veins. And in spirits it was the same. Johnny was jaded, worn out, without resilence, while his younger brother seemed bursting and spilling over with exuberance.

The mocking chant rose louder and louder. Will leaned closer as he danced, thrusting out his tongue. Johnny's left arm shot out and caught the other around the neck. At the same time he rapped his bony fist to the other's nose. It was a pathetically bony fist; but that it was sharp to hurt was evidenced by the squeal of pain it produced. The other children were uttering frightened cries, while Johnny's sister, Jennie, had dashed into the house.

He thrust Will from him, kicked him savagely on the shins, then reached for him and slammed him face downward in the dirt. Nor did he release him till the face had been rubbed into the dirt several times. Then the mother arrived, an anæmic whirlwind of solicitude and maternal wrath.

"Why can't he leave me alone?" was Johnny's reply to her upbraiding. "Can't he see I'm tired?"

"I'm as big as you," Will raged in her arms, his face a mess of tears, dirt and blood. "I'm as big as you now, an' I'm goin' to git bigger. Then I'll lick you—see if I don't."

"You ought to be to work, seein' how big you are," Johnny snarled. "That's what's the matter with you. You ought to be to work."

"But he's too young," she protested. "He's only a little boy."

"I was younger'n him when I started to work."

Johnny's mouth was open, further to express the sense of unfairness that he felt, but the mouth closed with a snap. He turned gloomily on his heel and stalked into the house and to bed. The door of his room was open to let in warmth from the kitchen. As he undressed in the semi-darkness he could hear his mother talking with a neighbor woman who had dropped in. His mother was crying, and her speech was punctuated with spiritless sniffles.

"I can't make out what's gittin' into Johnny," he could hear her say. "He didn't used to be this way. He was a patient little angel.

"An' he *is* a good boy," she hastened to defend. "He's worked faithful, an' he did go to work too young. But it wasn't my fault. I do the best I can, I'm sure."

Prolonged sniffling from the kitchen, and Johnny murmured to himself as his eyelids closed down, "You betcher life I've worked faithful."

The next morning he was torn bodily by his mother from the grip of sleep. Then came the meagre breakfast, the tramp through the dark, and the pale glimpse of day across the housetops as he turned his back on it and went in through the factory gate. It was another day, of all the days, and all the days were alike.

And yet there had been variety in his life—at the times he changed from one job to another, or was taken sick. When he was six, he was little mother and father to Will and the other children still younger. At seven he went into the mills—winding bobbins. When he was eight, he got work in another mill. His new job was marvellously easy. All he had to do was to sit down with a little stick in his hand and guide a stream of cloth that flowed past him. This stream of cloth came out of the maw of a machine, passed over a hot roller, and went on its way elsewhere. But he sat always in the one place, beyond the reach of daylight, a gas-jet flaring over him, himself part of the mechanism.

He was very happy at that job, in spite of the moist heat, for he was still young and in possession of dreams and illusions. And wonderful dreams he dreamed as he watched the steaming cloth streaming endlessly by. But there was no exercise about the work, no call upon his mind, and he dreamed less and less, while his mind grew torpid and drowsy. Nevertheless, he earned two dollars a week, and two dollars represented the difference between acute starvation and chronic underfeeding.

But when he was nine, he lost his job. Measles was the cause of it. After he recovered, he got work in a glass factory. The pay was better, and the work demanded skill. It was piecework, and the more skillful he was, the bigger wages he earned. Here was incentive. And under this incentive he developed into a remarkable worker.

It was simple work, the tying of glass stoppers into small bottles. At his waist he carried a bundle of twine. He held the bottles between his knees so that he might work with both hands. Thus, in a sitting position and bending over his own knees, his narrow shoulders grew humped and his chest was contracted for ten hours each day. This was not good for the lungs, but he tied three hundred dozen bottles a day.

The superintendent was very proud of him, and brought visitors to look at him. In ten hours three hundred dozen bottles passed through his hands. This meant that he had attained machine-like perfection. All waste movements were eliminated. Every motion of his thin arms, every movement of a muscle in the thin fingers, was swift and accurate. He worked at high tension, and the result was that he grew nervous. At night his muscles twitched in his sleep, and in the daytime he could not relax and rest. He remained keyed up and his muscles continued to twitch. Also he grew sallow and his lint-cough grew worse. Then pneumonia laid hold of the feeble lungs within the contracted chest, and he lost his job in the glass-works.

Now he had returned to the jute mills where he had first begun with winding bobbins. But promotion was waiting for him. He was a good worker. He would next go on the starcher, and later he would go into the loom room. There was nothing after that except increased efficiency.

The machinery ran faster than when he had first gone to work, and his mind ran slower. He no longer dreamed at all, though his earlier years had been full of dreaming. Once he had been in love. It was when he first began guiding the cloth over the hot roller, and it was with the daughter of the superintendent. She was much older than he, a young woman, and he had seen her at a distance only a paltry half-dozen times. But that made no difference. On the surface of the cloth stream that poured past him he pictured radiant futures wherein he performed prodigies of toil, invented miraculous machines, won to the mastership of the mills, and in the end took her in his arms and kissed her soberly on the brow.

But that was all in the long ago, before he had grown too old and tired to love. Also, she had married and gone away, and his mind had gone to sleep. Yet it had been a wonderful experience, and he used often to look back upon it as other men and women look back upon the time they believed in fairies. He had never believed in fairies nor Santa Claus; but he had believed implicitly in the smiling future his imagination had wrought into the steaming cloth stream.

He had become a man very early in life. At seven, when he drew his first wages, began his adolescence. A certain feeling of independence crept up in him, and the relationship between him and his mother changed. Somehow, as an earner and breadwinner, doing his own work in the world, he was more like an equal with her. Manhood, full-blown manhood, had come when he was eleven, at which time he had gone to work on the night shift for six months. No child works on the night shift and remains a child.

There had been several great events in his life. One of these had been when his mother bought some California prunes. Two others had been the two times when she cooked custard. Those had been events. He remembered them kindly. And at that time his mother had told him of a blissful dish she would sometime make—"floating island," she had called it, "better than custard." For years he had looked forward to the day when he would sit down to the table with floating island before him, until at last he had relegated the idea of it to the limbo of unattainable ideals.

Once he found a silver quarter lying on the sidewalk. That, also, was a great event in his life, withal a tragic one. He knew his duty on the instant the silver flashed on his eyes, before even he had picked it up. At home, as usual, there was not enough to eat, and home he should have taken it as he did his wages every Saturday night. Right conduct in this case was obvious; but he never had any spending of his money, and he was suffering from candy hunger. He was ravenous for the sweets that only on red-letter days he had ever tasted in his life.

He did not attempt to deceive himself. He knew it was sin, and deliberately he sinned when he went on a fifteen-cent candy debauch. Ten cents he saved for a future orgy; but not being accustomed to the carrying of money, he lost the ten cents. This occurred at the time when he was suffering all the torments of conscience, and it was to him an act of divine retribution. He had a frightened sense of the closeness of an awful and wrathful God. God had seen, and God had been swift to punish, denying him even the full wages of sin.

In memory he always looked back upon that event as the one great criminal deed of his life, and at the recollection his conscience always awoke and gave him another twinge. It was the one skeleton in his closet. Also, being so made and circumstanced, he looked back upon the deed with regret. He was dissatisfied with the manner in which he had spent the quarter. He could have invested it better, and, out of his later knowledge of the quickness of God, he would have beaten God out by spending the whole quarter at one fell swoop. In retrospect he spent the quarter a thousand times, and each time to better advantage.

There was one other memory of the past, dim and faded, but stamped into his soul everlastingly by the savage feet of his father. It was more like a nightmare than a remembered vision of a concrete thing—more like the race-memory of man that makes him fall in his sleep and that goes back to his arboreal ancestry.

This particular memory never came to Johnny in broad daylight when he was wide awake. It came at night, in bed, at the moment that his consciousness was sinking down and losing itself in sleep. It always aroused him to frightened wakefulness, and for the moment, in the first sickening start, it seemed to him that he lay crosswise on the foot of the bed. In the bed were the vague forms of his father and mother. He never saw what his father looked like. He had but one impression of his father, and that was that he had savage and pitiless feet.

His earlier memories lingered with him, but he had no late memories. All days were alike. Yesterday or last year were the same as a thousand years—or a minute. Nothing ever happened. There were no events to mark the march of time. Time did not march. It stood always still. It was only the whirling machines that moved, and they moved nowhere—in spite of the fact that they moved faster.

When he was fourteen, he went to work on the starcher. It was a colossal event. Something had at last happened that could be remembered beyond a night's sleep or a week's pay-day. It marked an era. It was a machine Olympiad, a thing to date from. "When

I went to work on the starcher," or, "after," or "before I went to work on the starcher," were sentences often on his lips.

He celebrated his sixteenth birthday by going into the loom room and taking a loom. Here was an incentive again, for it was piece-work. And he excelled, because the clay of him had been moulded by the mills into the perfect machine. At the end of three months he was running two looms, and, later, three and four.

At the end of his second year at the looms he was turning out more yards than any other weaver, and more than twice as much as some of the less skilful ones. And at home things began to prosper as he approached the full stature of his earning power. Not, however, that his increased earnings were in excess of need. The children were growing up. They ate more. And they were going to school, and school-books cost money. And somehow, the faster he worked, the faster climbed the prices of things. Even the rent went up, though the house had fallen from bad to worse disrepair.

He had grown taller; but with his increased height he seemed leaner than ever. Also, he was more nervous. With the nervousness increased his peevishness and irritability. The children had learned by many bitter lessons to fight shy of him. His mother respected him for his earning power, but somehow her respect was tinctured with fear.

There was no joyousness in life for him. The procession of the days he never saw. The nights he slept away in twitching uncon-sciousness. The rest of the time he worked, and his consciousness was machine consciousness. Outside this his mind was a blank. He had no ideals, and but one illusion; namely, that he drank excellent coffee. He was a work-beast. He had no mental life whatever; yet deep down in the crypts of his mind, unknown to him, were being weighed and sifted every hour of his toil, every movement of his hands, every twitch of his muscles, and preparations were making for a future course of action that would amaze him and all his little world.

It was in the late spring that he came home from work one night aware of unusual tiredness. There was a keen expectancy in the air as he sat down to the table, but he did not notice. He went through the meal in moody silence, mechanically eating what was before him. The children um'd and ah'd and made smacking noises with their mouths. But he was deaf to them.

"D'ye know what you're eatin'?" his mother demanded at last, desperately.

He looked vacantly at the dish before him, and vacantly at her.

"Floatin' island," she announced triumphantly.

"Oh," he said.

"Floating island!" the children chorussed loudly.

"Oh," he said. And after two or three mouthsfuls, he added, "I guess I ain't hungry tonight."

He dropped the spoon, shoved back his chair, and arose wearily from the table.

"An' I guess I'll go to bed."

His feet dragged more heavily than usual as he crossed the kitchen floor. Undressing was a Titan's task, a monstrous futility, and he wept weakly as he crawled into bed, one shoe still on. He was aware of a rising, swelling something inside his head that made his brain thick and fuzzy. His lean fingers felt as big as his wrist, while in the ends of them was a remoteness of sensation vague and fuzzy like his brain. The small of his back ached intolerably. All his bones ached. He ached everywhere. And in his head began the shrieking, pounding, crashing, roaring of a million looms. All space was filled with flying shuttles. They darted in and out, intricately, amongst the stars. He worked a thousand looms himself, and ever they speeded up, faster and faster, and his brain unwound, faster and faster, and became the thread that fed the thousand flying shuttles.

He did not go to work next morning. He was too busy weaving colossally on the thousand looms that ran inside his head. His mother went to work, but first she sent for the doctor. It was a severe attack of la grippe, he said. Jennie served as nurse and carried out his instructions.

It was a very severe attack, and it was a week before Johnny dressed and tottered feebly across the floor. Another week, the doctor said, and he would be fit to return to work. The foreman of the loom room visited him on Sunday afternoon, the first day of his convalescence. The best weaver in the room, the foreman told his mother. His job would be held for him. He could come back to work a week from Monday.

"Why don't you thank 'im, Johnny?" his mother asked anxiously.

"He's ben that sick he ain't himself yet," she explained apologetically to the visitor.

Johnny sat hunched up and gazing steadfastly at the floor. He sat in the same position long after the foreman had gone. It was warm outdoors, and he sat on the stoop in the afternoon. Sometimes his lips moved. He seemed lost in endless calculations.

Next morning, after the day grew warm, he took his seat on the stoop. He had pencil and paper this time with which to continue his calculations, and he calculated painfully and amazingly.

"What comes after millions?" he asked at noon, when Will came home from school. "An' how d'ye work 'em?"

That afternoon finished his task. Each day, but without paper and pencil, he returned to the stoop. He was greatly absorbed in the one tree that grew across the street. He studied it for hours at a time, and was unusually interested when the wind swayed its branches and fluttered its leaves. Throughout the week he seemed lost in a great communion with himself. On Sunday, sitting on the stoop, he laughed aloud, several times, to the perturbation of his mother, who had not heard him laugh in years.

Next morning, in the early darkness, she came to his bed to rouse him. He had had his fill of sleep all week, and awoke easily. He made no struggle, nor did he attempt to hold on to the bedding when she stripped it from him. He lay quietly, and spoke quietly.

"It ain't no use, ma."

"You'll be late," she said, under the impression that he was still stupid with sleep.

"I'm awake, ma, an' I tell you it ain't no use. You might as well lemme alone. I ain't goin' to git up."

"But you'll lose your job!" she cried.

"I ain't goin' to git up," he repeated in a strange, passionless voice.

She did not go to work herself that morning. This was sickness beyond any sickness she had ever known. Fever and delirium she could understand; but this was insanity. She pulled the bedding up over him and sent Jennie for the doctor.

When that person arrived, Johnny was sleeping gently, and gently he awoke and allowed his pulse to be taken.

"Nothing the matter with him," the doctor reported. "Badly debilitated, that's all. Not much meat on his bones."

"He's always been that way," his mother volunteered.

"Now go 'way, ma, an' let me finish my snooze."

Johnny spoke sweetly and placidly, and sweetly and placidly he rolled over on his side and went to sleep.

At ten o'clock he awoke and dressed himself. He walked out into the kitchen, where he found his mother with a frightened expression on her face.

"I'm goin' away, ma," he announced, "an' I jes' want to say good-by."

She threw her apron over her head and sat down suddenly and wept. He waited patiently.

"I might a-known it," she was sobbing.

"Where?" she finally asked, removing the apron from her head and gazing up at him with a stricken face in which there was little curiosity.

"I don't know—anywhere."

As he spoke, the tree across the street appeared with dazzling brightness on his inner vision. It seemed to lurk just under his eyelids, and he could see it whenever he wished.

"An' your job?" she quavered.

"I ain't never goin' to work again."

"My God, Johnny!" she wailed, "don't say that!"

What he had said was blasphemy to her. As a mother who hears her child deny God, was Johnny's mother shocked by his words.

"What's got into you, anyway?" she demanded, with a lame attempt at imperativeness.

"Figures," he answered. "Jes' figures. I've ben doin' a lot of figurin' this week, an' it's most surprisin'."

"I don't see what that's got to do with it," she sniffled.

Johnny smiled patiently, and his mother was aware of a distinct shock at the persistent absence of his peevishness and irritability.

"I'll show you," he said. "I'm plum' tired out. What makes me tired? Moves. I've ben movin' ever since I was born. I'm tired of movin', an' I ain't goin to move any more. Remember when I worked in the glass-house? I used to do three hundred dozen a day. Now I reckon I made about ten different moves to each bottle. That's thirty-six thousan' moves a day. Ten days, three hundred an' sixty thousan' moves a day. One month, one million an' eighty thousan' moves. Chuck out the eighty thousan'—" he spoke with the complacent beneficence of a philanthropist—"chuck out the eighty thousan', that leaves a million moves a month—twelve million moves a year.

"At the looms I'm movin' twic'st as much. That makes twenty-five million moves a year, an' it seems to me I've been a movin' that way 'most a million years.

"Now this week I ain't moved at all. I ain't made one move in hours an' hours. I tell you it was swell, jes' settin' there, hours an' hours, an' doin nothin'. I ain't never ben happy before. I never had any time. I've ben movin' all the time. That ain't no way to be happy. An' I ain't goin' to do it any more. I'm jes' goin' to set, an' set, an' rest, an' rest, and then rest some more."

"But what's goin' to come of Will an' the children?" she asked despairingly.

"That's it, 'Will an' the children,' " he repeated.

But there was no bitterness in his voice. He had long known his mother's ambition for the younger boy, but the thought of it no longer rankled. Nothing mattered any more. Not even that.

"I know, ma, what you've been plannin' for Will—keepin' him in school to make a bookkeeper out of him. But it ain't no use, I've quit. He's got to go to work."

"An' after I have brung you up the way I have," she wept, starting to cover her head with the apron and changing her mind.

"You never brung me up," he answered with sad kindliness. "I brung myself up, ma, an' I brung up Will. He's bigger'n me, an' heavier, an' taller. When I was a kid, I reckon I didn't git enough to eat. When he come along an' was a kid, I was workin' an' earnin' grub for him too. But that's done with. Will can go to work, same as me, or he can go to hell, I don't care which. I'm tired. I'm goin' now. Ain't you goin' to say good-by?"

She made no reply. The apron had gone over her head again, and she was crying. He paused a moment in the doorway.

"I'm sure I done the best I knew how," she was sobbing.

He passed out of the house and down the street. A wan delight came into his face at the sight of the lone tree. "Jes' ain't goin' to do nothin'," he said to himself, half aloud, in a crooning voice. He glanced wistfully up at the sky, but the bright sun dazzled and blinded him.

It was a long walk he took, and he did not walk fast. It took him past the jute-mill. The muffled roar of the loom room came to his ears, and he smiled. It was a gentle, placid smiled. He hated no one, not even the pounding, shrieking machines. There was no bitterness in him, nothing but an inordinate hunger for rest.

The houses and factories thinned out and the open spaces increased as he approached the country. At last the city was behind him, and he was walking down a leafy lane beside the railroad track. He did not walk like a man. He did not look like a man. He was a travesty of the human. It was a twisted and stunted and nameless piece of life that shambled like a sickly ape, arms loose-hanging, stoop-shouldered, narrow-chested, grotesque and terrible.

He passed by a small railroad station and lay down in the grass under a tree. All afternoon he lay there. Sometimes he dozed, with muscles that twitched in his sleep. When awake, he lay without movement, watching the birds or looking up at the sky through the branches of the tree above him. Once or twice he laughed aloud, but without relevance to anything he had seen or felt.

After twilight had gone, in the first darkness of the night, a freight train rumbled into the station. When the engine was switching cars on to the side-track, Johnny crept along the side of the train. He pulled open the side-door of an empty box-car and awkwardly and laboriously climbed in. He closed the door. The engine whistled. Johnny was lying down, and in the darkness he smiled.

FOUR HORSES AND A SAILOR

(*Sunset Magazine*, September, 1911)

The year 1911 was one of domesticity and relative tranquility for the restless Jack London. After his return from the *Snark* voyage to the South Seas in the summer of 1909, he had turned his energies to building up his "Beauty Ranch" at Glen Ellen, experimenting in all manner of farming methods, and working feverishly on the design and construction of his "Wolf House" mansion.

Nineteen-eleven was also his most productive year as a short story writer—twenty-four stories published in the twelve months, including the stories for such collections as *Smoke Bellew*, *A Son of the Sun* and *The Night-Born*, and such masterpieces as "War" and "The Strength of the Strong."

On June 12, 1911, London, his wife Charmian and Nakata Yoshimatsu, the personal servant Jack had hired in Hawaii during the *Snark* voyage, made a 1,350-mile trip up the California coast in a light Studebaker trap pulled by four horses, crossing the Oregon border on July 25 and returning to Glen Ellen on September 5.

"Four Horses and a Sailor" is Jack's light-hearted account of the trip, with a picturesque view of some of the most gorgeous countryside—then, as now—in America.

FOUR HORSES AND A SAILOR

"HUH! DRIVE FOUR horses! I wouldn't sit behind you—not for a thousand dollars—over them mountain roads."

So said Henry, and he ought to have known, for he drives four horses himself.

Said another Glen Ellen friend: "What? London? He drive four horses? Can't drive one!"

And the best of it is that he was right. Even after managing to get a few hundred miles with my four horses, I don't know how to drive one. Just the other day, swinging down a steep mountain road and rounding an abrupt turn, I came full tilt on a horse and buggy being driven by a woman up the hill. We could not pass on the narrow road, where was only a foot to spare, and my horses did not know how to back, especially up hill. About two hundred yards down the hill was a spot where we could pass. The driver of the buggy said she didn't dare back down because she was not sure of the brake. And as I didn't know how to tackle one horse, I didn't try it. So we unhitched her horse and backed down by hand. Which was very well, till it came to hitching the horse to the buggy again. She didn't know how. I didn't either, and I had depended on her knowledge. It took us about half an hour, with frequent debates and consultations, though it is an absolute certainty that never in its life was that horse hitched in that particular way.

No; I can't harness up one horse. But I can four, which compels me to back up again to get to my beginning. Having selected Sonoma Valley for our abiding place, Charmian and I decided it was about time we knew what we had in our own county and the neighboring ones. How to do it, was the first question. Among our many weaknesses is the one of being old-fashioned. We don't mix with gasoline very well. And, as true sailors should, we naturally gravitate toward horses. Being one of those lucky individuals who carries his office under his hat, I should have to take a typewriter and a load of books along. This put saddle-horses out of the running. Charmian suggested driving a span. She had faith in me; besides, she could drive a span herself. But when I thought of the many mountains to cross, and of crossing them for three months with a poor tired span, I vetoed the proposition and said we'd have to come back to gasoline after all. This she vetoed just as emphatically, and a deadlock obtained until I received inspiration.

"Why not drive four horses?" I said.

"But you don't know how to drive four horses," was her objection."

I threw my chest out and my shoulders back. "What man has done, I can do," I proclaimed grandly. "And please don't forget that when we sailed on the *Snark* I knew nothing of navigation, and that I taught myself as I sailed."

"Very well," she said. (And there's faith for you!) "They shall be four saddle horses, and we'll strap our saddles on behind the rig."

It was my turn to object. "Our saddles horses are not broken to harness."

"Then break them."

And what I knew about horses, much less about breaking them, was just about as much as any sailor knows. Having been kicked, bucked off, fallen over backward upon, and thrown out and run over, on very numerous occasions, I had a mighty vigorous respect for horses; but a wife's faith must be lived up to, and I went at it.

King was a polo pony from St. Louis, and Prince a many-gaited love-horse from Pasadena. The hardest thing was to get them to dig in and pull. They rollicked along on the levels and galloped down the hills, but when they struck an up-grade and felt the weight of the breaking-cart, they stopped and turned around and looked at me. But I passed them, and my troubles began. Milda was fourteen years old, an unadulterated broncho, and in temperament was a combination of mule and jack-rabbit blended equally. If you pressed your hand on her flank and told her to get over, she lay down on you. If you got her by the head and told her to back, she walked forward over you. And if you got behind her and shoved and told her to "Giddap!" she sat down on you. Also, she wouldn't walk. For endless weary miles I strove with her, but never could I get her to walk a step. Finally, she was a manger-glutton. No matter how near or far from the stable, when six o'clock came around she bolted for home and never missed the directest cross-road. Many times I rejected her.

The fourth and most rejected horse of all was the Outlaw. From the age of three to seven she had defied all horse-breakers and broken a number of them. Then a long, lanky cowboy, with a fifty-pound saddle and a Mexican bit had got her proud goat. I was the next owner. She was my favourite riding horse. Charmian said I'd have to put her in as a wheeler where I would have more control over her. Now Charmian had a favourite riding mare called Maid.

I suggested Maid as a substitute. Charmian pointed out that my mare was a branded range horse, while hers was a near-thorough-bred, and that the legs of her mare would be ruined forever if she were driven for three months. I acknowledged her mare's thoroughbredness, and at the same time defied her to find any thoroughbred with as small and delicately-viciously pointed ears as my Outlaw. She indicated Maid's exquisitely thin shinbone. I measured the Outlaw's. It was equally thin, although, I insinuated, possibly more durable. This stabbed Charmian's pride. Of course her near-thoroughbred Maid, carrying the blood of "old" Lexington, Morella, and a streak of the super-enduring Morgan, could run, walk, and work my unregistered Outlaw into the ground; and that was the very precise reason why such a paragon of a saddle animal should not be degraded by harness.

So it was that Charmian remained obdurate, until, one day, I got her behind the Outlaw for a forty-mile drive. For every inch of those forty miles the Outlaw kicked and jumped, in between the kicks and jumps finding time and space in which to seize its teammate by the back of the neck and attempt to drag it to the ground. Another trick the Outlaw developed during that drive was suddenly to turn at right angles in the traces and endeavor to butt its teammate over the grade. Reluctantly and nobly did Charmian give and and consent to the use of Maid. The Outlaw's shoes were pulled off, and she was turned out on range.

Finally, the four horses were hooked to the rig—a light Studebaker trap. With two hours and a half of practice, in which the excitement was not abated by several jackpoles and numerous kicking matches, I announced myself as ready for the start. Came the morning, and Prince, who was to have been a wheeler with Maid, showed up with a badly kicked shoulder. He did not exactly show up; we had to find him, for he was unable to walk. His leg swelled and continually swelled during the several days we waited for him. Remained only the Outlaw. In from pasture she came, shoes were nailed on, and she was harnessed into the wheel. Friends and relatives strove to press accident policies on me, but Charmian climbed up alongside, and Nakata got into the rear seat with the typewriter—Nakata, who sailed cabin-boy on the *Snark* for two years and who has shown himself afraid of nothing, not even of me and

my amateur jamborees in experimenting with new modes of loco-
motion. And we did very nicely, thank you, especially after the first
house or so, during which time the Outlaw had kicked about fifty
various times, chiefly to the damage of her own legs and the paint-
work, and after she had bitten a couple of hundred times, to the
damage of Maid's neck and Charmian's temper. It was hard enough
to have her favourite mare in the harness without also enduring the
spectacle of its being eaten alive.

Our leaders were joys. King being a polo pony and Milda a rabbit,
they rounded curves beautifully and darted ahead like coyotes out
of the way of the wheelers. Milda's besetting weakness was a frantic
desire not to have the lead-bar strike her hocks. When this happened, one of three things occurred; either she sat down on the
lead-bar, kicked it up in the air until she got her back under it, or
exploded in a straight-ahead, harness-disrupting jump. Not until
she carried the lead-bar clean away and danced a break-down on
it and the traces, did she behave decently. Nakata and I made the
repairs with good old-fashioned bale-rope, which is stronger than
wrought-iron any time, and we went on our way.

In the meantime I was learning—I shall not say to tool a four-in-
hand—but just simply to drive four horses. Now it is all right enough
to begin with four work-horses pulling a load of several tons. But
to begin with four light horses, all running, and a light rig that seems
to outrun them—well, when things happen they happen quickly.
My weakness was total ignorance. In particular, my fingers lacked
training, and I made the mistake of depending on my eyes to handle
the reins. This brought me up against a disastrous optical illusion.
The bight of the off head-line, being longer and heavier than that
of the off wheel-line, hung lower. In a moment requiring quick
action, I invariably mistook the two lines. Pulling on what I thought
was the wheel-line, in order to straighten the team, I would see the
leaders swing abruptly around into a jack-pole. Now for sensations
of sheer impotence, nothing can compare with a jack-pole, when
the horrified driver beholds his leaders prancing gaily up the road
and his wheelers jogging steadily down the road, all at the same
time and all harnessed together and to the same rig.

I no longer jack-pole, and I don't mind admitting how I got out
of the habit. It was my eyes that enslaved my fingers into ill practices.

So I shut my eyes and let the fingers go it alone. Today my fingers are independent of my eyes and work automatically. I do not see what my fingers do. They just do it. All I see is the satisfactory result.

Still we managed to get over the ground that first day—down sunny Sonoma Valley to the old town of Sonoma, founded by General Vallejo as the remotest outpost on the northern frontier for the purpose of holding back the Gentiles, as the wild Indians of those days were called. Here history was made. Here the last Spanish mission was reared; here the Bear flag was raised; and here Kit Carson, and Fremont, and all our early adventurers came and rested in the days before the days of gold.

We swung on over the low, rolling hills, through miles of dairy farms and chicken ranches where every blessed hen is white, and down the slopes to Petaluma Valley. Here, in 1776, Captain Quiros came up Petaluma Creek from San Pablo Bay in quest of an outlet to Bodega Bay on the coast. And here, later, the Russians, with Alaskan hunters, carried ski boats across from Fort Ross to poach for sea-otters on the Spanish preserve of San Francisco Bay. Here, too, still later, General Vallejo built a fort, which still stands—one of the finest examples of Spanish adobe that remain to us. And here, at the old fort, to bring the chronicle up to date, our horses proceeded to make peculiarly personal history with astonishing success and dispatch. King, our peerless polo-pony leader, went lame. So hopelessly lame did he go that no expert, then and afterward, could determine whether the lameness was in his frogs, hoofs, legs, shoulders, or head. Maid picked up a nail and began to limp. Milda, figuring the day already sufficiently spent and maniacal with manger gluttony, began to rabbit-jump. All that held her was the bale rope. And the Outlaw, game to the last, exceeded all previous exhibitions of skin-removing, paint-marring, and horse-eating.

At Petaluma we rested over while King was returned to the ranch and Prince sent to us. Now Prince had proved himself an excellent wheeler, yet he had to go into the lead and let the Outlaw retain his old place. There is an axiom that a good wheeler is a poor leader. I object to the last adjective. A good wheeler makes an infinitely worse kind of a leader than that. I know . . . now. I ought to know. Since that day I have driven Prince a few hundred miles in the lead.

He is neither any better nor any worse than the first mile he ran in the lead; and his worst is even extremely worse than what you are thinking. Not that he is vicious. He is merely a good-natured rogue who shakes hands for sugar, steps on your toes out of sheer excessive friendliness, and just goes on loving you in your harshest moments.

But he won't get out of the way. Also, whenever he is reproved for being in the wrong, he accuses Milda of it and bites the back of her neck. So bad has this become that whenever I yell "Prince!" in a loud voice, Milda immediately rabbit-jumps to the side, straight ahead, or sits down on the lead-bar. All of which is quite disconcerting. Picture it yourself. You are swinging a sharp, down-grade, mountain curve, at a fast trot. The rock wall is the outside of the curve. The inside of the curve is a precipice. The continuance of the curve is a narrow, unrailed bridge. You hit the curve, throwing the leaders in against the wall and making the polehorse do the work. All is lovely. The leaders are hugging the wall like nestling doves. But the moment comes in the evolution when the leader must shoot out ahead. They really must shoot, or else they'll hit the wall and miss the bridge. Also, behind them are the wheelers, and the rig, and you have just eased into the manœuvre. If ever teamwork is required, now is the time. Milda tries to shoot. She does her best, but Prince, bubbling over with roguishness, lags behind. He knows the trick. Milda is half a length ahead of him. He times it to the fraction of a second. Maid, in the wheel, over-running him, naturally bites him. This disturbs the Outlaw, who has been behaving beautifully, and she immediately reaches across for Maid. Simultaneously, with a fine display of firm conviction that it's all Milda's fault, Prince sinks his teeth into the back of Milda's defenceless neck. The whole thing has occurred in less than a second. Under the surprise and pain of the bite, Milda either jumps ahead to the imminent peril of harness and lead-bar, or smashes into the wall, stops short with the lead-bar over her back, and emits a couple of hysterical kicks. The Outlaw invariably selects this moment to remove paint. And after things are untangled and you have had time to appreciate the close shave, you go up to Prince and reprove him with your choicest vocabulary. And Prince, gazelle-eyed and tender, offers to shake hands with you for sugar. I leave it to any one: a boat would never act that way.

We have some history north of the Bay. Nearly three centuries and a half ago, that doughty pirate and explorer, Sir Francis Drake, combing the Pacific for Spanish galleons, anchored in the bight formed by Point Reyes, on which today is one of the richest dairy regions in the world. Here, less than two decades after Drake, Sebastien Carmenon piled up on the rocks with a silk-laden galleon from the Philippines. And in this same bay of Drake, long afterward, the Russian fur-poachers rendezvous'd their *bidarkes* and stole in through the Golden Gate to the forbidden waters of San Francisco Bay.

Farther up the coast, in Sonoma County, we pilgrimaged to the sites of the Russian settlements. At Bodega Bay, south of what to-day is called Russian River, was their anchorage, while north of the river they built their fort. And much of Fort Ross still stands. Log-bastions, church, and stables hold their own, and so well, with rusty hinges creaking, that we warmed ourselves at the hundred-years-old double fireplace and slept under the hand-hewn roof beams still held together by spikes of hand-wrought iron.

We went to see where history had been made, and we saw scenery as well. One of our stretches in a day's drive was from beautiful Inverness on Tomales Bay, down the Olema Valley to Bolinas Bay, along the eastern shore of that body of water to Willow Camp, and up over the sea-bluffs, around the bastions of Tamalpais, and down to Sausalito. From the head of Bolinas Bay to Willow Camp the drive on the edge of the beach, and actually, for half-mile stretches, in the waters of the bay itself, was a delightful experience. The wonderful part was to come. Very few San Franciscans, much less Californians, know of that drive from Willow Camp, to the south and east, along the poppy-blown cliffs, with the sea thundering in the sheer depths hundreds of feet below and the Golden Gate opening up ahead, disclosing smoky San Francisco on her many hills. Far off, blurred on the breast of the sea, can be seen the Farallones, which Sir Francis Drake passed on a S.W. course in the thick of what he describes as a "stynking fog." Well might he call it that, and a few other names, for it was the fog that robbed him of the glory of discovering San Francisco Bay.

It was on this part of the drive that I decided at last I was learning real mountain-driving. To confess the truth, for delicious titillation of one's nerve, I have since driven over no mountain road that was worse, or better, rather, than that piece.

And then the contrast! From Sausalito, over excellent, park-like boulevards, through the splendid redwoods and homes of Mill Valley, across the blossomed hills of Marin County, along the knoll-studded picturesque marshes, past San Rafael resting warmly among her hills, over the divide and up the Petaluma Valley, and on to the grassy feet of Sonoma Mountain and home. We covered fifty-five miles that day. Not so bad, eh, for Prince the Rogue, the paint-removing Outlaw, the thin-shanked thorough-bred, and the rabbit-jumper? And they came in cool and dry, ready for their mangers and the straw.

Oh, we didn't stop. We considered we were just starting, and that was many weeks ago. We have kept on going over six counties which are comfortably large, even for California, and we are still going. We have twisted and doubled, criss-crossed our tracks, made fascinating and lengthy drives into the interior valleys in the hearts of Napa and Lake Counties, travelled the coast for hundreds of miles on end, and are now in Eureka, on Humboldt Bay, which was discovered by accident by the gold-seekers, who were trying to find their way to and from the Trinity diggings. Even here, the white-man's history preceded them, for dim tradition says that the Russians once anchored here and hunted sea-otter before the first Yankee trader rounded the Horn, or the first Rocky Mountain trapper thirsted across the "Great American Desert" and trickled down the snowy Sierras to the sunkissed land. No; we are not resting our horses here on Humboldt Bay. We are writing this article, gorging on abalones and mussels, digging clams, and catching record-breaking sea-trout and rock-cod in the intervals in which we are not sailing, motor-boating, and swimming in the most temperately equable climate we have ever experienced.

These comfortably large counties! They are veritable empires. Take Humboldt, for instance. It is three times as large as Rhode Island, one and a half times as large as Delaware, almost as large as Connecticut, and half as large as Massachusetts. The pioneer has done his work in this north of the bay region, the foundations are laid, and all is ready for the inevitable inrush of population and adequate development of resources which so far have been no more than skimmed, and casually and carelessly skimmed at that. This region of the six counties alone will some day support a population of millions. In the meanwhile, O you home-seekers, you wealth-seekers, and, above all, you climate-seekers, now is the time to get in on the ground floor.

Robert Ingersoll once said that the genial climate of California would in a fairly brief time evolve a race resembling the Mexicans, and that in two or three generations the Californians would be seen of a Sunday morning on their way to a cockfight with a rooster under each arm. Never was made a rasher generalisation, based on so absolute an ignorance of facts. It is to laugh. Here is a climate that breeds vigour, with just sufficient geniality to prevent the expenditure of most of that vigour in fighting the elements. Here is a climate where a man can work three hundred and sixty-five days in the year without the slightest hint of enervation, and where for three hundred and sixty-five nights he must perforce sleep under blankets. What more can one say? I consider myself somewhat of a climate expert, having adventured among most of the climates of five out of the six zones. I have not yet been in the Antarctic, but whatever climate obtains there will not deter me from drawing the conclusion that nowhere is there a climate to compare with that of this region. Maybe I am as wrong as Ingersoll was. Nevertheless I take my medicine by continuing to live in this climate. Also, it is the only medicine I ever take.

But to return to the horses. There is some improvement. Milda has actually learned to walk. Milda has proved her thoroughbredness by never tiring on the longest days, and, while being the strongest and highest spirit of all, by never causing any trouble save for an occasional kick at the Outlaw. And the Outlaw rarely gallops, no longer butts, only periodically kicks, comes in to the pole and does her work without attempting to vivisect Maid's medulla oblongata, and—marvel of marvels—is really and truly getting lazy. But Prince remains the same incorrigible, loving and lovable rogue he has always been.

And the country we've been over! The drives through Napa and Lake Counties! One, from Sonoma Valley, via Santa Rosa, we could not refrain from taking several ways, and on all the ways we found the roads excellent for machines as well as horses. One route, and a more delightful one for an automobile cannot be found, is out from Santa Rosa, past old Altruria and Mark West Springs, then to the right and across to Calistoga in Napa Valley. By keeping to the left, the drive holds on up the Russian River Valley, through the miles of the noted Asti Vineyards to Cloverdale, and then by way of Pieta, Witter, and Highland Springs to Lakeport. Still another way we took, was down Sonoma Valley, skirting San Pablo Bay, and up the lovely Napa Valley. From Napa were side excursions through Pope and Berryessa Valleys, on to Ætna Springs, and still on, into Lake County, crossing the famous Langtry Ranch.

Continuing up the Napa Valley, walled on either hand by great rock palisades and redwood forests and carpeted with endless vineyards, and crossing the many stone bridges for which the County is noted and which are a joy to the beauty-loving eyes as well as to the four-horse tyro driver, past Calistoga with its old mud-baths and chicken soup springs, with St. Helena and its giant saddle ever towering before us, we climbed the mountains on a good grade and dropped down past the quicksilver mines to the canyon of the Geysers. After a stop over night and an exploration of the miniature-grand volcanic scene, we pulled on across the canyon and took the grade where the cicadas simmered audibly in the noon sunshine among the hillside manzanitas. Then, higher, came the big cattle-dotted upland pastures, and the rocky summit. And here on the summit, abruptly, we caught a vision, or what seemed a mirage. The ocean we had left long days before, yet far down and away shimmered a blue sea, framed on the farther shore by rugged mountains, on the near shore by fat and rolling farm lands. Clear Lake was before us, and like proper sailors we returned to our sea, going for a sail, a fish, and a swim ere the day was done and turning into tired Lakeport blankets in the early evening. Well has Lake County been called the Walled-in County. But the railroad is coming. They say the approach we made to Clear Lake is similar to the approach to Lake Lucerne. Be that as it may, the scenery, with its distant snowcapped peaks, can well be called Alpine.

And what can be more exquisite than the drive out from Clear Lake to Ukiah by way of the Blue Lakes chain!—every turn bringing into view a picture of breathless beauty; every glance backward revealing some perfect composition in line and colour, the intense blue of the water margined with splendid oaks, green fields, and swaths of orange poppies. But those side glances and backward glances were provocative of trouble. Charmian and I disagreed as to which way the connecting stream of water ran. We still disagree, for at the hotel, where we submitted the affair to arbitration, the hotel manager and the clerk likewise disagreed. I assume, now, that we never will know which way that stream runs. Charmian suggests "both ways." I refuse such a compromise. No stream of water I every saw could accomplish that feat at one and the same time. The greatest concession I can make is that sometimes it may run one way and sometimes the other, and that in the meantime we should both consult an oculist.

More valley from Ukiah to Willits, and then we turned westward through the virgin Sherwood Forest of magnificent redwood, stopping at Alpine for the night and continuing on through Mendocino County to Fort Bragg and "salt water." We also came to Fort Bragg up the coast from Fort Ross, keeping our coast journey intact from the Golden Gate. The coast weather was cool and delightful, the coast driving superb. Especially in the Fort Ross section did we find the roads thrilling, while all the way along we followed the sea. At every stream, the road skirted dizzy cliff-edges, dived down into lush growths of forest and ferns and climbed out along the cliff-edges again. The way was lined with flowers—wild lilac, wild roses, poppies, and lupins. Such lupins!—giant clumps of them, of every lupin shade and colour. And it was along the Mendocino roads that Charmian caused many delays by insisting on getting out to pick the wild blackberries, strawberries, and thimbleberries which grew so profusely. And ever we caught peeps, far down, of steam schooners loading lumber in the rocky coves; ever we skirted the cliffs, day by day, crossing stretches of rolling farm lands and passing through thriving villages and saw-mill towns. Memorable was our launch-trip from Mendocino City up Big River, where the steering gears of the launches work the reverse of anywhere else in the world; where we saw a stream of logs, of six to twelve and fifteen feet in diameter, which filled the river bed for miles to the obliteration of any sign of water; and where we were told of a white or albino redwood tree. We did not see this last, so we cannot vouch for it.

All the streams were filled with trout, and more than once we saw the side-hill salmon on the slopes. No, side-hill salmon is not a peripatetic fish; it is a deer out of season. But the trout! At Gualala Charmian caught her first one. Once before in my life I had caught two . . . on angleworms. On occasion I had tried fly and spinner and never got a strike, and I had come to believe that all this talk of fly-fishing was just so much nature-faking. But on the Gualala River I caught trout—a lot of them—on fly and spinners; and I was beginning to feel quite an expert, until Nakata, fishing on bottom with a pellet of bread for bait, caught the biggest trout of all. I now affirm there is nothing in science nor in art. Nevertheless, since that day poles and baskets have been added to our baggage, we tackle every stream we come to, and we no longer are able to remember the grand total of our catch.

At Usal, many hilly and picturesque miles north of Fort Bragg, we turned again into the interior of Mendocino, crossing the ranges and coming out in Humboldt County on the south fork of Eel River at Garberville. Throughout the trip, from Marin County north, we had been warned of "bad roads ahead." Yet we never found those bad roads. We seemed always to be just ahead of them or behind them. The farther we came the better the roads seemed, though this was probably due to the fact that we were learning more and more what four horses and a light rig could do on a road. And thus do I save my face with all the counties. I refuse to make invidious road comparisons. I can add that while, save in rare instances on steep pitches, I have trotted my horses down all the grades, I have never had one horse fall down nor have I had to send the rig to a blacksmith shop for repairs.

Also, I am learning to throw leather. If any tyro thinks it is easy to take a short-handled, long-lashed whip, and throw the end of that lash just where he wants it, let him put on automobile goggles and try it. On reconsideration, I would suggest the substitution of a wire fencing-mask for the goggles. For days I looked at that whip. It fascinated me, and the fascination was composed mostly of fear. At my first attempt, Charmian and Nataka became afflicted with the same sort of fascination, and for a long time afterward, whenever they saw me reach for the whip, they closed their eyes and shielded their heads with their arms.

Here's the problem. Instead of pulling honestly, Prince is lagging back and manœuvreing for a bite at Milda's neck. I have four reins in my hands. I must put these four reins into my left hand, properly gather the whip handle and the bight of the lash in my right hand, and throw that lash past Maid without striking her and into Prince. If the lash strikes Maid, her thoroughbredness will go up in the air and I'll have a case of horse hysteria on my hands for the next half hour. But follow. The whole problem is not yet stated. Suppose that I miss Maid and reach the intended target. The instant the lash cracks, the four horses jump, Prince most of all, and his jump, with spread wicked teeth, is for the back of Milda's neck. She jumps to escape—which is her second jump, for the first one came when the lash exploded. The Outlaw reaches for Maid's neck, and Maid, who had already jumped and tried to bolt, tries to bolt harder. And all this infinitesimal fraction of time I am trying to hold the four animals with my left hand, while my whip-lash writhing through the air, is coming back to me. Three simultaneous things I must do: keep hold of the four hands with my left hand; slam on the brake with my foot; and on the rebound catch that flying lash in the hollow of my right arm and get the bight of it safely into my right hand. Then I must get two of the four lines back into my right hand and keep the horses from running away or going over the grade. Try it some time. You will find life anything but wearisome. Why, the first time I hit the mark and made the lash go off like a revolver shot, I was so astounded and delighted that I was paralysed. I forgot to do any of the multitudinous other things, tangled the whip-lash in Maid's harness, and was forced to call upon Charmian for assistance. And now, confession. I carry a few pebbles handy. They're great for reaching Prince in a tight place. But just the same I'm learning that whip every day, and before I get home I hope to discard the pebbles. And as long as I rely on pebbles, I cannot truthfully speak of myself as "tooling a four-in-hand."

From Garberville, where we ate eel to repletion and got acquainted with the aborigines, we drove down the Eel River Valley for two days through the most unthinkably glorious body of redwood timber to be seen anywhere in California. From Dyerville on to Eureka, we caught glimpses of railroad construction and of great concrete bridges in the course of building, which advertised that at least Humboldt County was going to be linked to the rest of the world.

We still consider our trip is just begun. As soon as this is mailed from Eureka, it's heigh ho! for the horses and pull on. We shall continue up the coast, turn in for Hoopa Reservation and the gold mines, and shoot down the Trinity and Klamath rivers in Indian canoes to Requa. After that, we shall go on through Del Norte County and into Oregon. The trip so far has justified us in taking the attitude that we won't go home until the winter rains drive us in. And, finally, I am going to try the experiment of putting the Outlaw in the lead and relegating Prince to his old position in the near wheel. I won't need any pebbles then.[1]

[1]In the Spring of 1916, Sonoma Maid, mother of two fine colts, died in giving birth to a third. Also, during this year, Prince contracted an incurable rheumatism, and Milda began to show an incurable agedness. Jack had always said that the team should never leave the ranch, and so, following his own death in November, 1916, we laid away Prince the Love Horse, and Milda the Rabbit, on our hillside in the Valley of the Moon. Gert the Outlaw still flourishes upon her master's acres, and is the mother of three fine colts—C. K. L.

UTAH

MOUNTAIN MEADOWS
MASSACRE

(From *The Star Rover*, 1915)

In Joan London's 1939 biography of her father, *Jack London and His Times*, she expresses the belief that in his 1915 synoptic masterpiece, *The Star Rover*, London flung a handful of jewels that may have originally been ideas for entire novels—a story set in the time of Christ, another in ancient Korea, another of a shipwrecked sailor, yet another based upon an infamous massacre at Mountain Meadows in southern Utah in 1857.

The Star Rover, one of the least studied and most interesting of all London's twenty-two novels, hinges on the adventures of a condemned murderer, Darrell Standing, in San Quentin prison. Standing, considered an incorrigible, is bound tightly in a straitjacket and flung into solitary confinement where his only company is his mind—a formidable one, as it happens. Coached by another prisoner who has used the trick, Standing learns he can leave his terrestrial body and travel among the stars—and through human history, living random experiences of humankind.

One such experience is that of Jesse Fancher, a young Arkansas boy with a wagon train of settlers headed for Southern California. Jesse's father, Captain Fancher, leads the trek through the Mormon country of Utah Territory. There is inexplicable hostility everywhere: they are taunted, denied food and provisions, even milk for their babies, driven south from Salt Lake City to Fillmore, where

235

Jesse sees for the first time their chief nemesis, a tall blue-eyed man named Lee.

Captain Fancher is anxious to leave Utah behind and move on to the myth-land of California, but at Mountain Meadows . . .

What takes place in this chilling story is historically grounded. There *was* a wagon train of one-hundred-twenty men, women and children, led by Captain Alexander Fancher through Utah Territory in the fall of 1857, and what London describes as the fate of that train is accurate.

There was a Major Higbee and he did give the fatal order, "Do your duty!"

And the man who, more than any other, was responsible for the tragedy at Mountain Meadows, was a certain Mormon zealot named John D. Lee.

And history records that on March 23, 1877, almost twenty years after the events described here by Jack London, Lee was executed by rifle fire at the precise site in Mountain Meadows where the Fancher party met its fate.

London, it is certain, made use of Josiah Gibbs' *The Mountain Meadows Massacre* (1910) for the historical backdrop of this story. Charmian London's father, Captain Willard Kittredge, was a Union Army provost marshal at Fort Douglas, near Salt Lake City, and this bloody episode of Utah's recent past was surely known to him and perhaps passed on to his daughter. And finally, chances are that Jack examined the fateful Meadows himself either in 1905, when he and Charmian visited the state, or in 1911, when they were again in Utah, headed east to Baltimore where they were to board the four-masted barque *Dirigo* for a 148-day voyage around Cape Horn to Seattle.

This then is chapter 13 of *The Star Rover*: a complete story of its own, one of the few pieces of historical fiction in the Jack London canon.

MOUNTAIN MEADOWS

LONG BEFORE DAYLIGHT the camp of Nephi was astir. The cattle were driven out to water and pasture. While the men unchained the wheels and drew the wagons apart and clear for yoking in, the women cooked forty breakfasts over forty fires. The children, in the chill of dawn, clustered about the fires, sharing places, here and there, with the last relief of the night watch waiting sleepily for coffee.

It requires time to get a large train such as ours under way, for its speed is the speed of the slowest. So the sun was an hour high and the day was already uncomfortably hot when we rolled out of Nephi and on into the sandy barrens. No inhabitant of the place saw us off. All chose to remain indoors, thus making our departure as ominous as they had made our arrival the night before.

Again it was long hours of parching heat and biting dust, sagebrush and sand, and a land accursed. No dwellings of men, neither cattle nor fences, nor any sign of human kind, did we encounter all that day; and at night we made our wagon-circle beside an empty stream, in the damp sand of which we dug many holes that filled slowly with water seepage.

Our subsequent journey is always a broken experience to me. We made camp so many times, always with the wagons drawn in circle, that to my child mind a weary long time passed after Nephi. But always, strong upon all of us, was that sense of drifting to an impending and certain doom.

We averaged about fifteen miles a day. I know, for my father had said it was sixty miles to Fillmore, the next Mormon settlement, and we made three camps on the way. This meant four days of travel. From Nephi to the last camp of which I have any memory, we must have taken two weeks or a little less.

At Fillmore, the inhabitants were hostile, as all had been since Salt Lake. They laughed at us when we tried to buy food, and were not above taunting us with being Missourians.

When we entered the place, hitched before the largest house of the dozen houses that composed the settlement were two saddle horses, dusty, streaked with sweat, and drooping. The old man I have mentioned, the one with long sunburned hair and buckskin shirt and who seemed a sort of aide or lieutenant to Father, rode close to our wagon and indicated the jaded saddle animals with a cock of his head.

"Not sparin' horseflesh, Captain," he muttered in a low voice.

"An' what in the name of Sam Hill are they hard-riding for if it ain't for us?"

But my father had already noted the condition of the two animals, and my eager eyes had seen him. And I had seen his eyes flash, his lips tighten, and haggard lines form for a moment on his dusty face. That was all. But I put two and two together, and knew that the two tired saddle horses were just one more added touch of ominousness to the situation.

"I guess they're keeping an eye on us, Laban," was my father's sole comment.

It was at Fillmore that I saw a man that I was to see again. He was a tall, broad-shouldered man, well on in middle age, with all the evidence of good health and immense strength—strength not alone of body but of will. Unlike most men I was accustomed to about me, he was smooth-shaven. Several days' growth of beard showed that he was already well grayed. His mouth was unusually wide, with thin lips tightly compressed as if he had lost many of his front teeth. His nose was large, square, and thick. So was his face square, wide between the cheekbones, underhung with massive jaws, and topped with a broad, intelligent forehead. And the eyes, rather small, a little more than the width of an eye apart, were the bluest blue I had ever seen.

It was at the flour mill at Fillmore that I first saw this man. Father, with several of our company, had gone there to try to buy flour and I, disobeying my mother in my curiosity to see more of our enemies, had tagged along unperceived. This man was one of four or five who stood in a group with the miller during the interview.

"You seen that smooth-faced old cuss?" Laban said to Father, after we had got outside and were returning to camp.

Father nodded.

"Well, that's Lee," Laban continued. "I seen'm in Salt Lake. He's a regular son-of-a-gun. Got nineteen wives and fifty children, they all say. An' he's rank crazy on religion. Now what's he followin' us up for through this Godforsaken country?"

Our weary, doomed drifting went on. The little settlements, wherever water and soil permitted, were from twenty to fifty miles apart. Between stretched the barrenness of sand and alkali and drought. And at every settlement our peaceful atempts to buy food were vain. They denied us harshly, and wanted to know who of us had sold them food when we drove them from Missouri. It was useless on our part to tell them we were from Arkansas. From Arkansas we truly were, but they insisted on our being Missourians.

At Beaver, five days' journey south from Fillmore, we saw Lee again. And again we saw hard-ridden horses tethered before the houses. But we did not see Lee at Parowan.

Cedar City was the last settlement. Laban, who had ridden on ahead, came back and reported to Father. His first news was significant.

"I seen that Lee skeedaddling out as I rid in, Captain. An' there's more menfolk an' horses in Cedar City than the size of the place'd warrant."

But we had no trouble at the settlement. Beyond refusing to sell us food, they left us to ourselves. The women and children stayed in the houses and, though some of the men appeared in sight, they did not, as on former occasions, enter our camp and taunt us.

It was at Cedar City that the Wainwright baby died. I remember Mrs. Wainwright weeping and pleading with Laban to try to get some cow's milk.

"It may save the baby's life," she said. "And they've got cow's milk. I saw fresh cows with my own eyes. Go on, please, Laban. It won't hurt you to try. They can only refuse. But they won't. Tell them it's for a baby, a wee little baby. Mormon women have mother's hearts. They couldn't refuse a cup of milk for a wee little baby."

And Laban tried. But as he told father afterward, he did not get to see any Mormon women. He saw only the Mormen men, who turned him away.

This was the last Mormon outpost. Beyond lay the waste desert with, on the other side of it, the dream-land, ay, the myth-land, of California. As our wagons rolled out of the place in the early morning, I, sitting beside my father on the driver's seat, saw Laban give expression to his feelings. We had gone perhaps half a mile, and were topping a low rise that would sink Cedar City from view, when Laban turned his horse around, halted it, and stood up in the stirrups. Where he had halted was a new-made grave, and I knew it for the Wainwright baby's—not the first of our graves since we had crossed the Wasatch Mountains.

He was a weird figure of a man. Aged and lean, long-faced, hollow-cheeked, with matted, sunburned hair that fell below the shoulders of his buckskin shirt, his face was distorted with hatred and helpless rage. Holding his long rifle in his bridle hand, he shook his free fist at Cedar City.

"God's curse on all of you!" he cried out. "On your children, and on your babes unborn. May drought destroy your crops. May you eat sand seasoned with the venom of rattlesnakes. May the sweet water of your springs turn to bitter alkali. May . . ."

Here his words became indistinct as our wagons rattled on; but his heaving shoulders and brandishing fist attested that he had only begun to lay the curse. That he expressed the general feeling in our train was evidenced by the many women who leaned from the wagons, thrusting out gaunt forearms and shaking bony, labor-mal-formed fists at the last of Mormondom. A man, who walked in the sand and goaded the oxen of the wagon behind ours, laughed and waved his goad. It was unusual, that laugh, for there had been no laughter in our train for many days.

"Give'm hell, Laban," he encouraged. "Them's my sentiments."

And as our train rolled on, I continued to look back at Laban, standing in his stirrups by the baby's grave. Truly, he was a weird figure with his long hair, his moccasins, and fringed leggings. So old and weather-beaten was his buckskin shirt that ragged filaments, here and there, showed where proud fringes once had been. He was a man of flying tatters. I remember, at his waist, dangled dirty tufts of hair that, far back in the journey, after a shower of rain, were wont to show glossy black. These I know were Indian scalps, and the sight of them always thrilled me.

"It will do him good," Father commended, more to himself than to me. "I've been looking for days for him to blow up."

"I wish he'd go back and take a couple of scalps," I volunteered.

My father regarded me quizzically.

"Don't like the Mormons, eh, son?"

I shook my head and felt myself swelling with the inarticulate hate that possessed me.

"When I grow up," I said after a minute, "I'm goin' gunning for them."

"You, Jesse!" came my mother's voice from inside the wagon.

"Shut your mouth instanter." And to my father: "You ought to be ashamed, letting the boy talk on like that."

Two days' journey brought us to Mountain Meadows, and here, well beyond the last settlement, for the first time we did not form the wagon circle. The wagons were roughly in a circle, but there were many gaps, and the wheels were not chained. Preparations were made to stop a week. The cattle must be rested for the real desert, though this was desert enough in all seeming. The same low hills of sand were about us, but sparsely covered with scrub brush. The flat was sandy, but there was some grass—more than we had encountered in many days. Not more than a hundred feet from camp was a weak spring that barely supplied human needs. But farther along the bottom various other weak springs emerged from the hillsides, and it was at these that the cattle watered.

We made camp early that day and, because of the program to stay a week, there was a general overhauling of soiled clothes by the women, who planned to start washing on the morrow. Everybody worked till nightfall. While some of the men mended harness, others repaired the frames and ironwork of the wagons. There was much heating and hammering of iron and tightening of bolts and nuts. And I remember coming upon Laban, sitting cross-legged in the shade of a wagon and sewing away till nightfall on a new pair of moccasins. He was the only man in our train who wore moccasins and buckskin, and I have an impression that he had not belonged to our company when it left Arkansas. Also, he had neither wife, nor family, nor wagon of his own. All he possessed was his horse, his rifle, the clothes he stood up in, and a couple of blankets that were hauled in the Mason wagon.

Next morning it was that our doom fell. Two days' journey beyond the last Mormon outpost, knowing that no Indians were about and apprehending nothing from the Indians on any count, for the first time we had not chained our wagons in the solid circle, placed guards on the cattle, nor set a night watch.

My awakening was like a nightmare. It came as a sudden blast of sound. I was only stupidly awake for the first moments and did nothing except to try to analyze and identify the various noises that went to compose the blast that continued without letup. I could hear near and distant explosions of rifles, shouts and curses of men, women screaming and children bawling. Then I could make out the thuds and squeals of bullets that hit wood and iron in the wheels and under-construction of the wagon. Whoever it was that was shooting, the aim was too low.

When I started to rise, my mother, evidently just in the act of dressing, pressed me down with her hand. Father, already up and about, at this stage erupted into the wagon.

"Out of it!" he shouted. "Quick! To the ground!"

He wasted no time. With a hook-like clutch that was almost a blow, so swift was it, he flung me bodily out of the rear end of the wagon. I had barely time to crawl out from under when Father, Mother, and the baby came down pell mell where I had been.

"Here, Jesse!" Father shouted to me, and I joined him in scooping out sand behind the shelter of a wagon wheel. We worked barehanded and wildly. Mother joined in.

"Go ahead and make it deeper, Jesse," Father ordered.

He stood up and rushed away in the gray light, shouting commands as he ran. (I had learned by now my surname. I was Jesse Fancher. My father was Captain Fancher.)

"Lie down!" I could hear him. "Get behind the wagon wheels and burrow in the sand! Family men, get the women and children out of the wagons! Hold your fire! No more shooting! Hold your fire and be ready for the rush when it comes! Single men, join Laban at the right, Cochrane at the left, and me in the center! Don't stand up! Crawl for it!"

But no rush came. For a quarter of an hour the heavy and irregular firing continued. Our damage had come in the first moments of surprise when a number of the early-rising men were caught exposed in the light of the campfires they were building. The Indians—for Indians Laban declared them to be—had attacked us from the open, and were lying down and firing at us. In the growing light Father made ready for them. His position was near to where I lay in the burrow with Mother so that I heard him when he cried out:

"Now! —All together!"

From left, right, and center, our rifles loosed in a volley. I had popped my head up to see, and I could make out more than one stricken Indian. Their fire immediately ceased, and I could see them scampering back on foot across the open, dragging their dead and wounded with them.

All was work with us on the instant. While the wagons were being dragged and chained into the circle with tongues inside—I saw women and little boys and girls flinging their strength on the wheel spokes to help—we took toll of our losses. First, and gravest of all, our last animal had been run off. Next, lying about the fires they had been building, were seven of our men. Four were dead, and three were dying. Other men, wounded, were being cared for by the women. Little Rish Hardacre had been struck in the arm by a heavy ball. He was no more than six, and I remember looking on with mouth agape while his mother held him on her lap and his father set about bandaging the wound. Little Rish had stopped crying. I could see the tears on his cheeks while he stared wonderingly at a sliver of broken bone sticking out of his forearm.

Granny White was found dead in the Foxwell wagon. She was a fat and helpless old woman who never did anything but sit down all the time and smoke a pipe. She was the mother of Abby Foxwell. And Mrs. Grant had been killed. Her husband sat beside her body. He was very quiet. There were no tears in his eyes. He just sat there, his rifle across his knees, and everybody left him alone.

Under Father's directions the company was working like so many beavers. The men dug a big rifle pit in the center of the corral, forming a breastwork out of the displaced sand. Into this pit the women dragged bedding, food, and all sorts of necessaries from the wagons. All the children helped. There was no whimpering, and little or no excitement. There was work to be done, and all of us were folks born to work.

The big rifle pit was for the women and children. Under the wagons, completely around the circle, a shallow trench was dug and an earthwork thrown up. This was for the fighting men.

Laban returned from a scout. He reported that the Indians had withdrawn the matter of half a mile and were holding a powwow. Also, he had seen them carry six of their number off the field, three of which, he said, were deaders.

From time to time, during the morning of that first day, we observed clouds of dust that advertised the movements of considerable bodies of mounted men. These clouds of dust came toward us, hemming us in on all sides. But we saw no living creature. One cloud of dust only, moved away from us. It was a large cloud, and everybody said it was our cattle being driven off. And our forty great wagons that had rolled over the Rockies and half across the continent stood in a helpless circle. Without cattle, they could roll no farther.

At noon Laban came in from another scout. He had seen fresh Indians arriving from the south, showing that we were being closed in. It was at this time that we saw a dozen white men ride out on the crest of a low hill to the east and look down on us.

"That settles it," Laban said to Father. "The Indians have been put up to it."

"They're white like us," I heard Abby Foxwell complain to Mother. "Why don't they come in to us?"

"They ain't whites," I piped up, with a wary eye for the swoop of Mother's hand. "They're Mormons."

That night, after dark, three of our young men stole out of camp. I saw them go. They were Will Aden, Abel Milliken, and Timothy Grant.

"They are heading for Cedar City to get help," Father told Mother while he was snatching a hasty bite of supper.

Mother shook her head.

"There's plenty of Mormons within calling distance of camp," she said. "If they won't help, and they haven't shown any signs, then the Cedar City ones won't either."

"But there are good Mormons and bad Mormons—" Father began

"We haven't found any good ones so far," she shut him off.

Not until morning did I hear of the return of Abel Milliken and Timothy Grant, but I was not long in learning. The whole camp was downcast by reason of their report. The three had gone only a few miles when they were challenged by white men. As soon as Will Aden spoke up, telling that they were from the Fancher Company, going to Cedar City for help, he was shot down. Milliken and Grant escaped back with the news, and the news settled the last hope in the hearts of our company. The whites were behind the Indians, and the doom so long apprehended was upon us.

This morning of the second day, our men, going for water, were fired upon. The spring was only a hundred feet outside our circle, but the way to it was commanded by the Indians who now occupied the low hill to the east. It was close range, for the hill could not have been more than fifteen rods away. But the Indians were not good shots, evidently, for our men brought in the water without being hit.

Beyond an occasional shot into camp, the morning passed quietly. We had settled down in the rifle pit and, being used to rough living, were comfortable enough. Of course, it was bad for the families of those who had been killed, and there was the taking care of the wounded. I was forever stealing away from Mother in my insatiable curiosity to see everything that was going on, and I managed to see pretty much of everything. Inside the corral, to the south of the big rifle pit, the men dug a hole and buried the seven men and two women all together. Only Mrs. Hastings, who had lost her husband and father, made much trouble. She cried and screamed out, and it took the other women a long time to quiet her.

On the low hill to the east the Indians kept up a tremendous powwowing and yelling. But beyond an occasional harmless shot, they did nothing.

"What's the matter with the ornery cusses?" Laban impatiently wanted to know. "Can't they make up their minds what they're goin' to do, an' then do it?"

It was hot in the corral that afternoon. The sun blazed down out of a cloudless sky, and there was no wind. The men, lying with their rifles in the trench under the wagons, were partly shaded; but the big rifle pit, in which were over a hundred women and children, was exposed to the full power of the sun. Here too were the wounded men, over whom we erected awnings of blankets. It was crowded and stifling in the pit, and I was forever stealing out of it to the firing line and making a great to-do at carrying messages for Father.

Our grave mistake had been in not forming the wagon circle so as to enclose the spring. This had been due to the excitement of the first attack, when we did not know how quickly it might be followed by a second one. And now it was too late. At fifteen rods' distance from the Indian position on the hill, we did not dare unchain our wagons. Inside the corral, south of the graves, we constructed a latrine and, north of the rifle pit in the center, a couple of men were told off by Father to dig a well for water.

In the mid-afternoon of that day, which was the second day, we saw Lee again. He was on foot, crossing diagonally over the meadow to the northwest just out of rifle shot from us. Father hoisted one of Mother's sheets on a couple of ox goads lashed together. This was our white flag. But Lee took no notice of it, continuing on his way.

Laban was for trying a long shot at him, but Father stopped him, saying that it was evident the whites had not made up their minds what they were going to do with us, and that a shot at Lee might hurry them into making up their minds the wrong way.

"Here, Jesse," Father said to me, tearing a strip from the sheet and fastening it to an ox goad. "Take this and go out and try to talk to that man. Don't tell him anything about what's happened to us. Just try to get him to come in and talk with us."

As I started to obey, my chest swelling with pride in my mission, Jed Dunham cried out that he wanted to go with me. Jed was about my own age.

"Can your boy go with Jesse?" Father asked Jed's father. "Two's better'n one. They'll keep each other out of mischief."

So Jed and I, two youngsters of nine, went out under the white flag to talk with the leader of our enemies. But Lee would not talk. When he saw us coming, he started to sneak away. We never got within calling distance of him, and after a while he must have hidden in the brush; for we never laid eyes on him again, and we knew he couldn't have got clear away.

Jed and I beat up the brush for hundreds of yards all around. They hadn't told us how long we were to be gone, and since the Indians did not fire on us we kept on going. We were away over two hours, though had either of us been alone we would have been back in a quarter of the time. But Jed was bound to out-brave me, and I was equally bound to out-brave him.

Our foolishness was not without profit. We walked boldly about under our white flag, and learned how thoroughly our camp was beleaguered. To the south of our train, not more than half a mile away, we made out a large Indian camp. Beyond, on the meadow, we could see Indian boys riding herd on their horses.

Then there was the Indian position on the hill to the east. We managed to climb a low hill so as to look into this position. Jed and I spent half an hour trying to count them, and concluded, with much guessing, that there must be at least a couple of hundred. Also, we saw white men with them and doing a great deal of talking.

Northeast of our train, not more than four hundred yards from it, we discovered a large camp of whites behind a low rise of ground. And beyond we could see fifty or sixty saddle horses grazing. And a mile or so away, to the north, we saw a tiny cloud of dust approaching. Jed and I waited until we saw a single man, riding fast, gallop into the camp of the whites.

When we got back into the corral, the first thing that happened to me was a smack from Mother for having stayed away so long; but Father praised Jed and me when we gave our report.

"Watch for an attack now maybe, Captain," Aaron Cochrane said to Father. "That man the boys seen has rid in for a purpose. The whites are holding the Indians till they get orders from higher up. Maybe that man brung the orders one way or the other. They ain't sparing horseflesh, that's one thing sure."

Half an hour after our return, Laban attempted a scout under a white flag. But he had not gone twenty feet outside the circle when the Indians opened fire on him and sent him back on the run.

Just before sundown I was in the rifle pit holding the baby, while Mother was spreading the blankets for a bed. There were so many of us that we were packed and jammed. So little room was there, that many of the women the night before had sat up and slept with their heads bowed on their knees. Right alongside of me, so near that when he tossed his arms about he struck me on the shoulder, Silas Dunlap was dying. He had been shot in the head in the first attack, and all the second day was out of his head and raving and singing doggerel. One of his songs, that he sang over and over, until it made Mother frantic nervous, was:

> "Said the first little devil to the second little devil,
> 'Give me some tobaccy from your old tobaccy box.'
> Said the second little devil to the first little devil,
> 'Stick close to your money and close to your rocks,
> An' you'll always have tobaccy in your old tobaccy box.'"

I was sitting directly alongside of him, holding the baby, when the attack burst on us. It was sundown, and I was staring with all my eyes at Silas Dunlap, who was just in the final act of dying. His wife Sarah had one hand resting on his forehead. Both she and her Aunt Martha were crying softly. And then it came—explosions and bullets from hundreds of rifles. Clear around from east to west by way of the north, they had strung out in half a circle and were pumping lead into our position. Everybody in the rifle pit flattened down. Lots of the younger children set up a squalling, and it kept the women busy hushing them. Some of the women screamed at first, but not many.

Thousands of shots must have rained in on us in the next few minutes. How I wanted to crawl out to the trench under the wagons where our men were keeping up a steady but irregular fire! Each was shooting on his own whenever he saw a man to pull trigger on. But Mother suspected me, for she made me crouch down and keep right on holding the baby.

I was just taking a look at Silas Dunlap—he was still quivering—when the little Castleton baby was killed. Dorothy Castleton, herself only about ten, was holding it, so that it was killed in her arms. She was not hurt at all. I heard them talking about it, and they conjectured that the bullet must have struck high up on one of the wagons and been deflected down into the rifle pit. It was just an accident, they said, and that except for such accidents we were safe where we were.

When I looked again, Silas Dunlap was dead, and I suffered distinct disappointment in being cheated out of witnessing that particular event. I had never been lucky enough to see a man actually die before my eyes.

Dorothy Castleton got hysterics over what had happened, and yelled and screamed for a long time, and she set Mrs. Hastings going again. Altogether, such a row was raised that Father sent Watt Cummings crawling back to us to find out what was the matter.

Well along into twilight the heavy firing ceased, although there were scattering shots during the night. Two of our men were wounded in this second attack, and were brought into the rifle pit. Bill Tyler was killed instantly and they buried him, Silas Dunlap, and the Castleton baby in the dark, alongside of the others.

All during the night men relieved one another at sinking the well deeper; but the only sign of water they got was damp sand. Some of the men fetched a few pails of water from the spring, but were fired upon, and they gave it up when Jeremy Hopkins had his left hand shot off at the wrist.

Next morning, the third day, it was hotter and drier than ever. We awoke thirsty, and there was no cooking. So dry were our mouths that we could not eat. I tried a piece of stale bread Mother gave me, but had to give it up. The firing rose and fell. Sometimes there were hundreds shooting into the camp. At other times came lulls in which not a shot was fired. Father was continually cautioning our men not to waste shots because we were running short of ammunition.

And all the time the men went on digging the well. It was so deep that they were hoisting the sand up in buckets. The men who hoisted were exposed, and one of them was wounded in the shoulder. He was Peter Bromley, who drove oxen for the Bloodgood wagon, and he was engaged to marry Jane Bloodgood. She jumped out of the rifle pit and ran right to him while the bullets were flying and led him back into shelter. About midday the well caved in, and there was lively work digging out the couple who were buried in the sand. Amos Wentworth did not come to for an hour. After that they timbered the well with bottom boards from the wagons and wagon tongues, and the digging went on. But all they would get, and they were twenty-feet down, was damp sand. The water would not seep.

By this time the conditions in the rifle pit were terrible. The children were complaining for water, and the babies, hoarse from much crying, went on crying. Robert Carr, another wounded man, lay about ten feet from Mother and me. He was out of his head, and kept thrashing his arms about and calling for water. And some of the women were almost as bad, and kept raving against the Mormons and Indians. Some of the women prayed a great deal, and the three grown Demdike sisters with their mother sang gospel hymns. Other women got damp sand that was hoisted out of the bottom of the well, and packed it against the bare bodies of the babies to try to cool and soothe them.

The two Fairfax brothers couldn't stand it any longer and, with pails in their hands, crawled out under a wagon and made a dash for the spring. Giles never got halfway, when he went down. Roger made it there and back without being hit. He brought two pails part full, for some splashed out when he ran. Giles crawled back, and when they helped him into the rifle pit he was bleeding at the mouth and coughing.

Two part-pails of water could not go far among over a hundred of us, not counting the men. Only the babies, and the very little children, and the wounded men, got any. I did not get a sip, although Mother dipped a bit of cloth into the several spoonfuls she got for the baby and wiped my mouth out. She did not even do that for herself, for she left me the bit of damp rag to chew.

The situation grew unspeakably worse in the afternoon. The quiet sun blazed down through the clear windless air and made a furnace of our hole in the sand. And all about us were the explosions of rifles and yells of the Indians. Only once in a while did Father permit a single shot from the trench, and that only by our best marksmen, such as Laban and Timothy Grant. But a steady stream of lead poured into our position all the time. There were no more disastrous ricochets, however; and our men in the trench, no longer firing lay low and escaped damage. Only four were wounded, and only one of them very badly.

Father came in from the trench during a lull in the firing. He sat for a few minutes alongside Mother and me without speaking. He seemed to be listening to all the moaning and crying for water that was going up. Once he climbed out of the rifle pit and went over to investigate the well. He brought back only damp sand, which he plastered thick on the chest and shoulders of Robert Carr. Then he went to where Jed Dunham and his mother were, and sent for Jed's father to come in from the trench. So closely packed were we that when anybody moved about inside the rifle pit he had to crawl carefully over the bodies of those lying down.

After a time, Father came crawling back to us.

"Jesse," he asked, "are you afraid of the Indians?"

I shook my head emphatically, guessing that I was to be sent on another proud mission.

"Are you afraid of the damned Mormons?"

"Not of any damned Mormon," I answered, taking advantage of the opportunity to curse our enemies without fear of the avenging back of Mother's hand.

I noted the little smile that curled his tired lips for the moment, when he heard my reply.

"Well, then, Jesse," he said, "will you go with Jed to the spring for water?"

I was all eagerness.

"We're going to dress the two of you up as girls," he continued, "so that maybe they won't fire on you."

I insisted on going as I was, as a male human that wore pants; but I surrendered quickly enough when Father suggested that he would find some other boy to dress up and go along with Jed.

A chest was fetched in from the Chattox wagon. The Chattox girls were twins and of about a size with Jed and me. Several of the women got around to help. They were the Sunday dresses of the Chattox twins, and had come in the chest all the way from Arkansas.

In her anxiety, Mother left the baby with Sarah Dunlap, and came as far as the trench with me. There, under a wagon and behind the little breastwork of sand, Jed and I received our last instructions. Then we crawled out and stood up in the open. We were dressed precisely alike—white stockings, white dresses with big blue sashes, and white sunbonnets. Jed's right and my left hand were clasped together. In each of our free hands we carried two small pails.

"Take it easy," Father cautioned as we began our advance. "Go slow. Walk like girls.'

Not a shot was fired. We made the spring safely, filled our pails, and lay down and took a good drink ourselves. With a full pail in each hand we made the return trip. And still not a shot was fired.

I cannot remember how many journeys we made—fully fifteen or twenty. We walked slowly, always going out with hands clasped, always coming back slowly with four pails of water. It was astonishing how thirsty we were. We lay down several times and took long drinks.

But it was too much for our enemies. I cannot imagine that the Indians would have withheld their fire for so long, girls or no girls, had they not obeyed instructions from the whites who were with them. At any rate, Jed and I were just starting on another trip when a rifle went off from the Indian hill, and then another.

"Come back!" Mother cried out.

I looked at Jed, and found him looking at me. I knew he was stubborn and had made up his mind to be the last one in. So I started to advance, and at the same instant he started.

"You! —Jesse!" cried my mother. And there was more than a smacking in the way she said it.

Jed offered to clasp hands, but I shook my head.

"Run for it," I said.

And while we hotfooted it across the sand, it seemed all the rifles on Indian hill were turned loose on us. I got to the spring a little ahead, so that Jed had to wait for me to fill my pails.

"Now run for it," he told me; and from the leisurely way he went about filling his own pails I knew he was determined to be in last.

So I crouched down and, while I waited, watched the puffs of dust raised by the bullets. We began the return side by side and running.

"Not so fast," I cautioned him, "or you'll spill half the water."

That stung him, and he slacked back perceptibly. Midway I stumbled and fell headlong. A bullet, striking directly in front of me, filled my eyes with sand. For the moment I thought I was shot.

"Done it a-purpose," Jed sneered, as I scrambled to my feet. He had stood and waited for me.

I caught his idea. He thought I had fallen deliberately in order to spill my water and go back for more. This rivalry between us was a serious matter—so serious, indeed, that I immediately took advantage of what he had imputed and raced back to the spring. And Jed Dunham, scornful of the bullets that were puffing dust all around him, stood there upright in the open and waited for me. We came in side by side, with honors even in our boy's foolhardiness. But when we delivered the water, Jed had only one pailful. A bullet had gone through the other pail close to the bottom.

Mother took it out on me with a lecture on disobedience. She must have known, after what I had done, that Father wouldn't let her smack me; for while she was lecturing, Father winked at me across her shoulder. It was the first time he had ever winked at me.

Back in the rifle pit Jed and I were heroes. The women wept and blessed us, and kissed us and mauled us. And I confess I was proud of the demonstration, although, like Jed, I let on that I did not like all such making-over. But Jeremy Hopkins, a great bandage about the stump of his left wrist, said we were the stuff white men were made out of—men like Daniel Boone, like Kit Carson and Davy Crockett. I was prouder of that than all the rest.

The remainder of the day I seem to have been bothered principally with the pain of my right eye caused by the sand that had been kicked into it by the bullet. The eye was bloodshot, Mother said; and to me it seemed to hurt just as much whether I kept it open or closed. I tried both ways.

Things were quieter in the rifle pit, because all had had water; though strong upon us was the problem of how the next water was to be procured. Coupled with this was the known fact that our ammunition was almost exhausted. A thorough overhauling of the wagons by Father had resulted in finding five pounds of powder. A very little more was in the flasks of the men.

I remembered the sundown attack of the night before, and anticipated it this time by crawling to the trench before sunset. I crept into a place alongside of Laban. He was busy chewing tobacco, and did not notice me. For some time I watched him, fearing that when he discovered me he would order me back. He would take a long squint out between the wagon wheels, chew steadily a while, and then spit carefully into a little depression he had made in the sand.

"How's tricks?" I asked finally. It was the way he always addressed me.

"Fine," he answered. "Most remarkable fine, Jesse, now that I can chew again. My mouth was that dry that I couldn't chew from sun-up to when you brung the water."

Here, a man showed head and shoulders over the top of the little hill to the northeast occupied by the whites. Laban sighted his rifle on him for a long minute. Then he shook his head.

"Four hundred yards. Nope, I don't risk it. I might get him, and then again I mightn't, an' your dad is mighty anxious about the powder."

"What do you think our chances are?" I asked, man-fashion, for after my water exploit I was feeling very much the man.

Laban seemed to consider carefully for a space, ere he replied. "Jesse, I don't mind tellin' you we're in a damned bad hole. But we'll get out, oh, we'll get out, you can bet your bottom dollar."

"Some of us ain't going to get out," I objected.

"Who for instance?" he queried.

"Why, Bill Tyler, and Mrs. Grant, and Silas Dunlap, and all the rest."

"Aw, shucks, Jesse—they're in the ground already. Don't you know everybody has to bury their dead as they traipse along. They've ben doin' it for thousands of years, I reckon, and there's just as many alive as ever they was. You see, Jesse, birth and death go hand in hand. And they're born as fast as they die—faster, I reckon, because they've increased and multiplied. Now you, you might a-got killed this afternoon packin' water. But you're here, ain't you, a-gassin' with me an' likely to grow up an' be the father of a fine large family in Californy. They say everything grows large in Californy."

This cheerful way of looking at the matter encouraged me to dare sudden expression of a long covetousness.

"Say, Laban, supposin' you got killed here—"

"Who? —me?" he cried.

"I'm just sayin' supposin'," I explained.

"Oh, all right then. Go on. Supposin' I am killed?"

"Will you give me your scalps?"

"Your ma'll smack you if she catches you a-wearin' them," he temporized.

"I don't have to wear them when she's around. Now if you got killed, Laban, somebody'd have to get them scalps. Why not me?"

"Why not?" he repeated. "That's correct, and why not you? All right, Jesse. I like you and your pa. The minute I'm killed the scalps is yourn, and the scalpin' knife, too. And there's Timothy Grant for witness.—Did you hear, Timothy?"

Timothy said he had heard, and I lay there speechless in the stifling trench, too overcome by my greatness of good fortune to be able to utter a word of gratitude.

I was rewarded for my foresight in going to the trench. Another general attack was made at sundown, and thousands of shots were fired into us. Nobody on our side was scratched. On the other hand, although we fired barely thirty shots, I saw Laban and Timothy Grant each get an Indian. Laban told me that from the first only the Indians had done the shooting. He was certain that no white had fired a shot. All of which sorely puzzled him. The whites neither offered us aid nor attacked us, and all the while were on visiting terms with the Indians who were attacking us.

Next morning found the thirst harsh upon us. I was out at the first hint of light. There had been a heavy dew, and men, women, and children were lapping it up with their tongues from off the wagon tongues, brake blocks, and wheel tires.

There was talk that Laban had returned from a scout just before daylight; that he had crept close to the position of the whites; that they were already up; and that in the light of their campfires he had seen them praying in a large circle. Also, he reported from what few words he caught that they were praying about us and what was to be done with us.

"May God send them the light then," I heard one of the Demdike sisters say to Abby Foxwell.

"And soon," said Abby Foxwell, "for I don't know what we'll do a whole day without water, and our powder is about gone."

Nothing happened all morning. Not a shot was fired. Only the sun blazed down through the quiet air. Our thirst grew, and soon the babies were crying and the younger children whimpering and complaining. At noon, Will Hamilton took two large pails and started for the spring. But before he could crawl under the wagon, Ann Demdike ran and got her arms around him and tried to hold him back. But he talked to her and kissed her and went on. Not a shot was fired, nor was any fired all the time he continued to go out and bring back water.

"Praise God!" cried old Mrs. Demdike. "It is a sign. They have relented."

This was the opinion of many of the women.

About two o'clock, after we had eaten and felt better, a white man appeared, carrying a white flag. Will Hamilton went out and talked to him, came back and talked with Father and the rest of our men, and then went out to the stranger again. Farther back we could see a man standing and looking on whom we recognized as Lee.

With us, all was excitement. The women were so relieved that they were crying and kissing one another, and old Mrs. Demdike and others were hallelujahing and blessing God. The proposal, which our men had accepted, was that we would put ourselves under the flag of truce and be protected from the Indians.

"We had to do it," I heard Father tell Mother.

He was sitting, droop-shouldered and dejected, on a wagon tongue.

"But what if they intend treachery?" Mother asked.

He shrugged his shoulders.

"We've got to take the chance that they don't," he said. "Our ammunition is gone."

Some of our men were unchaining one of our wagons and rolling it out of the way. I ran across to see what was happening. In came Lee himself, followed by two empty wagons, each driven by one man. Everybody crowded around Lee. He said that they had had a hard time with the Indians keeping them off of us, and that Major Higbee with fifty of the Mormon militia were ready to take us under their charge.

But what made Father and Laban and some of the men suspicious was when Lee said that we must put all our rifles into one of the wagons so as not to arouse the animosity of the Indians. By so doing we would appear to be the prisoners of the Mormon militia.

Father straightened up and was about to refuse when he glanced to Laban, who replied in an undertone:

"They ain't no more use in our hands than in the wagon, seein' as the powder's gone."

Two of our wounded men who could not walk were put into the wagons, and along with them were put all the little children. Lee seemed to be picking them out over eight and under eight. Jed and I were large for our age, and we were nine, besides; so Lee put us with the older bunch and told us we were to march with the women on foot.

When he took our baby from Mother and put it in a wagon, she started to object. Then I saw her lips draw tightly together, and she gave in. She was a gray-eyed, strong-featured, middle-aged woman, large-boned and fairly stout. But the long journey and hardship had told on her, so that she was hollow-cheecked and gaunt, and like all the women in the company she wore an expression of brooding, never-ceasing anxiety.

It was when Lee described the order of march that Laban came to me. Lee said that the women and the children that walked should go first in line, following behind the two wagons. Then the men, in single file, should follow the women. When Laban heard this, he came to me, untied the scalps from his belt, and fastened them to my waist.

"But you ain't killed yet," I protested.

"You bet your life I ain't," he answered lightly. "I've just reformed, that's all. This scalp-wearin' is a vain thing and heathen." He stopped a moment as if he had forgotten something, then, as he turned abruptly on his heel to regain the men of our company, he called over his shoulder, "Well, so long, Jesse."

I was wondering why he should say good-bye, when a white man came riding into the corral. He said Major Higbee had sent him to tell us to hurry up, because the Indians might attack at any moment.

So the march began, the two wagons first. Lee kept along with the women and walking children. Behind us, after waiting until we were a couple of hundred feet in advance, came our men. As we emerged from the corral we could see the militia just a short distance away. They were leaning on their rifles and standing in a long line about six feet apart. As we passed them, I could not help noticing how solemn-faced they were. The looked like men at a funeral. So did the women notice this, and some of them began to cry.

I walked right behind my mother. I had chosen this position so that she would not catch sight of my scalps. Behind me came the three Demdike sisters, two of them helping the old mother. I could hear Lee calling all the time to the men who drove the wagons not to go so fast. A man that one of the Demdike girls said must be Major Higbee sat on a horse watching us go by. Not an Indian was in sight.

By the time our men were just abreast of the militia—I had just looked back to try to see where Jed Dunham was—the thing happened. I heard Major Higbee cry out in a loud voice, "Do your duty!" All the rifles of the militia seemed to go off at once, and our men were falling over and sinking down. All the Demdike women went down at one time. I turned quickly to see how Mother was, and she was down. Right alongside of us, out of the bushes, came hundreds of Indians, all shooting. I saw the two Dunlap sisters start on the run across the sand, and took after them, for whites and Indians were all killing us. And as I ran, I saw the driver of one of the wagons shooting the two wounded men. The horses of the other wagon were plunging and rearing and their driver was trying to hold them.

It was when the little boy that was I was running after the Dunlap girls that blackness came upon him. All memory there ceases, for

Jesse Fancher there ceased and, as Jesse Fancher, ceased forever. The form that was Jesse Fancher, the body that was his, being matter and apparitional, like an apparition passed and was not. But the imperishable spirit did not cease. It continued to exist and, in its next incarnation, became the residing spirit of that apparitional body known as Darrell Standing and which soon is to be taken out and hanged and sent into the nothingness whither all apparitions go.

There is a lifer here in Folsom, Matthew Davies, of old pioneer stock, who is trusty of the scaffold and execution chamber. He is an old man, and his folks crossed the plains in the early days. I have talked with him, and he has verified the massacre in which Jesse Fancher was killed. When this old lifer was a child, there was much talk in his family of the Mountain Meadows Massacre. The children in the wagons, he said, were saved, because they were too young to tell tales.

All of which I submit. Never, in my life of Darrell Standing, have I read a line or heard a word spoken of the Fancher Company that perished at Mountain Meadows. Yet, in the jacket in San Quentin prison, all this knowledge came to me. I could not create this knowledge out of nothing, any more than could I create dynamite out of nothing. This knowledge and these facts I have related have but one explanation. They are out of the spirit content of me—the spirit that, unlike matter, does not perish.

In closing this chapter, I must state that Matthew Davies also told me that some years after the massacre Lee was taken by United States government officials to the Mountain Meadows and there executed on the site of our old corral.

MEXICO

THE MEXICAN

(Saturday Evening Post, August 19, 1911)

Ranked among the dozen best stories Jack London ever wrote, "The Mexican" can be read as a splendid example of revolutionary propaganda or as one of the best examples in a genre—the prizefight story—which Earle Labor says (in his *Jack London*, 1974) that London "virtually invented."

Jack, an amateur boxer himself, loved the prize-ring, and wrote eloquently of it as a journalist at ringside (most notably at the Jack Johnson–Jim Jeffries heavyweight championship match in Reno in July, 1910), as a novelist (*The Game*, 1905, in which the hero is killed in the ring—this book was greatly admired by heavyweight champion Gene Tunney—and *The Abysmal Brute*, 1913), and as a short story writer, as in the oft-anthologized "A Piece of Steak" (1909) and the present story.

As revolutionary literature, specifically for the 1910 Mexican Revolution, the story has even greater impact. Felipe Rivera, the mysterious young protagonist from Rio Blanco, works for a Baja California junta that is dedicated to overthrowing dictator Porfirio Diaz. Rivera *is* the revolution, "pitiless as steel, keen and cold as frost . . . the breath of Death," and when the junta needs $5,000 for guns to wage its war, Rivera fights a *gringo* named Danny Ward, winner taking all, for the cause.

In truth, London did a radical *volte face* in his attitude toward the revolution in Mexico. He wrote "The Mexican" before he saw the revolution with his own eyes. In April, 1914, three years after the story was published, he traveled to Galveston, Texas, thence to Vera Cruz and Tampico, representing *Collier's* magazine (at a salary of $1,100 per week) as war correspondent. He fell ill with dysentery, was frustrated at finding no "war" to report, and sent home articles reflecting a growing contempt for the revolution and expressing a belief that it was the duty of the United States to police, organize, and manage the country.

Joan London, a socialist herself, in her biography *Jack London and His Times* (1939), states that her father was not, as commonly held by his critics, a captive to or being subsidized by American oil and businessmen in Mexico. To Joan London, her father's conflict was his drift away from the social revolutionary beliefs of his youth and toward a life-style of capitalistic luxury on his Northern California ranch. "His was a more tragic sellout," she candidly wrote, "for he had been subsidized, bought body and soul, by the kind of life he had thought he wanted, and it was destroying him."

Whatever these implications, "The Mexican" is Jack London in top storytelling form: gritty, strong of character and impact, polished, memorable.

THE MEXICAN

I

NOBODY KNEW HIS history—they of the Junta least of all. He was their "little mystery," their "big patriot," and in his way he worked as hard for the coming Mexican Revolution as did they. They were tardy in recognizing this, for not one of the Junta liked him. The day he first drifted into their crowded, busy rooms, they all suspected him of being a spy—one of the bought tools of the Diaz secret service. Too many of the comrades were in civil and military prisons scattered over the United States, and others of them, in irons, were even then being taken across the border to be lined up against adobe walls and shot.

At the first sight the boy did not impress them favorably. Boy he was, not more than eighteen and not over large for his years. He announced that he was Felipe Rivera, and that it was his wish to work for the Revolution. That was all—not a wasted word, no further explanation. He stood waiting. There was no smile on his lips, no geniality in his eyes. Big dashing Paulino Vera felt an inward shudder. Here was something forbidding, terrible, inscrutable. There was something venomous and snakelike in the boy's black eyes. They burned like cold fire, as with a vast, concentrated bitterness. He flashed them from the faces of the conspirators to the typewriter which little Mrs. Sethby was industriously operating. His eyes rested on hers but an instant—she had chanced to look up—and she, too, sensed the nameless something that made her pause. She was compelled to read back in order to regain the swing of the letter she was writing.

Paulino Vera looked questioningly at Arrellano and Ramos, and questioningly they looked back and to each other. The indecision of doubt brooded in their eyes. This slender boy was the Unknown, vested with all the menace of the Unknown. He was unrecognizable, something quite beyond the ken of honest, ordinary revolutionists whose fiercest hatred for Diaz and his tyranny after all was only that of honest and ordinary patriots. Here was something else, they knew not what. But Vera, always the most impulsive, the quickest to act, stepped into the breach.

"Very well," he said coldly. "You say you want to work for the Revolution. Take off your coat. Hang it over there. I will show you—come—where are the buckets and cloths. The floor is dirty. You will begin by scrubbing it, and by scrubbing the floors of the other rooms. The spittoons need to be cleaned. Then there are the windows."

"Is it for the Revolution?" the boy asked.

"It is for the Revolution," Vera answered.

Rivera looked cold suspicion at all of them, then proceeded to take off his coat.

"It is well," he said.

And nothing more. Day after day he came to his work—sweeping, scrubbing, cleaning. He emptied the ashes from the stoves, brought up the coal and kindling, and lighted the fires before the most energetic one of them was at his desk.

"Can I sleep here?" he asked once.

Ah, ha! So that was it—the hand of Diaz showing through! To sleep in the rooms of the Junta meant access to their secrets, to the lists of names, to the addresses of comrades down on Mexican soil. The request was denied, and Rivera never spoke of it again. He slept they knew not where, and ate they knew not where nor how. Once, Arrellano offered him a couple of dollars. Rivera declined the money with a shake of the head. When Vera joined in and tried to press it upon him, he said:

"I am working for the Revolution."

It takes money to raise a modern revolution. and always the Junta was pressed. The members starved and toiled, and the longest day was none too long. and yet there were times when it appeared as if the Revolution stood or fell on no more than the matter of a few dollars. Once, the first time, when the rent of the house was two months behind and the landlord was threatening dispossession, it was Felipe Rivera, the scrub-boy in the poor, cheap clothes, worn and threadbare, who laid sixty dollars in gold on May Sethby's desk. There were other times. Three hundred letters, clicked out on the busy typewriters (appeals for assistance, for sanctions from the organized labor groups, requests for square news deals to the editors of newspapers, protests against the high-handed treatment of revolutionists by the United States courts), lay unmailed, awaiting postage. Vera's watch had disappeared—the old-fashioned gold repeater that had been his father's. Likewise had gone the plain gold band from May Sethby's third finger. Things were desperate. Ramos and Arrellano pulled their long mustaches in despair. The letters must go off, and the Post Office allowed no credit to purchasers of stamps. Then it was that Rivera put on his hat and went out. When he came back he laid a thousand two-cent stamps on May Sethby's desk.

"I wonder if it is the cursed gold of Diaz?" said Vera to the comrades.

They elevated their brows and could not decide. And Felipe Rivera, the scrubber for the Revolution, continued, as occasion arose, to lay down gold and silver for the Junta's use.

And still they could not bring themselves to like him. They did not know him. His ways were not theirs. He gave no confidences. He repelled all probing. Youth that he was, they could never nerve themselves to dare to question him.

"A great and lonely spirit, perhaps, I do not know, I do not know," Arrellano said helplessly.

"He is not human," said Ramos.

"His soul has been seared," said May Sethby. "Light and laughter have been burned out of him. He is like one dead, and yet he is fearfully alive."

"He has been through hell," said Vera. "No man could look like that who has not been through hell—and he is only a boy."

Yet they could not like him. He never talked, never inquired, never suggested. He would stand listening, expressionless, a thing dead, save for his eyes, coldly burning, while their talk of the Revolution ran high and warm. From face to face and speaker to speaker his eyes would turn, boring like gimlets of incandescent ice, disconcerting and perturbing.

"He is no spy," Vera confided to May Sethby. "He is a patriot—mark me, the greatest patriot of us all. I know it, I feel it, here in my heart and head I feel it. But him I know not at all."

"He has a bad temper," said May Sethby.

"I know," said Vera, with a shudder. "He has looked at me with those eyes of his. They do not love; they threaten; they are savage as a wild tiger's. I know, if I should prove unfaithful to the Cause, that he would kill me. He has no heart. He is pitiless as steel, keen and cold as frost. He is like moonshine in a winter night when a man freezes to death on some lonely mountain top. I am not afraid of Diaz and all his killers; but this boy, of him am I afraid. I tell you true. I am afraid. He is the breath of death."

Yet Vera it was who persuaded the others to give the first trust to Rivera. The line of communication between Los Angeles and Lower California had broken down. Three of the comrades had dug their own graves and been shot into them. Two more were United States prisoners in Los Angeles. Juan Alvarado, the Federal commander, was a monster. All their plans did he checkmate. They could no longer gain access to the active revolutionists, and the incipient ones, in Lower California.

Young Rivera was given his instructions and dispatched south. When he returned, the line of communication was reëstablished, and Juan Alvarado was dead. He had been found in bed, a knife hilt-deep in his breast. This had exceeded Rivera's instructions, but they of the Junta knew the times of his movements. They did not ask him. He said nothing. But they looked at one another and conjectured.

"I have told you," said Vera. "Diaz has more to fear from this youth than from any man. He is implacable. He is the hand of God."

The bad temper, mentioned by May Sethby, and sensed by them all, was evidence by physical proofs. Now he appeared with a cut lip, a blackened cheek, or a swollen ear. It was patent that he brawled, somewhere in that outside world where he ate and slept, gained money, and moved in ways unknown to them. As the time passed, he had come to set type for the little revolutionary sheet they published weekly. There were occasions when he was unable to set type, when his knuckles were bruised and battered, when his thumbs were injured and helpless, when one arm or the other hung wearily at his side while his face was drawn with unspoken pain.

"A wastrel," said Arrellano.

"A frequenter of low places," said Ramos.

"But where does he get the money?" Vera demanded. "Only today, just now, have I learned that he paid the bill for white paper—one hundred and forty dollars."

"There are his absences," said May Sethby. "He never explains them."

"We should set a spy upon him," Ramos propounded.

"I should not care to be that spy," said Vera. "I fear you would never see me again, save to bury me. He has a terrible passion. Not even God would he permit to stand between him and the way of his passion."

"I feel like a child before him," Ramos confessed.

"To me he is power—he is the primitive, the wild wolf,—the striking rattlesnake, the stinging centipede," said Arrellano.

"He is the Revolution incarnate," said Vera. "He is the flame and the spirit of it, the insatiable cry for vengeance that makes no cry but that slays noiselessly. He is a destroying angel moving through the still watches of the night."

"I could weep over him," said May Sethby. "He knows nobody. He hates all people. Us he tolerates, for we are the way of his desire. He is alone . . . lonely." Her voice broke in a half sob and there was dimness in her eyes.

Rivera's ways and times were truly mysterious. There were periods when they did not see him for a week at a time. Once, he was away a month. These occasions were always capped by his return, when, without advertisement or speech, he laid gold coins on May Sethby's desk. Again, for days and weeks, he spent all his time with the Junta. And yet again, for irregular periods, he would disappear through the heart of each day, from early morning until late afternoon. At such times he came early and remained late. Arrellano had found him at midnight, setting type with fresh swollen knuckles, or mayhap it was his lip, new-split, that still bled.

II

THE TIME OF the crisis approached. Whether or not the Revolution would be depended upon the Junta, and the Junta was hard-pressed. The need for money was greater than ever before, while money was harder to get. Patriots had given their last cent and now could give no more. Section gang laborers—fugitive peons from Mexico—were contributing half their scanty wages. But more than that was needed. The heart-breaking, conspiring, undermining toil of years approached fruition. The time was ripe. The Revolution hung on the balance. One shove more, one last heroic effort, and it would tremble across the scales to victory. They knew their Mexico. Once started, the Revoltuion would take care of itself. The whole Diaz machine would go down like a house of cards. The border was ready to rise. One Yankee, with a hundred I. W. W. men, waited the word to cross over the border and begin the conquest of Lower California. But he needed guns. And clear across to the Atlantic, the Junta in touch with them all and all of them needing guns, mere adventurers, soldiers of fortune, bandits, disgruntled American union men, socialists, anarchists, rough-necks, Mexican exiles, peons escaped from bondage, whipped miners from the bull-pens of Cœur d'Alene and Colorado who desired only the more vindictively to fight—all the flotsam and jetsam of wild spirits from the madly complicated modern world. And it was guns and ammunition, ammunition and guns—the unceasing and eternal cry.

Fling this heterogeneous, bankrupt, vindictive mass across the border, and the Revolution was on. The custom house, the northern ports of entry, would be captured. Diaz could not resist. He dared not throw the weight of his armies against them, for he must hold the south. And through the south the flame would spread despite. The people would rise. The defenses of city after city would crumple up. State after state would totter down. And at last, from every side, the victorious armies of the Revolution would close in on the city of Mexico itself, Diaz's last stronghold.

But the money. They had the men, impatient and urgent, who would use the guns. They knew the traders who would sell and deliver the guns. But to culture the Revolution thus far had exhausted the Junta. The last dollar had been spent, the last resource and the last starving patriot milked dry, and the great adventure still trembled on the scales. Guns and ammunition! The ragged battalions must be armed. But how? Ramos lamented his confiscated estates. Arrellano wailed the spendthriftness of his youth. May Sethby wondered if it would have been different had they of the Junta been more economical in the past.

"To think that the freedom of Mexico should stand or fall on a few paltry thousands of dollars," said Paulino Vera.

Despair was in all their faces. José Amarillo, their last hope, a recent convert, who had promised money, had been apprehended at his hacienda in Chihuahua and shot against his own stable wall. The news had just come through.

Rivera, on his knees, scrubbing, looked up, with suspended brush, his bare arms flecked with soapy, dirty water.

"Will five thousand do it?" he asked.

They looked their amazement. Vera nodded and swallowed. He could not speak, but he was on the instant invested with a vast faith.

"Order the guns," Rivera said, and thereupon was guilty of the longest flow of words they had ever heard him utter. "The time is short. In three weeks I shall bring you the five thousand. It is well. The weather will be warmer for those who fight. Also, it is the best I can do."

Vera fought his faith. It was incredible. Too many fond hopes had been shattered since he had begun to play the revolution game. He believed this threadbare scrubber of the Revolution, and yet he dared not believe.

"You are crazy," he said.

"In three weeks," said Rivera. "Order the guns."

He got up, rolled down his sleeves, and put on his coat.

"Order the guns," he said. "I am going now."

III

AFTER HURRYING AND scurrying, much telephoning and bad language, a night session was held in Kelly's office. Kelly was rushed with business; also, he was unlucky. He had brought Danny Ward out from New York, arranged the fight for him with Billy Carthey, the date was three weeks away, and for two days now, carefully concealed from the sporting writers, Carthey had been lying up, badly injured. There was no one to take his place. Kelly had been burning the wires East to every eligible lightweight, but they were tied up with dates and contracts. And now hope had revived, though faintly.

"You've got a hell of a nerve," Kelly addressed Rivera, after one look, as soon as they got together.

Hate that was malignant was in Rivera's eyes, but his face remained impassive.

"I can lick Ward," was all he said.

"How do you know? Ever see him fight?"

Rivera shook his head.

"He can beat you up with one hand and both eyes closed."

Rivera shrugged his shoulders.

"Haven't you got anything to say?" the fight promoter snarled.

"I can lick him."

"Who'd you ever fight, anyway?" Michael Kelly demanded. Michael was the promoter's brother, and ran the Yellowstone pool rooms where he made goodly sums on the fight game.

Rivera favored him with a bitter, unanswering stare.

The promoter's secretary, a distinctively sporty young man, sneered audibly.

"Well, you know Roberts," Kelly broke the hostile silence. "He ought to be here. I've sent for him. Sit down and wait, though from the looks of you, you haven't got a chance. I can't throw the public down with a bum fight. Ringside seats are selling at fifteen dollars, you know that."

When Roberts arrived, it was patent that he was mildly drunk. He was a tall, lean, slack-jointed individual, and his walk, like his talk, was a smooth and languid drawl.

Kelly went straight to the point.

"Look here, Roberts, you've been braggin' you discovered this little Mexican. You know Carthey's broke his arm. Well, this little yellow streak has the gall to blow in today and say he'll take Carthey's place. What about it?"

"It's all right, Kelly," came the slow response. "He can put up a fight."

"I suppose you'll be sayin' next that he can lick Ward," Kelly snapped.

Roberts considered judicially.

"No, I won't say that. Ward's a top-notcher and a ring general. But he can't hashhouse Rivera in short order. I know Rivera. Nobody can get his goat. He ain't got a goat that I could ever discover. And he's a two-handed fighter. He can throw in the sleep-makers from any position."

"Never mind that. What kind of a show can he put up? You've been conditioning and training fighters all your life. I take off my hat to your judgment. Can he give the public a run for its money?"

"He sure can, and he'll worry Ward a mighty heap on top of it. You don't know that boy. I do. I discovered him. He ain't got a goat. He's a devil. He's a wizzy-wooz if anybody should ask you. He'll make Ward sit up with a show of local talent that'll make the rest of you sit up. I won't say he'll lick Ward, but he'll put up such a show that you'll all know he's a comer."

"All right." Kelly turned to his secretary. "Ring up Ward. I warned him to show up if I thought it worth while. He's right across at the Yellowstone, throwin' chests and doing the popular." Kelly turned back to the conditioner. "Have a drink?"

Roberts sipped his highball and unburdened himself.

"Never told you how I discovered the little cuss. It was a couple of years ago he showed up out at the quarters. I was getting Prayne ready for his fight with Delaney. Prayne's wicked. He ain't got a tickle of mercy in his make-up. He'd chopped up his pardners something cruel, and I couldn't find a willing boy that'd work with him. I'd noticed this little starved Mexican kid hanging around, and I was desperate. So I grabbed him, slammed on the gloves, and put him in. He was tougher'n rawhide, but weak. And he didn't know the first letter in the alphabet of boxing. Prayne chopped him to ribbons. But he hung on for two sickening rounds, when he fainted. Starvation, that was all. Battered? You couldn't have recognized him. I gave him half a dollar and a square meal. You oughta seen him wolf it down. He hadn't had a bite for a couple of days. That's the end of him, thinks I. But next day he showed up, stiff an' sore, ready for another half and a square meal. And he done better as time went by. Just a born fighter, and tough beyond belief. He hasn't a heart. He's a piece of ice. And he never talked eleven words in a string since I know him. He saws wood and does his work."

"I've seen 'm," the secretary said. "He's worked a lot for you."

"All the big little fellows has tried out on him," Roberts answered. "And he's learned from 'em. I've seen some of them he could lick. But his heart wasn't in it. I reckoned he never liked the game. He seemed to act that way."

"He's been fighting some before the little clubs the last few months," Kelly said.

"Sure. But I don't know what struck 'm. All of a sudden his heart got into it. He just went out like a streak and cleaned up all the little local fellows. Seemed to want the money, and he's won a bit, though his clothes don't look it. He's peculiar. Nobody knows his business. Nobody knows how he spends his time. Even when he's on the job, he plumb up and disappears most of each day soon as his work is done. Sometimes he just blows away for weeks at a time. But he don't take advice. There's a fortune in it for the fellow that gets the job of managin' him, only he won't consider it. And you watch him hold out for the cash money when you get down to terms."

It was at this stage that Danny Ward arrived. Quite a party it was. His manager and trainer were with him, and he breezed in like a gusty draught of geniality, good-nature, and all-conqueringness. Greetings flew about, a joke here, a retort there, a smile or a laugh for everybody. Yet it was his way, and only partly sincere. He was a good actor, and he had found geniality a most valuable asset in the game of getting on in the world. But down underneath he was the deliberate, cold-blooded fighter and business man. The rest was a mask. Those who knew him or trafficked with him said that when it came to brass tacks he was Danny-on-the-Spot. He was invariably present at all business discussions, and it was urged by some that his manager was a blind whose only function was to serve as Danny's mouth-piece.

Rivera's way was different. Indian blood, as well as Spanish, was in his veins, and he sat back in a corner, silent, immobile, only his black eyes passing from face to face and noting everything.

"So that's the guy," Danny said, running an appraising eye over his proposed antagonist. "How de do, old chap."

Rivera's eyes burned venomously, but he made no sign of acknowledgment. He disliked all Gringos, but this Gringo he hated with an immediacy that was unusual even in him.

"Gawd!" Danny protested facetiously to the promoter. "You ain't expectin' me to fight a deef mute." When the laughter subsided, he made another hit. "Los Angeles must be on the dink when this is the best you can scare up. What kindergarten did you get'm from?"

"He's a good little boy, Danny, take it from me," Roberts defended. "Not as easy as he looks."

"And half the house is sold already," Kelly pleaded. "You'll have to take 'm on, Danny. It's the best we can do."

Danny ran another careless and unflattering glance over Rivera and sighed.

"I gotta be easy with 'm, I guess. If only he don't blow up."

Roberts snorted.

"You gotta be careful," Danny's manager warned. "No taking chances with a dub that's likely to sneak a lucky one across."

"Oh, I'll be careful all right, all right," Danny smiled. "I'll get 'm at the start an' nurse 'm along for the dear public's sake. What d' ye say to fifteen rounds, Kelly— An' then the hay for him?"

"That'll do," was the answer. "As long as you make it realistic."

"Then let's get down to biz." Danny paused and calculated. "Of course, sixty-five per cent. of gate receipts, same as with Carthey. But the split'll be different. Eighty will just about suit me." And to his manager, "That right?"

The manager nodded.

"Here, you, did you get that?" Kelly asked Rivera.

Rivera shook his head.

"Well, it's this way," Kelly exposited. "The purse'll be sixty-five per cent. of the gate receipts. You're a dub, and an unknown. You and Danny split, twenty per cent. goin' to you, an' eighty to Danny. That's fair, isn't it, Roberts?"

"Very fair, Rivera," Roberts agreed. "You see, you ain't got a reputation yet."

"What will sixty-five per cent. of the gate receipts be?" Rivera demanded.

"Oh, maybe five thousand, maybe as high as eight thousand," Danny broke in to explain. "Something like that. Your share'll come to something like a thousand or sixteen hundred. Pretty good for takin' a licking from a guy with my reputation. What d' ye say?"

Then Rivera took their breaths away.

"Winner takes all," he said with finality.

A dead silence prevailed.

"It's like candy from a baby," Danny's manager proclaimed.

Danny shook his head.

"I've been in the game too long," he explained. "I'm not casting reflections on the referee, or the present company. I'm not sayin' nothing about book-makers an' frame-ups that sometimes happen. But what I do say is that it's poor business for a fighter like me. I play safe. There's no tellin'. Mebbe I break my arm, eh? Or some guy slips me a bunch of dope?" He shook his head solemnly. "Win or lose, eighty is my split. What d' ye say, Mexican?"

Rivera shook his head.

Danny exploded. He was getting down to brass tacks now.

"Why, you dirty little greaser! I've a mind to knock your block off right now."

Roberts drawled his body to interposition between hostilities.

"Winner takes all," Rivera repeated sullenly.

"Why do you stand out that way?" Danny asked.

"I can lick you," was the straight answer.

Danny half started to take off his coat. But, as his manager knew, it was a grandstand play. The coat did not come off, and Danny allowed himself to be placated by the group. Everybody sympathized with him. Rivera stood alone.

"Look here, you little fool," Kelly took up the argument. "You're nobody. We know what you've been doing the last few months—putting away little local fighters. But Danny is class. His next fight after this will be for the championship. And you're unknown. Nobody ever heard of you out of Los Angeles."

"They will," Rivera answered with a shrug, "after this fight."

"You think for a second you can lick me?" Danny blurted in.

Rivera nodded.

"Oh, come; listen to reason," Kelly pleaded. "Think of the advertising."

"I want the money," was Rivera's answer.

"You couldn't win from me in a thousand years," Danny assured him.

"Then what are you holding out for?" Rivera countered. "If the money's that easy, why don't you go after it?"

"I will, so help me!" Danny cried with abrupt conviction. "I'll beat you to death in the ring, my boy—you monkeyin' with me this way. Make out the articles, Kelly. Winner take all. Play it up in the sportin' columns. Tell 'em it's a grudge fight. I'll show this fresh kid a few."

Kelly's secretary had begun to write, when Danny interrupted.

"Hold on!" He turned to Rivera. "Weights?"

"Ringside," came the answer

"Not on your life, Fresh Kid. If winner takes all, we weigh in at ten A.M."

"And winner takes all?" Rivera queried.

Danny nodded. That settled it. He would enter the ring in his full ripeness of strength.

"Weigh in at ten," Rivera said.

The secretary's pen went on scratching.

"It means five pounds," Roberts complained to Rivera. "You've given too much away. You've thrown the fight right there. Danny'll be as strong as a bull. You're a fool. He'll lick you sure. You ain't got the chance of a dewdrop in hell."

Rivera's answer was a calculated look of hatred. Even this Gringo he despised, and him had he found the whitest Gringo of them all.

IV

BARELY NOTICED WAS Rivera as he entered the ring. Only a very slight and very scattering ripple of half-hearted hand-clapping greeted him. The house did not believe in him. He was the lamb led to slaughter at the hands of the great Danny. Besides, the house was disappointed. It had expected a rushing battle between Danny Ward and Billy Carthey, and here it must put up with this poor little tyro. Still further, it had manifested its disapproval of the change by betting two, and even three, to one on Danny. And where a betting audience's money is, there is its heart.

The Mexican boy sat down in his corner and waited. The slow minutes lagged by. Danny was making him wait. It was an old trick, but ever it worked on the young, new fighters. They grew frightened, sitting thus and facing their own apprehensions and a callous, tobacco-smoking audience. But for once the trick failed. Roberts was right. Rivera had no goat. He, who was more delicately coördinated, more finely nerved and strung than any of them, had no nerves of this sort. The atmosphere of fore-doomed defeat in his own corner had no effect on him. His handlers were Gringos and strangers. Also they were scrubs—the dirty driftage of the fight game, without honor, without efficiency. And they were chilled, as well, with certitude that theirs was the losing corner.

"Now you gotta be careful," Spider Hagerty warned him. Spider was his chief second. "Make it last as long as you can—them's my instructions from Kelly. If you don't, the papers'll call it another bum fight and give the game a bigger black eye in Los Angeles."

All of which was not encouraging. But Rivera took no notice. He despised prize fighting. It was the hated game of the hated Gringo. He had taken up with it, as a chopping block for others in the training quarters, solely because he was starving. The fact that he was marvelously made for it, had meant nothing. He hated it. Not until he had come in to the Junta, had he fought for money, and he had found the money easy. Not first among the sons of men had he been to find himself successful at a despised vocation.

He did not analyze. He merely knew that he must win this fight. There could be no other outcome. For behind him, nerving him to this belief, were profounder forces than any the crowded house dreamed. Danny Ward fought for money, and for the easy ways of life that money would bring. But the things Rivera fought for burned in his brain—blazing and terrible visions, that, with eyes wide open, sitting lonely in the corner of the ring and waiting for his tricky antagonist, he saw as clearly as he had lived them.

He saw the white-walled, water-power factories of Rio Blanco. He saw the six thousand workers, starved and wan, and the little children, seven and eight years of age, who toiled long shifts for ten cents a day. He saw the perambulating corpses, the ghastly death's heads of men who labored in the dye-rooms. He remembered that he had heard his father call the dye-rooms the "suicide-holes," where a year was death. He saw the little patio, and his mother cooking and moiling at crude housekeeping and finding time to caress and love him. And his father he saw, large, big-moustached and deep-chested, kindly above all men, who loved all men and whose heart was so large that there was love to overflowing still left for the mother and the little muchacho playing in the corner of the patio. In those days his name had not been Felipe Rivera. It had been Fernandez, his father's and mother's name. Him had they called Juan. Later, he had changed it himself, for he had found the name of Fernandez hated by prefects of police, *jefes politicos*, and *rurales*.

Big, hearty Joaquin Fernandez! A large place he occupied in Rivera's visions. He had not understood at the time, but looking back he could understand. He could see him setting type in the little printery, or scribbling endless hasty, nervous lines on the much-cluttered desk. And he could see the strange evenings, when workmen, coming secretly in the dark like men who did ill deeds, met with his father and talked long hours where he, the muchacho, lay not always asleep in the corner.

As from a remote distance he could hear Spider Hagerty saying to him: "No layin' down at the start. Them's instructions. Take a beatin' an' earn your dough."

Ten minutes had passed, and he still sat in his corner. There were no signs of Danny, who was evidently playing the trick to the limit.

But more visions burned before the eye of Rivera's memory. The strike, or, rather, the lockout, because the workers of Rio Blanco had helped their striking brothers of Puebla. The hunger, the expeditions in the hills for berries, the roots and herbs that all ate and that twisted and pained the stomachs of all of them. And then, the nightmare; the waste of ground before the company's store; the thousands of starving workers; General Rosalio Martinez and the soldiers of Porfirio Diaz; and the death-spitting rifles that seemed never to cease spitting, while the workers' wrongs were washed and washed again in their own blood. And that night! He saw the flat cars, piled high with the bodies of the slain, consigned to Vera Cruz, food for the sharks of the bay. Again he crawled over the grisly heaps, seeking and finding, stripped and mangled, his father and his mother. His mother he especially remembered—only her face projecting, her body burdened by the weight of dozens of bodies. Again the rifles of the soldiers of Porfirio Diaz cracked, and again he dropped to the ground and slunk away like some hunted coyote of the hills.

To his ears came a great roar, as of the sea, and he saw Danny Ward, leading his retinue of trainers and seconds, coming down the center aisle. The house was in wild uproar for the popular hero who was bound to win. Everybody proclaimed him. Everybody was for him. Even Rivera's own seconds warmed to something akin to cheerfulness when Danny ducked jauntily through the ropes and entered the ring. His face continually spread to an unending succession of smiles, and when Danny smiled he smiled in every feature, even to the laughter-wrinkles of the corners of the eyes and into the depths of the eyes themselves. Never was there so genial a fighter. His face was a running advertisement of good feeling, of good fellowship. He knew everybody. He joked, and laughed, and greeted his friends through the ropes. Those farther away, unable to suppress their admiration, cried loudly: "Oh, you Danny!" It was a joyous ovation of affection that lasted a full five minutes.

Rivera was disregarded. For all that the audience noticed, he did not exist. Spider Hagerty's bloated face bent down close to his.

"No gettin' scared," the Spider warned. "An' remember instructions. You gotta last. No layin' down. If you lay down, we got instructions to beat you up in the dressing rooms. Savve? You just gotta fight."

The house began to applaud. Danny was crossing the ring to him. Danny bent over, caught Rivera's right hand in both his own and shook it with impulsive heartiness. Danny's smile-wreathed face was close to his. The audience yelled its appreciation of Danny's display of sporting spirit. He was greeting his opponent with the fondness of a brother. Danny's lips moved, and the audience, interpreting the unheard words to be those of a kindly-natured sport, yelled again. Only Rivera heard the low words.

"You little Mexican rat," hissed from between Danny's gaily smiling lips, "I'll fetch the yellow outa you."

Rivera made no move. He did not rise. He merely hated with his eyes.

"Get up, you dog!" some man yelled through the ropes from behind.

The crowd began to hiss and boo him for his unsportsmanlike conduct, but he sat unmoved. Another great outburst of applause was Danny's as he walked back across the ring.

When Danny stripped, there was ohs! and ahs! of delight. His body was perfect, alive with easy suppleness and health and strength. The skin was white as a woman's, and as smooth. All grace, and resilience, and power resided therein. He had proved it in scores of battles. His photographs were in all the physical culture magazines.

A groan went up as Spider Hagerty peeled Rivera's sweater over his head. His body seemed leaner, because of the swarthiness of the skin. He had muscles, but they made no display like his opponent's. What the audience neglected to see was the deep chest. Nor could it guess the toughness of the fiber of the flesh, the instantaneousness of the cell explosions of the muscles, the fineness of the nerves that wired every part of him into a splendid fighting mechanism. All the audience saw was a brown-skinned boy of eighteen with what seemed the body of a boy. With Danny it was different. Danny was a man of twenty-four, and his body was a man's body. The contrast was still more striking as they stood together in the center of the ring receiving the referee's last instructions.

Rivera noticed Roberts sitting directly behind the newspaper men. He was drunker than usual, and his speech was correspondingly slower.

"Take it easy, Rivera," Roberts drawled. "He can't kill you, remember that. He'll rush you at the go-off, but don't get rattled. You just cover up, and stall, and clinch. He can't hurt you much. Just make believe to yourself that he's choppin' out on you at the trainin' quarters."

Rivera made no sign that he had heard.

"Sullen little devil," Roberts muttered to the man next to him. "He always was that way."

But Rivera forgot to look his usual hatred. A vision of countless rifles blinded his eyes. Every face in the audience, far as he could see, to the high dollar-seats, was transformed into a rifle. And he saw the long Mexican border arid and sun-washed and aching, and along it he saw the ragged bands that delayed only for the guns.

Back in his corner he waited, standing up. His seconds had crawled out through the ropes, taking the canvas stool with them. Diagonally across the squared ring, Danny faced him. The gong struck, and the battle was on. The audience howled its delight. Never had it seen a battle open more convincingly. The papers were right. It was a grudge fight. Three-quarters of the distance Danny covered in the rush to get together, his intention to eat up the Mexican lad plainly advertised. He assailed with not one blow, nor two, nor a dozen. He was a gyroscope of blows, a whirlwind of destruction. Rivera was nowhere. He was overwhelmed, buried beneath avalanches of punches delivered from every angle and position by a past master in the art. He was overborne, swept back against the ropes, separated by the referee, and swept back against the ropes again.

It was not a fight. It was a slaughter, a massacre. Any audience, save a prize fighting one, would have exhausted its emotions in that first minute. Danny was certainly showing what he could do—a splendid exhibition. Such was the certainty of the audience, as well as its excitement and favoritism, that it failed to take notice that the Mexican still stayed on his feet. It forgot Rivera. It rarely saw him, so closely was he enveloped in Danny's man-eating attack. A minute of this went by, and two minutes. Then, in a separation, it caught a clear glimpse of the Mexican. His lip was cut, his nose was bleeding. As he turned and staggered into a clinch, the welts of oozing blood, from his contacts with the ropes, showed in red bars across his back. But what the audience did not notice was that his chest was not heaving and that his eyes were coldly burning as ever. Too many aspiring champions, in the cruel welter of the training camps, had practiced this man-eating attack on him. He had learned to live through for a compensation of from half a dollar a go up to fifteen dollars a week—a hard school, and he was schooled hard.

Then happened the amazing thing. The whirling, blurring mix-up ceased suddenly. Rivera stood alone. Danny, the redoubtable

Danny, lay on his back. His body quivered as consciousness strove to return to it. He had not staggered and sunk down, nor had he gone over in a long slumping fall. The right hook of Rivera had dropped him in midair with the abruptness of death. The referee shoved Rivera back with one hand, and stood over the fallen glad- iator counting the seconds. It is the custom of prizefighting audi- ences to cheer a clean knock-down blow. But this audience did not cheer. The thing had been too unexpected. It watched the toll of the seconds in tense silence, and through this silence the voice of Roberts rose exultantly:

"I told you he was a two-handed fighter!"

By the fifth second, Danny was rolling over on his face, and when seven was counted, he rested on one knee, ready to rise after the count of nine and before the count of ten. If his knee still touched the floor at "ten," he was considered "down," and also "out." The instant his knee left the floor, he was considered "up," and in that instant it was Rivera's right to try and put him down again. Rivera took no chances. The moment that knee left the floor he would strike again. He circled around, but the referee circled in between, and River knew that the seconds he counted were very slow. All Gringos were against him, even the referee.

At "nine" the referee gave Rivera a sharp thrust back. It was unfair, but it enabled Danny to rise, the smile back on his lips. Doubled partly over, with arms wrapped about face and abdomen, he cleverly stumbled into a clinch. By all the rules of the game the referee should have broken it, but he did not, and Danny clung on like a surf-battered barnacle and moment by moment recuperated. The last minute of the round was going fast. If he could live to the end, he would have a full minute in his corner to revive. And live to the end he did, smiling through all desperateness and extremity.

"The smile that won't come off!" somebody yelled, and the au- dience laughed loudly in its relief.

"The kick that Greaser's got is something God-awful," Danny gasped in his corner to his adviser while his handlers worked frant- ically over him.

The second and third rounds were tame. Danny, a tricky and consummate ring general, stalled and blocked and held on, devoting himself to recovering from that dazing first-round blow. In the fourth round he was himself again. Jarred and shaken, nevertheless his good condition had enabled him to regain his vigor. But he tried no man-eating tactics. The Mexican had proved a tartar. Instead, he brought to bear his best fighting powers. In tricks and skill and experience he was the master, and though he could land nothing vital, he proceeded scientifically to chop and wear down his opponent. He landed three blows to Rivera's one, but they were punishing blows only, and not deadly. It was the sum of many of them that constituted deadliness. He was respectful of this two-handed dub with the amazing short-arm kicks in both his fists.

In defense, Rivera developed a disconcerting straight-left. Again and again, attack after attack he straight-lefted away from him with accumulated damage to Danny's mouth and nose. But Danny was protean. That was why he was the coming champion. He could change from style to style of fighting at will. He now devoted himself to infighting. In this he was particularly wicked, and it enabled him to avoid the other's straight-left. Here he set the house wild repeatedly, capping it with a marvelous lock-break and lift of an inside uppercut that raised the Mexican in the air and dropped him to the mat. Rivera rested on one knee, making the most of the count, and in the soul of him he knew the referee was counting short seconds on him.

Again, in the seventh, Danny achieved the diabolical inside uppercut. He succeeded only in staggering Rivera, but, in the ensuing moment of defenseless helplessness, he smashed him with another blow through the ropes. Rivera's body bounced on the heads of the newspaper men below, and they boosted him back to the edge of the platform outside the ropes. Here he rested on one knee, while the referee raced off the seconds. Inside the ropes, through which he must duck to enter the ring, Danny waited for him. Nor did the referee intervene or thrust Danny back.

The house was beside itself with delight.

"Kill'm, Danny, kill'm!" was the cry.

Scores of voices took it up until it was like a war-chant of wolves.

Danny did his best, but Rivera, at the count of eight, instead of nine, came unexpectedly through the ropes and safely into a clinch. Now the referee worked, tearing him away so that he could be hit, giving Danny every advantage that an unfair referee can give.

But Rivera lived, and the daze cleared from his brain. It was all of a piece. They were the hated Gringos and they were all unfair. And in the worst of it visions continued to flash and sparkle in his brain—long lines of railroad track that simmered across the desert; *rurales* and American constables; prisons and calabooses; tramps at water tanks—all the squalid and painful panorama of his odyssey after Rio Blanco and the strike. And, resplendent and glorious, he saw the great, red Revolution sweeping across his land. The guns were there before him. Every hated face was a gun. It was for the guns he fought. He was the guns. He was the Revolution. He fought for all Mexico.

The audience began to grow incensed with Rivera. Why didn't he take the licking that was appointed him? Of course he was going to be licked, but why should he be so obstinate about it? Very few were interested in him, and they were the certain, definite percentage of a gambling crowd that plays long shots. Believing Danny to be the winner, nevertheless they had put their money on the Mexican at four to ten and one to three. More than a trifle was up on the point of how many rounds Rivera could last. Wild money had appeared at the ringside proclaiming that he could not last seven rounds, or even six. The winners of this, now that their cash risk was happily settled, had joined in cheering on the favorite.

Rivera refused to be licked. Through the eighth round his opponent strove vainly to repeat the uppercut. In the ninth, Rivera stunned the house again. In the midst of a clinch he broke the lock with a quick, lithe movement, and in the narrow space between their bodies his right lifted from the waist. Danny went to the floor and took the safety of the count. The crowd was appalled. He was being bested at his own game. His famous right-uppercut had been worked back on him. Rivera made no attempt to catch him as he arose at "nine." The referee was openly blocking that play, though he stood clear when the situation was reversed and it was Rivera who desired to rise.

Twice in the tenth, Rivera put through the right-uppercut, lifted from waist to opponent's chin. Danny grew desperate. The smile never left his face, but he went back to his man-eating rushes. Whirlwind as he would, he could not damage Rivera, while Rivera, through the blur and whirl, dropped him to the mat three times in succession. Danny did not recuperate so quickly now, and by the eleventh round he was in a serious way. But from then till the fourteenth he put up the gamest exhibition of his career. He stalled and blocked, fought parsimoniously, and strove to gather strength. Also, he fought as foully as a successful fighter knows how. Every trick and device he employed, butting in the clinches with the seeming of accident, pinioning Rivera's glove between arm and body, heeling his glove on Rivera's mouth to clog his breathing. Often, in the clinches, through his cut and smiling lips he snarled insults unspeakable and vile in Rivera's ear. Everybody, from the referee to the house, was with Danny and was helping Danny. And they knew what he had in mind. Bested by this surprise-box of an unknown, he was pinning all on a single punch. He offered himself for punishment, fished, and feinted, and drew, for that one opening that would enable him to whip a blow through with all his strength and turn the tide. As another and greater fighter had done before him, he might do—a right and left, to solar plexus and across the jaw. He could do it, for he was noted for the strength of punch that remained in his arms as long as he could keep his feet.

Rivera's seconds were not half-caring for him in the intervals between rounds. Their towels made a showing, but drove little air into his panting lungs. Spider Hagerty talked advice to him, but Rivera knew it was wrong advice. Everybody was against him. He was surrounded by treachery. In the fourteenth round he put Danny down again, and himself stood resting, hands dropped at side, while the referee counted. In the other corner Rivera had been noting suspicious whisperings. He saw Michael Kelly make his way to Roberts and bend and whisper. Rivera's ears were a cat's, desert-trained, and he caught snatches of what was said. He wanted to hear more, and when his opponent arose he maneuvered the fight into a clinch over against the ropes.

"Got to," he could hear Michael, while Roberts nodded. "Danny's got to win—I stand to lose a mint—I've got a ton of money covered—my own—If he last the fifteenth I'm bust—The boy'll mind you. Put something across."

And thereafter Rivera saw no more visions. They were trying to job him. Once again he dropped Danny and stood resting, his hands at his side. Roberts stood up.

"That settled him," he said. "Go to your corner."

He spoke with authority, as he had often spoken to Rivera at the training quarters. But Rivera looked hatred at him and waited for Danny to rise. Back in his corner in the minute interval, Kelly, the promoter, came and talked to Rivera.

"Throw it, damn you," he rasped in a harsh low voice. "You gotta lay down, Rivera. Stick with me and I'll make your future. I'll let you lick Danny next time. But here's where you lay down."

Rivera showed with his eyes that he heard, but he made neither sign of assent nor dissent.

"Why don't you speak?" Kelly demanded angrily.

"You lose, anyway," Spider Hagerty supplemented. "The referee'll take it away from you. Listen to Kelly, and lay down."

"Lay down, kid," Kelly pleaded, "and I'll help you to the championship."

Rivera did not answer.

"I will, so help me, kid."

At the strike of the gong Rivera sensed something impending. The house did not. Whatever it was it was there inside the ring with him and very close. Danny's earlier surety seemed returned to him. The confidence of his advance frightened Rivera. Some trick was about to be worked. Danny rushed, but Rivera refused the encounter. He side-stepped away into safety. What the other wanted was a clinch. It was in some way necessary to the trick. Rivera backed and circled away, yet he knew, sooner or later, the clinch and the trick would come. Desperately he resolved to draw it. He made as if to effect the clinch with Danny's next rush. Instead, at the last instant, just as their bodies should have come together, Rivera darted nimbly back. And in the same instant Danny's corner raised a cry of foul. Rivera had fooled them. The referee paused irresolutely. The decision that trembled on his lips was never uttered, for a shrill, boy's voice from the gallery piped, "Raw work!"

Danny cursed Rivera openly, and forced him, while Rivera danced away. Also, Rivera made up his mind to strike no more blows at the body. In this he threw away half his chance of winning, but he knew if he was to win at all it was with the outfighting that remained to him. Given the least opportunity, they would lay a foul on him. Danny threw all caution to the winds. For two rounds he tore after and into the boy who dared not meet him at close quarters. Rivera was struck again and again; he took blows by the dozens to avoid the perilous clinch. During this supreme final rally of Danny's the audience rose to its feet and went mad. It did not understand. All it could see was that its favorite was winning after all.

"Why don't you fight?" it demanded wrathfully of Rivera. "You're yellow! You're yellow!" "Open up, you cur! Open up!" "Kill'm, Danny! Kill'm!" "You sure got'm! Kill'm!"

In all the house, bar none, Rivera was the only cold man. By temperament and blood he was the hottest-passioned there; but he had gone through such vastly greater heats that this collective passion of ten thousand throats, rising surge on surge, was to his brain no more than the velvet cool of a summer twilight.

Into the seventeenth round Danny carried his rally. Rivera, under a heavy blow, drooped and sagged. His hands dropped helplessly as he reeled backward. Danny thought it was his chance. The boy was at his mercy. Thus Rivera, feigning, caught him off his guard, lashing out a clean drive to the mouth. Danny went down. When he arose, Rivera felled him with a down-chop of the right on neck and jaw. Three times he repeated this. It was impossible for any referee to call these blows foul.

"Oh, Bill! Bill!" Kelly pleaded to the referee.

"I can't," that official lamented back. "He won't give me a chance."

Danny, battered and heroic, still kept coming up. Kelly and others near to the ring began to cry out to the police to stop it, though Danny's corner refused to throw in the towel. Rivera saw the fat police captain starting awkwardly to climb through the ropes, and was not sure what it meant. There were so many ways of cheating in this game of the Gringos. Danny, on his feet, tottered groggily and helplessly before him. The referee and the captain were both reaching for Rivera when he struck the last blow. There was no need to stop the fight, for Danny did not rise.

"Count!" Rivera cried hoarsely to the referee.

And when the count was finished, Danny's seconds gathered him up and carried him to his corner.

"Who wins?" Rivera demanded.

Reluctantly, the referee caught his gloved hand and held it aloft. There were no congratulations for Rivera. He walked to his corner unattended, where his seconds had not yet placed his stool. He leaned backward on the ropes and looked his hatred at them, swept it on and about him till the whole ten thousand Gringos were included. His knees trembled under him, and he was sobbing from exhaustion. Before his eyes the hated faces swayed back and forth in the giddiness of nausea. Then he remembered they were the guns. The guns were his. The Revolution could go on.

THE
ROAD

HOBOES THAT PASS IN THE NIGHT

(*Cosmopolitan*, December, 1907)

In 1894, a San Franciscan named Charles T. Kelly organized an "Industrial Army" of unemployed workers and announced his plans to meet with "General" Jacob S. Coxey of Massillon, Ohio, for a march on Washington, D.C. Coxey, a quarry and scrap-iron businessman left Massillon in March of the year with about one hundred of a ragtag "army" and an idea that the federal government could solve the economic crisis by lending legal tender notes to communities which, in turn, would use them to pay the unemployed for labor in such public works as building roads.

Jack London, with a chum from Oakland named Frank Davis, joined "Kelly's Army" in April, 1894, only a few weeks before Coxey's contingent, swollen to five hundred men, reached the capital. Jack dutifully traveled with Kelly's band from Council Bluffs, Iowa, to Hannibal, Missouri, then deserted. He traveled by rail to Chicago where he visited the site of the Columbian Exposition, then on to New York City, Niagara Falls, and Buffalo. In Niagara Falls he was arrested as a vagrant and spent a month in the Erie County Penitentiary. After his release, he traveled down to Washington, to Baltimore, back to New York, to Boston, Montreal, Ottawa, and Vancouver where he earned his passage back to San Francisco by working as a coal stoker on the freighter *Umatilla*.

His six months as a tramp he saw as the turning point of his life and for the rest of his life took great pride in his knowledge of "the

Road"—of Skysail Jack, "side-door Pullmans" (the freight cars in which hobos stole rides), bulls, stiffs, and men with "monicas" such as Leary Joe, Painter Red, Pacific Slim, and Frisco Sheeny.

"Hoboes That Pass in the Night" is included in London's book of his hobo days, *The Road* (1907), a book that has put the author among the forefront of American writers (Jim Tully, now unjustly forgotten, is London's closest kinsman in this small but valuable genre) who chronicled, by firsthand knowledge, the tramp life.

HOBOES THAT PASS IN THE NIGHT

IN THE COURSE of my tramping I encountered hundreds of hoboes, whom I hailed or who hailed me, and with whom I waited at water-tanks, "boiled-up," cooked "mulligans," "battered" the "drag" of "privates," and beat trains, and who passed and were seen never again. On the other hand, there were hoboes who passed and re-passed with amazing frequency, and others, still, who passed like ghosts, close at hand, unseen, and never seen.

It was one of the latter that I chased clear across Canada over three thousand miles of railroad, and never once did I lay eyes on him. His "monica" was Skysail Jack. I first ran into it at Montreal. Carved with a jack-knife was the skysail-yard of a ship. It was per-fectly executed. Under it was "Skysail Jack." Above was "B.W. 9–15–94." This latter conveyed the information that he had passed through Montreal bound west, on October 15, 1894. He had one day the start of me. "Sailor Jack" was my monica at that particular time, and promptly I carved it alongside of his, along with the date and the information that I, too, was bound west.

I had misfortune in getting over the next hundred miles, and eight days later I picked up Skysail Jack's trail three hundred miles west of Ottawa. There it was, carved on a water-tank, and by the date I saw that he likewise had met with delay. He was only two days ahead of me. I was a "comet" and "tramp-royal," so was Skysail Jack; and it was up to my pride and reputation to catch up with him. I "railroaded" day and night, and I passed him; then turn about he passed me. Sometimes he was a day or so ahead, and sometimes

I was. From hoboes, bound east, I got word of him occasionally, when he happened to be ahead; and from them I learned that he had become interested in Sailor Jack and was making inquiries about me.

We'd have made a precious pair, I am sure, if we'd ever got together; but get together we couldn't. I kept ahead of him clear across Manitoba, but he led the way across Alberta, and early one bitter gray morning, at the end of a division just east of Kicking Horse Pass, I learned that he had been seen the night before between Kicking Horse Pass and Rogers' pass. It was rather curious the way the information came to me. I had been riding all night in a "side-door Pullman" (box-car), and nearly dead with cold had crawled out at the division to beg for food. A freezing fog was drifting past, and I "hit" some firemen I found in the round-house. They fixed me up with the leavings from their lunch-pails, and in addition I got out of them nearly a quart of heavenly "Java" (coffee). I heated the latter, and, as I sat down to eat, a freight pulled in from the west. I saw a side-door open and a road-kid climb out. Through the drifting fog he limped over to me. He was stiff with cold, his lips blue. I shared my Java and grub with him, learned about Skysail Jack, and then learned about him. Behold, he was from my own town, Oakland, California, and he was a member of the celebrated Boo Gang—a gang with which I had affiliated at rare intervals. We talked fast and bolted the grub in the half-hour that followed. Then my freight pulled out, and I was on it, bound west on the trail of Skysail Jack.

I was delayed between the passes, went two days without food, and walked eleven miles on the third day before I got any, and yet I succeeded in passing Skysail Jack along the Fraser River in British Columbia. I was riding "passengers" then and making time; but he must have been riding passengers, too, and with more luck or skill than I, for he got into Mission ahead of me.

Now Mission was a junction, forty miles east of Vancouver. From the junction one could proceed south through Washington and Oregon over the Northern Pacific. I wondered which way Skysail Jack would go, for I thought I was ahead of him. As for myself I was still bound west to Vancouver. I proceeded to the water-tank to leave that information, and there, freshy carved, with that day's date upon it, was Skysail Jack's monica. I hurried on into Vancouver. But he was gone. He had taken ship immediately and was still flying west on his world-adventure. Truly, Skysail Jack, you were a tramp-royal, and your mate was the "wind that tramps the world." I take off my hat to you. You were "blowed-in-the-glass" all right. A week later I, too, got my ship, and on board the steamship *Umatilla*, in the forecastle, was working my way down the coast to San Francisco. Skysail Jack and Sailor Jack—gee! if we'd ever got together.

Water-tanks are tramp directories. Not all in idle wantonness do tramps carve their monicas, dates, and courses. Often and often have I met hoboes earnestly inquiring if I had seen anywhere such and such a "stiff" or his monica. And more than once I have been able to give the monica of recent date, the water-tank, and the direction in which he was then bound. And promptly the hobo to whom I gave the information lit out after his pal. I have met hoboes who, in trying to catch a pal, had pursued clear across the continent and back again, and were still going.

"Monicas" are the *nom-de-rails* that hoboes assume or accept when thrust upon them by their fellows. Leary Joe, for instance, was timid, and was so named by his fellows. No self-respecting hobo would select Stew Bum for himself. Very few tramps care to remember their pasts during which they ignobly worked, so monicas based upon trades are very rare, though I remember having met the following: Moulder Blackey, Painter Red, Chi Plumber, Boiler-maker, Sailor Boy, and Printer Bo. "Chi" (pronounced *shy*), by the way, is the argot for "Chicago."

A favorite device of hoboes is to base their monicas on the localities from which they hail as: New York Tommy, Pacific Slim, Buffalo Smithy, Canton Tim, Pittsburgh Jack, Syracuse Shine, Troy Mickey, K. L. Bill, and Connecticut Jimmy. Then there was "Slim Jim from Vinegar Hill, who never worked and never will." A "shine" is always a negro, so called, possibly, from the high lights on his countenance. Texas Shine or Toledo Shine convey both race and nativity.

Among those that incorporated their race, I recollect the following: Frisco Sheeny, New York Irish, Michigan French, English Jack, Cockney Kid, and Milwaukee Dutch. Others seem to take their monicas in part from the color-schemes stamped upon them at birth, such as: Chi Whitey, New Jersey Red, Boston Blackey, Seattle

Browney, and Yellow Dick and Yellow Belly—the last a Creole from Mississippi, who, I suspect, had his monica thrust upon him.

Texas Royal, Happy Joe, Bust Connors, Burley Bo, Tornado Blackey, and Touch McCall used more imagination in rechristening themselves. Others, with less fancy, carry the names of their physical peculiarities, such as: Vancouver Slim, Detroit Shorty, Ohio Fatty, Long Jack, Big Jim, Little Joe, New York Blink, Chi Nosey, and Broken-backed Ben.

By themselves come the road-kids, sporting an infinite variety of monicas. For example, the following, whom here and there I have encountered: Buck Kid, Blind Kid, Midget Kid, Holy Kid, Bat Kid, Swift Kid, Cookey Kid, Monkey Kid, Iowa Kid, Corduroy Kid, Orator Kid (who could tell how it happened), and Lippy Kid (who was insolent, depend upon it).

On the water-tank at San Marcial, New Mexico, a dozen years ago, was the following hobo bill of fare:—

(1) Main-drag fair.
(2) Bulls not hostile.
(3) Round-house good for kipping.
(4) North-bound trains no good.
(5) Privates no good.
(6) Restaurants good for cooks only.
(7) Railroad House good for night-work only.

Number one conveys the information that begging for money on the main street is fair; number two, that the police will not bother hoboes; number three, that one can sleep in the round-house. Number four, however, is ambiguous. The north-bound trains may be no good to beat, and they may be no good to beg. Number five means that the residences are not good to beggars, and number six means that only hoboes that have been cooks can get grub from the restaurants. Number seven bothers me. I cannot make out whether the Railroad House is a good place for any hobo to beg at night, or whether it is good only for hobo-cooks to beg at night, or whether any hobo, cook or non-cook, can lend a hand at night, helping the cooks of the Railroad House with their dirty work and getting something to eat in payment.

But to return to the hoboes that pass in the night. I remember one I met in California. He was a Swede, but he had lived so long in the United States that one couldn't guess his nationality. He had to tell it on himself. In fact, he had come to the United States when no more than a baby. I ran into him first at the mountain town of Truckee. "Which way, Bo?" was our greeting, and "Bound east" was the answer each of us gave. Quite a bunch of "stiffs" tried to ride out the overland that night, and I lost the Swede in the shuffle. Also, I lost the overland.

I arrived in Reno, Nevada, in a box-car that was promptly side-tracked. It was Sunday morning, and after I threw my feet for breakfast, I wandered over to the Piute camp to watch the Indians gambling. And there stood the Swede, hugely interested. Of course we got together. He was the only acquaintance I had in that region, and I was his only acquaintance. We rushed together like a couple of dissatisfied hermits, and together we spent the day, threw our feet for dinner, and late in the afternoon tried to "nail" the same freight. But he was ditched, and I rode her out alone, to be ditched myself in the desert twenty miles beyond.

Of all desolate places, the one at which I was ditched was the limit. It was called a flag-station, and it consisted of a shanty dumped inconsequentially into the sand and sage-brush. A chill wind was blowing, night was coming on, and the solitary telegraph operator who lived in the shanty was afraid of me. I knew that neither grub nor bed could I get out of him. It was because of his manifest fear of me that I did not believe him when he told me that east-bound trains never stopped there. Besides, hadn't I been thrown off of an east-bound train right at that very spot not five minutes before? He assured me that it had stopped under orders, and that a year might go by before another was stopped under orders. He advised me that it was only a dozen or fifteen miles on to Wadsworth and that I'd better hike. I elected to wait, however, and I had the pleasure of seeing two west-bound freights go by without stopping, and one east-bound freight. I wondered if the Swede was on the latter. It was up to me to hit the ties to Wadsworth, and hit them I did, much to the telegraph operator's relief, for I neglected to burn his shanty and murder him. Telegraph operators have much to be thankful for. At the end of half a dozen miles, I had to get off the ties and let the east-bound overland go by. She was going fast, but I caught sight of a dim form on the first "blind" that looked like the Swede.

That was the last I saw of him for weary days. I hit the high places across those hundreds of miles of Nevada desert, riding the overlands at night, for speed, and in the day-time riding in box-cars and getting my sleep. It was early in the year, and it was cold in those upland pastures. Snow lay here and there on the level, all the mountains were shrouded in white, and at night the most miserable wind imaginable blew off from them. It was not a land in which to linger. And remember, gentle reader, the hobo goes through such a land, without shelter, without money, begging his way and sleeping at night without blankets. This last is something that can be realized only by experience.

In the early evening I came down to the depot at Ogden. The overland of the Union Pacific was pulling east, and I was bent on making connections. Out in the tangle of tracks ahead of the engine I encountered a figure slouching through the gloom. It was the Swede. We shook hands like long-lost brothers, and discovered that our hands were gloved. "Where'd ye glahm 'em?" I asked. "Out of an engine-cab," he answered; "and where did you?" "They belonged to a fireman," said I; "he was careless."

We caught the blind as the overland pulled out, and mighty cold we found it. The way led up a narrow gorge between snow-covered mountains, and we shivered and shook and exchanged confidences about how we had covered the ground between Reno and Ogden. I had closed my eyes for only an hour or so the previous night, and the blind was not comfortable enough to suit me for a snooze. At a stop, I went forward to the engine. We had on a "double-header" (two engines) to take us over the grade.

The pilot of the head engine, because it "punched the wind," I knew would be too cold; so I selected the pilot of the second engine, which was sheltered by the first engine. I stepped on the cowcatcher and found the pilot occupied. In the darkness I felt out the form of a young boy. He was sound asleep. By squeezing, there was room for two on the pilot, and I made the boy hudge over and crawled up beside him. It was a "good" night; the "shacks" (brakemen) didn't bother us, and in no time we were asleep. Once in a while hot cinders or heavy jolts aroused me, when I snuggled closer to the boy and dozed off to the coughing of the engines and the screeching of the wheels.

The overland made Evanston, Wyoming, and went no farther. A wreck ahead blocked the line. The dead engineer had been brought in, and his body attested the peril of the way. A tramp, also, had been killed, but his body had not been brought in. I talked with the boy. He was thirteen years old. He had run away from his folks in some place in Oregon, and was heading east to his grandmother. He had a tale of cruel treatment in the home he had left that rang true; besides, there was no need for him to lie 'to me, a nameless hobo on the track.

And that boy was going some, too. He couldn't cover the ground fast enough. When the division superintendents decided to send the overland back over the way it had come, then up on a cross "jerk" to the Oregon Short Line, and back along that road to tap the Union Pacific the other side of the wreck, that boy climbed upon the pilot and said he was going to stay with it. This was too much for the Swede and me. It meant travelling the rest of that frigid night in order to gain no more than a dozen miles or so. We said we'd wait till the wreck was cleared away, and in the meantime get a good sleep.

Now it is no snap to strike a strange town, broke, at midnight, in cold weather, and find a place to sleep. The Swede hadn't a penny. My total assets consisted of two dimes and a nickel. From some of the town boys we learned that beer was five cents, and that the saloons kept open all night. There was our meat. Two glasses of beer would cost ten cents, there would be a stove and chairs, and we could sleep it out till morning. We headed for the lights of a saloon, walking briskly, the snow crunching under our feet, a chill little wind blowing through us.

Alas, I had misunderstood the town boys. Beer was five cents in one saloon only in the whole burg, and we didn't strike that saloon. But the one we entered was all right. A blessed stove was roaring white-hot; there were cosey, cane-bottomed arm-chairs, and a none-too-pleasant-looking barkeeper who glared suspiciously at us as we came in. A man cannot spend continuous days and nights in his clothes, beating trains, fighting soot and cinders, and sleeping anywhere, and maintain a good "front." Our fronts were decidedly against us; but what did we care? I had the price in my jeans.

"Two beers," said I nonchalantly to the barkeeper, and while he

drew them, the Swede and I leaned against the bar and yearned
secretly for the arm-chairs by the stove.

The barkeeper set the two foaming glasses before us, and with
pride I deposited the ten cents. Now I was dead game. As soon as
I learned my error in the price I'd have dug up another ten cents.
Never mind if it did leave me only a nickel to my name, a stranger
in a strange land. I'd have paid it all right. But that barkeeper never
gave me a chance. As soon as his eyes spotted the dime I had laid
down, he seized the two glasses, one in each hand, and dumped
the beer into the sink behind the bar. At the same time, glaring at
us malevolently, he said:

"You've got scabs on your nose. You've got scabs on your nose.
You've got scabs on your nose. See!"

I hadn't either, and neither had the Swede. Our noses were all
right. The direct bearing of his words was beyond our comprehen-
sion, but the indirect bearing was clear as print: he didn't like our
looks, and beer was evidently ten cents a glass.

I dug down and laid another dime on the bar, remarking carelessly, "Oh, I thought this was a five-cent joint."

"Your money's no good here," he answered, shoving the two
dimes across the bar to me.

Sadly I dropped them back into my pocket, sadly we yearned
toward the blessed stove and the arm-chairs, and sadly we went out
the door into the frosty night.

But as we went out the door, the barkeeper, still glaring, called
after us, "You've got scabs on your nose, see!"

I have seen much of the world since then, journeyed among
strange lands and peoples, opened many books, sat in many lecture-
halls; but to this day, though I have pondered long and deep, I have
been unable to divine the meaning in the cryptic utterance of that
barkeeper in Evanston, Wyoming. Our noses *were* all right.

We slept that night over the boilers in an electric-lighting plant.
How we discovered that "kipping" place I can't remember. We
must have just headed for it, instinctively, as horses head for water
or carrier-pigeons head for the home-cote. But it was a night not
pleasant to remember. A dozen hoboes were ahead of us on top of
the boilers, and it was too hot for all of us. To complete our misery,
the engineer would not let us stand around down below. He gave
us our choice of the boilers or the outside snow.

"You said you wanted to sleep, and so, damn you, sleep," said he to me, when, frantic and beaten out by the heat, I came down into the fire-room.

"Water," I gasped, wiping the sweat from my eyes, "water."

He pointed out of doors and assured me that down there somewhere in the blackness I'd find the river. I started for the river, got lost in the dark, fell into two or three drifts, gave it up, and returned half-frozen to the top of the boilers. When I had thawed out, I was thirstier than ever. Around me the hoboes were moaning, groaning, sobbing, sighing, gasping, panting, rolling and tossing and floundering heavily in their torment. We were so many lost souls toasting on a griddle in hell, and the engineer, Satan Incarnate, gave us the sole alternative of freezing in the outer cold. The Swede sat up and anathematized passionately the wanderlust in man that sent him tramping and suffering hardships such as that.

"When I get back to Chicago," he perorated, "I'm going to get a job and stick to it till hell freezes over. Then I'll go tramping again."

And, such is the irony of fate, next day, when the wreck ahead was cleared, the Swede and I pulled out of Evanston in the ice-boxes of an "orange special," a fast freight laden with fruit from sunny California. Of course, the ice-boxes were empty on account of the cold weather, but that didn't make them any warmer for us. We entered them through hatchways in the top of the car; the boxes were constructed of galvanized iron, and in that biting weather were not pleasant to the touch. We lay there, shivered and shook, and with chattering teeth held a council wherein we decided that we'd stay by the ice-boxes day and night till we got out of the inhospitable plateau region and down into the Mississippi Valley.

But we must eat, and we decided that at the next division we would throw our feet for grub and make a rush back to our ice-boxes. We arrived in the town of Green River late in the afternoon, but too early for supper. Before meal-time is the worst time for "battering" back-doors; but we put on our nerve, swung off the side-ladders as the freight pulled into the yards, and made a run for the houses. We were quickly separated; but we had agreed to meet in the ice-boxes. I had bad luck at first; but in the end, with a couple of "hand-outs" poked into my shirt, I chased for the train. It was pulling out and going fast. The particular refrigerator-car in which we were to meet had already gone by, and half a dozen cars down the train from it I swung on to the side-ladders, went up on top hurriedly, and dropped down into an ice-box.

But a shack had seen me from the caboose, and at the next stop a few miles farther on, Rock Springs, the shack stuck his head into my box and said: "Hit the grit, you son of a toad! Hit the grit!" Also he grabbed me by the heels and dragged me out. I hit the grit all right, and the orange special and the Swede rolled on without me.

Snow was beginning to fall. A cold night was coming on. After dark I hunted around in the railroad yards until I found an empty refrigerator car. In I climbed—not into the ice-boxes, but into the car itself. I swung the heavy doors shut, and their edges, covered with strips of rubber, sealed the car air-tight. The walls were thick. There was no way for the outside cold to get in. But the inside was just as cold as the outside. How to raise the temperature was the problem. But trust a "profesh" for that. Out of my pockets I dug up three or four newspapers. These I burned, one at a time, on the floor of the car. The smoke rose to the top. Not a bit of the heat could escape, and, comfortable and warm, I passed a beautiful night. I didn't wake up once.

In the morning it was still snowing. While throwing my feet for breakfast, I missed an east-bound freight. Later in the day I nailed two other freights and was ditched from both of them. All afternoon no east-bound trains went by. The snow was falling thicker than ever, but at twilight I rode out on the first blind of the overland. As I swung aboard the blind from one side, somebody swung aboard from the other. It was the boy who had run away from Oregon.

Now the first blind of a fast train in a driving snowstorm is no summer picnic. The wind goes right through one, strikes the front of the car, and comes back again. At the first stop, darkness having come on, I went forward and interviewed the fireman. I offered to "shove" coal to the end of his run, which was Rawlins, and my offer was accepted. My work was out on the tender, in the snow, breaking the lumps of coal with a sledge and shovelling it forward to him in the cab. But as I did not have to work all the time, I could come into the cab and warm up now and again.

"Say," I said to the fireman, at my first breathing spell, "there's a little kid back there on the first blind. He's pretty cold."

The cabs on the Union Pacific engines are quite spacious, and we fitted the kid into a warm nook in front of the high seat of the fireman, where the kid promptly fell asleep. We arrived at Rawlins at midnight. The snow was thicker than ever. Here the engine was to go into the round-house, being replaced by the fresh engine. As the train came to a stop, I dropped off the engine steps plump into the arms of a large man in a large overcoat. He began asking me questions, and I promptly demanded who he was. Just as promptly he informed me that he was the sheriff. I drew in my horns and listened and answered.

He began describing the kid who was still asleep in the cab. I did some quick thinking. Evidently the family was on the trail of the kid, and the sheriff had received telegraphed instructions from Oregon. Yes, I had seen the kid. I had met him first in Ogden. The date tallied with the sheriff's information. But the kid was still behind somewhere, I explained, for he had been ditched from that very overland that night when it pulled out of Rock Springs. And all the time I was praying that the kid wouldn't wake up, come down out of the cab, and put the "kibosh" on me.

The sheriff left me in order to interview the shacks, but before he left he said:

"Bo, this town is no place for you. Understand? You ride this train out, and make no mistake about it. If I catch you after it's gone . . ."

I assured him that it was not through desire that I was in his town; that the only reason I was there was that the train had stopped there; and that he wouldn't see me for smoke the way I'd get out of his darn town.

While he went to interview the shacks, I jumped back into the cab. The kid was awake and rubbing his eyes. I told him the news and advised him to ride the engine into the round-house. To cut the story short, the kid made the same overland out, riding the pilot, with instructions to make an appeal to the fireman at the first stop for permission to ride in the engine. As for myself, I got ditched. The new fireman was young and not yet lax enough to break the rules of the Company against having tramps in the engine; so he turned down my offer to shove coal. I hope the kid succeeded with him, for all night on the pilot in that blizzard would have meant death.

Strange to say, I do not at this late day remember a detail of how I was ditched at Rawlins. I remember watching the train as it was immediately swallowed up in the snow-storm, and of heading for a saloon to warm up. Here was light and warmth. Everything was in full blast and wide open. Faro, roulette, craps, and poker tables were running, and some mad cow-punchers were making the night merry. I had just succeeded in fraternizing with them and was downing my first drink at their expense, when a heavy hand descended on my shoulder. I looked around and sighed. It was the sheriff.

Without a word he led me out into the snow.

"There's an orange special down there in the yards," said he.

"It's a damn cold night," said I.

"It pulls out in ten minutes," said he.

That was all. There was no discussion. And when that orange special pulled out, I was in the ice-boxes. I thought my feet would freeze before morning, and the last twenty miles into Laramie I stood upright in the hatchway and danced up and down. The snow was too thick for the shacks to see me, and I didn't care if they did.

My quarter of a dollar bought me a hot breakfast at Laramie, and immediately afterward I was on board the blind baggage of an overland that was climbing to the pass through the backbone of the Rockies. One does not ride blind baggages in the daytime; but in this blizzard at the top of the Rocky Mountains I doubted if the shacks would have the heart to put me off. And they didn't. They made a practice of coming forward at every stop to see if I was frozen yet.

At Ames' Monument, at the summit of the Rockies—I forget the altitude—the shack came forward for the last time.

"Say, Bo," he said, "you see that freight side-tracked over there to let us go by?"

I saw. It was on the next track, six feet away. A few feet more in that storm and I could not have seen it.

"Well, the 'after-push' of Kelly's Army is in one of them cars. They've got two feet of straw under them, and there's so many of them that they keep the car warm."

His advice was good, and I followed it, prepared, however, if it was a "con game" the shack had given me, to take the blind as the overland pulled out. But it was straight goods. I found the car—a big refrigerator car with the leeward door wide open for ventilation. Up I climbed and in. I stepped on a man's leg, next on some other man's arm. The light was dim, and all I could make out was arms and legs and bodies inextricably confused. Never was there such a tangle of humanity. They were all lying in the straw, and over, and under, and around one another. Eighty-four husky hoboes take up a lot of room when they are stretched out. The men I stepped on were resentful. Their bodies heaved under me like the waves of the sea, and imparted an involuntary forward movement to me. I could not find any straw to step upon, so I stepped upon more men. The resentment increased, so did my forward movement. I lost my footing and sat down with sharp abruptness. Unfortunately, it was on a man's head. The next moment he had risen on his hands and knees in wrath, and I was flying through the air. What goes up must come down, and I came down on another man's head.

What happened after that is very vague in my memory. It was like going through a threshing-machine. I was bandied about from one end of the car to the other. Those eighty-four hoboes winnowed me out till what little was left of me, by some miracle, found a bit of straw to rest upon. I was initiated, and into a jolly crowd. All the rest of that day we rode through the blizzard, and to while the time away it was decided that each man was to tell a story. It was stipulated that each story must be a good one, and, furthermore, that it must be a story no one had ever heard before. The penalty for failure was the threshing-machine. Nobody failed. And I want to say right here that never in my life have I sat at so marvellous a story-telling debauch. Here were eight-four men from all the world—I made eighty-five; and each man told a masterpiece. It had to be, for it was either masterpiece or threshing-machine.

Late in the afternoon we arrived in Cheyenne. The blizzard was at its height, and though the last meal of all of us had been breakfast, no man cared to throw his feet for supper. All night we rolled on through the storm, and next day found us down on the sweet plains of Nebraska and still rolling. We were out of the storm and the mountains. The blessed sun was shining over a smiling land, and we had eaten nothing for twenty-four hours. We found out that the freight would arrive about noon at a town, if I remember right, that was called Grand Island.

We took up a collection and sent a telegram to the authorities of that town. The text of the message was that eighty-five healthy, hungry hoboes would arrive about noon and that it would be a good idea to have dinner ready for them. The authorities of Grand Island had two courses open to them. They could feed us, or they could throw us in jail. In the latter event they'd have to feed us anyway, and they decided wisely that one meal would be the cheaper way.

When the freight rolled into Grand Island at noon, we were sitting on the tops of the cars and dangling our legs in the sunshine. All the police in the burg were on the reception committee. They marched us in squads to the various hotels and restaurants, where dinners were spread for us. We had been thirty-six hours without food, and we didn't have to be taught what to do. After that we were marched back to the railroad station. The police had thoughtfully compelled the freight to wait for us. She pulled out slowly, and the eighty-five of us, strung out along the track, swarmed up the side-ladders. We "captured" the train.

We had no supper that evening—at least the "push" didn't, but I did. Just at supper time, as the freight was pulling out of a small town, a man climbed into the car where I was playing pedro with three other stiffs. The man's shirt was bulging suspiciously. In his hand he carried a battered quart-measure from which arose steam. I smelled "Java." I turned my cards over to one of the stiffs who was looking on, and excused myself. Then, in the other end of the car, pursued by envious glances, I sat down with the man who had climbed aboard and shared his "Java" and the handouts that had bulged his shirt. It was the Swede.

At about ten o'clock in the evening, we arrived at Omaha.

"Let's shake the push," said the Swede to me.

"Sure," said I.

As the freight pulled into Omaha, we made ready to do so. But the people of Omaha were also ready. The Swede and I hung upon the side-ladders, ready to drop off. But the freight did not stop. Furthermore, long rows of policemen, their brass buttons and stars glittering in the electric lights, were lined up on each side of the track. The Swede and I knew what would happen to us if we ever dropped off into their arms. We stuck by the side-ladders, and the train rolled on across the Missouri River to Council Bluffs.

"General" Kelly, with an army of two thousand hoboes, lay in camp at Chautauqua Park, several miles away. The after-push we were with was General Kelly's rearguard, and, detraining at Council Bluffs, it started to march to camp. The night had turned cold, and heavy wind-squalls, accompanied by rain, were chilling and wetting us. Many police were guarding us and herding us to the camp. The Swede and I watched our chance and made a successful get-away.

The rain began coming down in torrents, and in the darkness, unable to see our hands in front of our faces, like a pair of blind men we fumbled about for shelter. Our instinct served us, for in no time we stumbled upon a saloon—not a saloon that was open and doing business, not merely a saloon that was closed for the night, and not even a saloon with a permanent address, but a saloon propped up on big timbers, with rollers underneath, that was being moved from somewhere to somewhere. The doors were locked. A squall of wind and rain drove down upon us. We did not hesitate. Smash went the door, and in we went.

I have made some tough camps in my time, "carried the banner" in infernal metropolises, bedded in pools of water, slept in the snow under two blankets when the spirit thermometer registered seventy-four degrees below zero (which is a mere trifle of one hundred and six degrees of frost); but I want to say right here that never did I make a tougher camp, pass a more miserable night, than that night I passed with the Swede in the itinerant saloon at Council Bluffs. In the first place, the building, perched up as it was in the air, had exposed a multitude of openings in the floor through which the wind whistled. In the second place, the bar was empty; there was no bottled fire-water with which we could warm ourselves and forget our misery. We had no blankets, and in our wet clothes, wet to the skin, we tried to sleep. I rolled under the bar, and the Swede rolled under the table. The holes and crevices in the floor made it impossible, and at the end of half an hour I crawled up on top the bar. A little later the Swede crawled up on top his table.

And there we shivered and prayed for daylight. I know, for one, that I shivered until I could shiver no more, till the shivering muscles exhausted themselves and merely ached horribly. The Swede moaned and groaned, and every little while, through chattering teeth, he muttered, "Never again; never again." He muttered this phrase repeatedly, ceaselessly, a thousand times; and when he dozed, he went on muttering it in his sleep.

At the first gray of dawn we left our house of pain, and outside, found ourselves in a mist, dense and chill. We stumbled on till we came to the railroad track. I was going back to Omaha to throw my feet for breakfast; my companion was going on to Chicago. The moment for parting had come. Our palsied hands went out to each other. We were both shivering. When we tried to speak, our teeth chattered us back into silence. We stood alone, shut off from the world; all that we could see was a short length of railroad track, both ends of which were lost in the driving mist. We stared dumbly at each other, our clasped hands shaking sympathetically. The Swede's face was blue with the cold, and I know mine must have been.

"Never again what?" I managed to articulate.

Speech strove for utterance in the Swede's throat; then, faint and distant, in a thin whisper from the very bottom of his frozen soul, came the words:

"Never again a hobo."

He paused, and, as he went on again, his voice gathered strength and huskiness as it affirmed his will.

"Never again a hobo. I'm going to get a job. You'd better do the same. Nights like this make rheumatism."

He wrung my hand.

"Good-by, Bo," said he.

"Good-by, Bo," said I.

The next we were swallowed up from each other by the mist. It was our final passing. But here's to you, Mr. Swede, wherever you are. I hope you got that job.

FAR TO
THE WEST

WAR

(The Nation, June 19, 1911)

". . . a little masterpiece," Earle Labor, in his *Jack London* (1974), says of this little-known gem of a tale, "which deserves to be ranked with the best war stories of Stephen Crane and Ernest Hemingway."

Indeed, and with the best of Ambrose Bierce as well, including his immortal "An Occurrence at Owl Creek Bridge," which "War" strangely resembles in its irony and quiet but bludgeoning impact.

"War" is quite simply unforgettable, a tale of such surpassing brilliance that it is a wonder that it is not better known among London's work. London has pared the details to the bone: the reader is given only the slightest clues as to where the story takes place, or when. The unnamed young cavalryman rides vaguely northward, scouting, apprehending something *from* the north, something he is looking for, some "work he had to do." He hears in the distance, but from the *west,* the boom of heavy guns. We know that the "pulse of war beats from the West" and that the war is a large one involving the "companionship of battling thousands." The terrain described *seems* western.

We know little else of consequence, nor do we need to know more, although we are anxious to know more: What is meant by "the detested tongue of the alien invaders"? What war *is* it? *Where* is it? *When* is it? Who *is* the mysterious man with the ginger-beard? Who were the hanged men and why were they executed?

Jack London scholar Russ Kingman, in his introduction to a limited edition printing of this story in 1985, wrote: "This unique story reads like an episode of the Civil War but we are left wondering whether it is a scene from a former war or one that is to occur in the future."

Kingman sees the story as an indictment of war, a comment on the futility and waste and tragedy of war.

Others have found a different interpretation: He who hesitates in time of war is lost.

But each reader's interpretation is as valid as these.

WAR

I

HE WAS A young man, not more than twenty-four or -five, and he might have sat his horse with the careless grace of his youth had he not been so catlike and tense. His black eyes roved everywhere, catching the movements of twigs and branches where small birds hopped, questing ever onward through the changing vistas of trees and brush, and returning always to the clumps of undergrowth on either side. And as he watched, so did he listen, though he rode on in silence, save for the boom of heavy guns from far to the west. This had been sounding monotonously in his ears for hours, and only its cessation would have aroused his notice. For he had business closer to hand. Across his saddle-bow was balanced a carbine.

So tensely was he strung, that a bunch of quail, exploding into fight from under his horse's nose, startled him to such an extent that automatically, instantly, he had reined in and fetched the carbine halfway to his shoulder. He grinned sheepishly, recovered himself, and rode on. So tense was he, so bent upon the work he had to do, that the sweat stung his eyes unwiped, and unheeded rolled down his nose and spattered his saddle pommel. The band of his cavalryman's hat was fresh-stained with sweat. The roan horse under him was likewise wet. It was high noon of a breathless day of heat. Even the birds and squirrels did not dare the sun, but sheltered in shady hiding places among the trees.

Man and horse were littered with leaves and dusted with yellow pollen, for the open was ventured no more than was compulsory.

They kept to the brush and trees, and invariably the man halted and peered out before crossing a dry glade or naked stretch of upland pasturage. He worked always to the north, though his way was devious, and it was from the north that he seemed most to apprehend that for which he was looking. He was no coward, but his courage was only that of the average civilized man, and he was looking to live, not die.

Up a small hillside he followed a cowpath through such dense scrub that he was forced to dismount and lead his horse. But when the path swung around to the west, he abandoned it and headed to the north again along the oak-covered top of the ridge.

The ridge ended in a steep descent—so steep that he zigzagged back and forth across the face of the slope, sliding and stumbling among the dead leaves and matted vines and keeping a watchful eye on the horse above that threatened to fall down upon him. The sweat ran from him, and the pollen-dust, settling pungently in mouth and nostrils, increased his thirst. Try as he would, nevertheless the descent was noisy, and frequently he stopped, panting in the dry heat and listening for any warning from beneath.

At the bottom he came out on a flat, so densely forested that he could not make out its extent. Here the character of the woods changed, and he was able to remount. Instead of the twisted hillside oaks, tall straight trees, big-trunked and prosperous, rose from the damp fat soil. Only here and there were thickets, easily avoided, while he encountered winding, park-like glades where the cattle had pastured in the days before war had run them off.

His progress was more rapid now, as he came down into the valley, and at the end of half an hour he halted at an ancient rail fence on the edge of a clearing. He did not like the openness of it, yet his path lay across to the fringe of trees that marked the banks of the stream. It was a mere quarter of a mile across that open, but the thought of venturing out in it was repugnant. A rifle, a score of them, a thousand, might lurk in that fringe by the stream.

Twice he essayed to start, and twice he paused. He was appalled by his own loneliness. The pulse of war that beat from the West suggested the companionship of battling thousands; here was naught but silence, and himself, and possible death-dealing bullets from a myriad ambushes. And yet his task was to find what he feared to find. He must go on, and on, till somewhere, some time, he encountered another man, or other men, from the other side, scouting, as he was scouting, to make report, as he must make report, of having come in touch.

Changing his mind, he skirted inside the woods for a distance, and again peeped forth. This time, in the middle of the clearing, he saw a small farmhouse. There were no signs of life. No smoke curled from the chimney, not a barnyard fowl clucked and strutted. The kitchen door stood open, and he gazed so long and hard into the black aperture that it seemed almost that a farmer's wife must emerge at any moment.

He licked the pollen and dust from his dry lips, stiffened himself, mind and body, and rode out into the blazing sunshine. Nothing stirred. He went on past the house, and approached the wall of trees and bushes by the river's bank. One thought persisted maddeningly. It was of the crash into his body of a high-velocity bullet. It made him feel very fragile and defenseless, and he crouched lower in the saddle.

Tethering his horse in the edge of the wood, he continued a hundred yards on foot till he came to the stream. Twenty feet wide it was, without perceptible current, cool and inviting, and he was very thirsty. But he waited inside his screen of leafage, his eyes fixed on the screen on the opposite side. To make the wait endurable, he sat down, his carbine resting on his knees. The minutes passed, and slowly his tenseness relaxed. At last he decided there was no danger; but just as he prepared to part the bushes and bend down to the water, a movement among the opposite bushes caught his eye.

It might be a bird. But he waited. Again there was an agitation of the bushes, and then, so suddenly that it almost startled a cry from him, the bushes parted and a face peered out. It was a face covered with several weeks' growth of ginger-colored beard. The eyes were blue and wide apart, with laughter-wrinkles in the corners that showed despite the tired and anxious expression of the whole face.

All this he could see with microscopic clearness, for the distance was no more than twenty feet. And all this he saw in such brief time, that he saw it as he lifted his carbine to his shoulder. He glanced along the sights, and knew that he was gazing upon a man who was as good as dead. It was impossible to miss at such point blank range.

But he did not shoot. Slowly he lowered the carbine and watched. A hand, clutching a water-bottle, became visible and the ginger beard bent downward to fill the bottle. He could hear the gurgle of the water. Then arm and bottle and ginger beard disappeared behing the closing bushes. A long time he waited, when, with thirst unslaked, he crept back to his horse, rode slowly across the sun-washed clearing, and passed into the shelter of the woods beyond.

II

ANOTHER DAY, HOT and breathless. A deserted farmhouse, large, with many outbuildings and an orchard, standing in a clearing. From the woods, on a roan horse, carbine across pommel, rode the young man with the quick black eyes. He breathed with relief as he gained the house. That a fight had taken place here earlier in the season was evident. Clips and empty cartridges, tarnished with verdigris, lay on the ground, which, while wet, had been torn up by the hoofs of horses. Hard by the kitchen garden were graves, tagged and numbered. From the oak tree by the kitchen door, in tattered, weather-beaten garments, hung the bodies of two men. The faces, shriveled and defaced, bore no likeness to the faces of men. The roan horse snorted beneath them, and the rider caressed and soothed it and tied it farther away.

Entering the house, he found the interior a wreck. He trod on empty cartridges as he walked from room to room to reconnoiter from the windows. Men had camped and slept everywhere, and on the floor of one room he came upon stains unmistakable where the wounded had been laid down.

Again outside, he led the horse around behind the barn and invaded the orchard. A dozen trees were burdened with ripe apples. He filled his pockets, eating while he picked. Then a thought came to him, and he glanced at the sun, calculating the time of his return to camp. He pulled off his shirt, tying the sleeves and making a bag. This he proceeded to fill with apples.

As he was about to mount his horse, the animal suddenly pricked up its ears. The man, too, listened, and heard, faintly, the thud of hoofs on soft earth. He crept to the corner of the barn and peered out. A dozen mounted men, strung out loosely, approaching from the opposite side of the clearing, were only a matter of a hundred yards or so away. They rode on to the house. Some dismounted, while others remained in the saddle as an earnest that their stay would be short. They seemed to be holding a council, for he could hear them talking excitedly in the detested tongue of the alien invader. The time passed, but they seemed unable to reach a decision. He put the carbine away in its boot, mounted, and waited impatiently, balancing the shirt of apples on the pommel.

He heard footsteps approaching, and drove his spurs so fiercely into the roan as to force a surprised groan from the animal as it leaped forward. At the corner of the barn he saw the intruder, a mere boy of nineteen or twenty for all of his uniform, jump back to escape being run down. At the same moment the roan swerved, and its rider caught a glimpse of the aroused men by the house. Some were springing from their horses, and he could see the rifles going to their shoulders. He passed the kitchen door and the dried corpses swinging in the shade, compelling his foes to run around the front of the house. A rifle cracked, and a second, but he was going fast, leaning forward, low in the saddle, one hand clutching the shirt of apples, the other guiding the horse.

The top bar of the fence was four feet high, but he knew his roan and leaped it at full career to the accompaniment of several scattered shots. Eight hundred yards straight away were the woods, and the roan was covering the distance with mighty strides. Every man was now firing. They were pumping their guns so rapidly that he no longer heard individual shots. A bullet went through his hat, but he was unaware, though he did know when another tore through the apples on the pommel. And he winced and ducked even lower when a third bullet, fired low, struck a stone between his horse's legs and ricochetted off through the air, buzzing and humming like some incredible insect.

The shots died down as the magazines were emptied, until, quickly, there was no more shooting. The young man was elated. Through that astonishing fusillade he had come unscathed. He glanced back. Yes, they had emptied their magazines. He could see several reloading. Others were running back behind the house for their horses. As he looked, two already mounted, came back into view around the corner, riding hard. And at the same moment, he saw the man with the unmistakable ginger beard kneel down on the ground, level his gun, and coolly take his time for the long shot.

The young man threw his spurs into the horse, crouched very low, and swerved in his flight in order to distract the other's aim. And still the shot did not come. With each jump of the horse, the woods sprang nearer. They were only two hundred yards away, and still the shot was delayed.

And then he heard it, the last thing he was to hear, for he was dead ere he hit the ground in the long crashing fall from the saddle. And they, watching at the house, saw him fall, saw his body bounce when it struck the earth, and saw the burst of red-cheeked apples that rolled about him. They laughed at the unexpected eruption of apples, and clapped their hands in applause of the long shot by the man with the ginger beard.

Jack London: A Chronology

1876   Born at 615 Third Street, San Francisco, California, January 12. Son of Flora Wellman (born Massillon, Ohio, August 17, 1843) and William Henry Chaney (born near present-day Chesterville, Maine, January 13, 1821). Chaney, an itinerant astrologer, lived with Flora Wellman during 1874-1875. Chaney deserted his common-law wife upon learning of her pregnancy and later (1897) denied to London that he could have been his father.

On September 7, Flora (who used the name Chaney) marries John London, a native of Pennsylvania and Union Army veteran, a widower with two daughters. John London accepts Flora's son as his own and he is named John Griffith London, the middle name deriving from a favorite nephew of Flora Wellman's, Griffith Everhard.

1891   Completes grammar school. Works in a cannery.

1892   Purchases the sloop *Razzle-Dazzle* with $300 borrowed from his former wet nurse "Mammy Jenny" Prentiss and becomes "Prince of the Oyster Pirates" on San Francisco Bay.
Serves as officer in the Fish Patrol on San Francisco Bay.

1893   Serves several months aboard the sealing schooner *Sophia Sutherland* in Bering Sea sealing waters and the North Pacific. Returns in summer and on November 12, wins first prize in the San Francisco *Call's* "Best Descriptive Article" contest for "Story of a Typhoon Off the Coast of Japan."

1894   Joins the western detachment of "Coxey's Army"—"Kelly's Army"—to march to Washington, D.C. Leaves the ragtag "army" in the Midwest and rides the rails eastward. Is arrested for vagrancy in Niagara Falls, N.Y., in June and serves one month in the Erie County Pen-

317

itentiary. These experiences he will later chronicle in *The Road* (1907)

1895 Finishes public school education at Oakland High School where he writes sketches and stories for the student magazine *Aegis*.

1896 Joins Socialist Labor Party. Passes entrance examinations and attends the University of California at Berkeley for one semester.

1897 Joins Klondike gold rush and spends the winter in the Yukon. John London dies in Oakland on October 14.

1898 Returns from Alaska via 2,000-mile boat trip down the Yukon River.

1899 Publishes first "professional" story, "To the Man on the Trail" in *Overland Monthly*. Begins writing for a living.
THE WHITE-SILENCE (*Overland Monthly*, February, 1899)
IN A FAR COUNTRY (*Overland Monthly*, June, 1899)
December 21, signs contract with Houghton Mifflin Co. for a book of short stories.

1900 "An Odyssey of the North" is published in *The Atlantic Monthly*. Marries Bessie Maddern on April 7; on the same day, his first published book, *The Son of the Wolf*, a collection of Northland fiction, appears.

1901 First daughter, Joan, is born.
THE LAW OF LIFE (*McClure's Magazine*, March, 1901)

1902 Travels to London where he lives six weeks in the city's East End ghetto, and there gathers material for his brilliant sociological study, *The People of the Abyss* (a phrase credited to H.G. Wells).
Second daughter, Bess, is born.
First novel, *A Daughter of the Snows*, is published by Lippincott's.

1903 W. H. Chaney dies on January 8 in Chicago.
The Kempton-Wace Letters, an epistolary exchange with co-author Anna Strunsky on the subject of love, is published by Macmillan.
Separates from Bessie London.
GOLD HUNTERS OF THE NORTH (*The Atlantic*, July, 1903)
The Call of the Wild is published, an instantaneous success.

1904 Sails for Japan and Korea as war correspondent for the Hearst Syndicate in the Russo-Japanese War.
The Sea Wolf is published, London's second most famous novel.
Divorces Bessie Maddern London.

1905 Marries Charmian Kittredge on November 20 in Chicago.
Purchases ranch near Glen Ellen, California.

Lectures in Midwest and East.
WHITE AND YELLOW *(The Youth's Companion,* February 16, 1905)
ALL GOLD CANYON *(The Century Magazine,* November, 1905)
LOVE OF LIFE *(McClure's Magazine,* December, 1905)

1906 Lectures at Yale in January on "The Coming Crisis."
Reports on the San Francisco earthquake and fire, April 18, for *Collier's.* Begins building the *Snark* (named after Lewis Carroll's creation), to sail around the world.
White Fang, written as a companion volume to *The Call of the Wild,* is published.
THE APOSTATE *(Woman's Home Companion,* September, 1906)

1907 Sails April 23 from San Francisco in *Snark,* visiting Hawaii—including the leper colony at Molokai—the Marquesas, and Tahiti.
HOBOES THAT PASS IN THE NIGHT *(Cosmopolitan,* December, 1907)

1908 Returns to California aboard the *Mariposa* to straighten out financial affairs. Continues *Snark* voyage to Samoa, Fiji Islands, New Hebrides, and the Solomon Islands.
The Iron Heel is published.
TO BUILD A FIRE *(The Century Magazine,* August, 1908)
LOST FACE (New York *Herald,* December 13, 1908)

1909 Is hospitalized in Sydney, Australia, with a series of tropical ailments. Abandons *Snark* voyage and returns to California on the Scotch collier *Tymeric* via Pitcairn Island, Ecuador, Panama, New Orleans and Arizona.
Arrives at Wake Robin Lodge on July 24.
Martin Eden, a semi-autobiographical novel, is published.

1910 Devotes energies, and funds, to building up his "Beauty Ranch." Wolf House, London's baronial mansion, is begun.
Birth and death of the Londons' first child, a daughter named Joy.

1911 With his wife and servant, drives a four-horse carriage through Northern California and Oregon.
THE TASTE OF THE MEAT *(Cosmopolitan,* June, 1911)
WAR *(The Nation,* June, 19, 1911)
THE MEXICAN *(Saturday Evening Post,* August 19, 1911)
FOUR HORSES AND A SAILOR *(Sunset Magazine,* September, 1911)

1912 Sails on March 2 from Baltimore around Cape Horn to Seattle aboard

the four-masted barque *Dirigo*, a 148-day voyage.
The Londons' second baby lost in miscarriage.

1913   Wolf House, on August 22, is mysteriously destroyed by fire, a $40,000 loss.
John Barleycorn, semi-autobiographical novel-treatise on alcoholism, is published.

1914   Becomes correspondent for *Collier's*, at $1,100 a week, in Mexican Revolution.

1915   Returns to Hawaii, this time for health purposes.
His last great work, *The Star Rover*, is published.
MOUNTAIN MEADOWS MASSACRE (*The Star Rover*, October, 1915)
Is warned by doctors of his excesses in drink and diet.

1916   Resigns from Socialist Party "because of its lack of fire and fight, and its loss of emphasis on the class struggle."
Dies at 7:45 P.M., November 22, of uremic poisoning.

1917   LIKE ARGUS OF THE ANCIENT TIMES (*Hearst's Magazine*, March, 1917)

1922   Flora Wellman London dies on January 4.

1947   Bess Maddern London dies on September 7.

1955   Charmian Kittredge London dies on January 13.

1965   *Letters from Jack London*, most important of all source books on London's life and thought, is published by Odyssey Press, edited by King Hendricks and Irving Shepard.

1970   *Jack London Reports*, a collection of London's war correspondence, prize-fight reporting and miscellaneous newspaper writing, is published by Doubleday, edited by King Hendricks and Irving Shepard.

1971   Joan London dies on January 19.